SING 'N' LEARN
MUSIC ACTIVITIES KIT

A Complete Sequential Program
in Basic Music Theory
for Grades 1–6

SING 'N' LEARN
MUSIC ACTIVITIES KIT

A Complete Sequential Program in Basic Music Theory for Grades 1–6

Malcolm Hines

Illustrated by the author

PARKER PUBLISHING COMPANY
West Nyack, New York 10995

10 9 8 7 6 5 4 3 2 1

Printed in the United States of America

Library of Congress Cataloging-in-Publication Data

Hines, Malcolm.
   Sing 'n' learn music activities kit : a complete sequential
program in basic music theory for grades 1–6 / Malcolm Hines;
illustrated by the author.
      p. cm.
   ISBN 0–13–809401–2
   1. Music—Theory, Elementary.   I. Title.   II. Title: Sing and
learn music activities kit.
MT7.H67 1990
372.87—dc20   89–22873
                                                              CIP
                                                               MN

ISBN 0-13-809401-2

PARKER PUBLISHING COMPANY
BUSINESS & PROFESSIONAL DIVISION
A division of Simon & Schuster
West Nyack, New York 10995

Dedicated to my grandmother,
Florence Quinn,
whose love of life and music will live on forever.

About the Author

Malcolm Hines holds a Bachelor of Music Degree majoring in Theory and Composition, a Bachelor of Education Degree in Elementary Education and Secondary School Music Education, and a Master of Music Degree in Literature and Performance granted by the University of Western Ontario, London, Canada. He also holds an Associate Diploma for Music Performance (saxophone), which was awarded by the Western Ontario Conservatory of Music. In addition, Mr. Hines has studied music at the Paris and Bordeaux Conservatories in France under a Canada Council Grant.

Mr. Hines has taught classroom music for 14 years in all grades at the elementary and secondary school levels, offering instruction in choral, string, and band music. He has also taught music for the University of Western Ontario, the University of Waterloo, Vancouver Community College, and Cambrian College. Mr. Hines has been active as a clinician for Ontario, British Columbia, and Alberta schools. Many of the groups that he has coached have won local, provincial, and national music competitions across Canada.

An active performing musician for over 25 years, Mr. Hines has participated equally in the classical and popular fields. He has been a CBC Talent Festival Semifinalist as a soloist and has led and performed in a host of varied musical groups. He has adjudicated for the Ontario Music Educators' Association, the Canadian Stage Band Association, and the Canadian Bandmasters' Association.

About This Resource

Every child's world is filled with radios, lavish music videos, and a never-ending list of musical groups. Young people want to be able to recreate the music they love, but their enthusiasm wanes at times when they discover that producing music is more difficult than they imagined. This is understandable because they must simultaneously learn music notation and related theory, master their instrument, and coordinate their performance with the conductor's expectations. Becoming musically literate *before* studying an instrument eliminates a major hurdle in students' struggles towards proficiency; only with the knowledge of music theory can a student perform artistically.

Sing 'n' Learn Music Activities Kit lets students achieve success in music while it greatly simplifies your role as teacher.

STORIES AND SONGS TEACH MUSIC THEORY

Each chapter begins with a fictional story having three central characters: a young boy, a young girl, and an endearing old man, Mr. Treble Clef, who guides these children and the reader through adventure and musical knowledge. The stories are sequential, which keeps your students wondering what will happen next. Students inadvertently learn music theory because it is cleverly woven into each tale. Creative illustrations accompany each story to increase student enjoyment and to assist in demonstrating musical concepts. Each imaginative fable evolves to introduce a rousing song that is to be performed by students.

The lyrics of the songs are music theory facts that require memorization. After students have sung a song a few times, they will have automatically committed music facts to memory without effort. These "teaching tunes" are written in a popular and upbeat style so that children will want to sing them often. Body motions are given and are meant to be performed while students sing the songs. This increases student involvement in rehearsals and facilitates the learning process. They also assist you in classroom control and add a visual dimension to the songs when performed for audiences. In concert, the songs have enjoyed extremely positive audience response. They assist in ending the cycle of theory lessons and concert rehearsals competing for precious class time.

THE QUIZZES: A PLEASURE FOR STUDENT AND TEACHER

The quizzes are progressively difficult and are meant to be reproduced and distributed to students. Included are puzzles, games, and pictures that students can color. "Mr. Treble Clef" is found throughout the quizzes in a myriad of appropriate transformations to excite student interest and make students feel that their "friend" is always there to help. "Boredom Busters" follow each quiz section. These are designed to reinforce the concepts students have learned through a wide variety of mind teasers.

STUDENT EVALUATION MADE EASY

All quizzes can be marked by the students themselves. Answer keys are provided, which can be duplicated and given to students, or you may want to make a transparency of an answer key for display on a large screen. Marks may be tabulated on the given student record sheets. All quizzes are out of a multiple of 25 marks which allows for easy averaging of a student's grade. An achievement grid is also included on which the student can color in his or her success level. Student participation in this evaluative process motivates students to achieve and, since the quizzes are creatively repetitive, most students continually enjoy an extremely high degree of success.

You can keep a record of the accomplishments of individual classes using the class progress sheets provided.

MUSIC ACTIVITIES ASSIST CLASS MANAGEMENT

Many helpful features have been incorporated into *Sing 'n' Learn* to assist you in managing your classes. There are hundreds of illustrations in the quiz sections that a student can color should he or she be the first to finish any activity. In addition, the students' achievement pages are meant to be colored by the children. The social games at the end of the chapters keep all of the students occupied in musical activities as do the body motions associated with the songs. The games can be completely student-run if you wish. Finally, a cassette is provided, in part, to allow you to step away from your role as accompanist and work with individual students.

NO PREPARATION NEEDED BY TEACHERS

Sing 'n' Learn Music Activities Kit provides a complete, sequenced course in basic music theory that can be easily used by anyone who teaches music to children. You will not have to do any advance planning. You simply read a story to the class, showing the pictures as they appear in the tale. In the margins are suggestions for teaching each story. Suggestions for teaching the songs are also included. Body motions for the songs are explained in detail in each chapter.

FOR MUSIC SPECIALISTS AND CLASSROOM TEACHERS

Sing 'n' Learn is designed to assist both the seasoned music specialist and the classroom teacher who has little or no musical training. The music specialist is offered a complete program that teaches rudimentary music theory. Complete piano accompaniments are provided for each song, as are chord symbols for guitar, autoharp, and ukulele use. The teacher who has little or no music background may utilize every component of *Sing 'n' Learn* to offer his or her students a first-rate program.

FOR THE PRIVATE MUSIC TEACHER

Sing 'n' Learn will be of great assistance to the private vocal and instrumental music teacher, too. The stories and quizzes add a refreshing and valuable component to the private lesson. The songs are well within the vocal range of youngsters and can be nicely incorporated into the students' repetoire. *Sing 'n' Learn* will also enable the private music teacher to give students a number of activities to complete at home in sequence. The private music teacher will then be able to spend the majority of lesson time on performance techniques since the student can practice music rudiments at home.

APPROPRIATE FOR GRADES 1–6

Sing 'n' Learn has proven to be most effective in grades 1–6. All of the book material can be used sequentially in grades 3–6. In grade 1, it is recommended that two or three stories and songs (with body motions) and a few games be used during the school year. In grade 2, you might work through two additional chapters and give two or three oral tests from any of the covered chapters. If you complete all of the material by grade 6, the students will be well prepared to be introduced to an instrumental music program by grade 7. Their acquired music literacy will also allow them to function as literate young musicians in a choral program.

A FINAL WORD

Sing 'n' Learn Music Activities Kit gives you a thorough, easy-to-use, and educationally sound music theory program. It is a lot of fun, so enjoy it with your students!

Malcolm Hines

Contents

Acknowledgment

To my wife, Catherine M. Hines, I express my deepest gratitude for her steadfast belief and immeasurable contribution from the creation to completion of this project.

Mac and Christina Meet
Mr. Treble Clef

Draw:

on the board

One golden Saturday morning, bright and early, Mac and Christina set out for their very first music lesson. As they were about to go across the street to the music school, Mac noticed a silver coin, shining up from inside the curb. He saw that the old coin had a backwards "S" written on it, which was very neatly drawn.

"That's a treble clef drawn on the coin," said Christina. "You find them written at the beginning of music lines."

Mac turned the coin over. Something was written on it but it was too dirty for him to read. Mac started to rub it clean and he was beginning to see what the coin read.

Mac slowly said, "The coin says, 'Rub this and . . . .' "

And poof! A cloud of glowing white smoke suddenly appeared. From inside the billowing smoke, two aging hands pulled the children right into it, and then the smoke disappeared. Nothing was left at all.

"Where are we?" asked Mac.

"I don't know!" answered Christina.

"Don't be afraid," an old man's voice said softly. "You two are visiting the beautiful *Musictown*, the land of the *Golden Pot* which is filled full of *musical knowledge*." With that, Mac and Christina found themselves standing in a lovely field surrounded in the distance by quaint buildings which were many different colors.

Smiling at them was a very old man with a pink tuxedo and top hat, sporting a full green beard and a *staff* which he leaned on for support. The staff was made of five straight sticks and a backwards "S" written at the beginning of the staff.

"Gee, hi!" sang the old man. "My name is Mr. Treble Clef. Some call me Mr. G. Clef too!"

"What's that you're leaning on?" asked Christina in a shaky voice.

"Why gee, this is my staff, and I write music on it! After I sign my *treble clef* on it, of course!"

Point out the treble clef on his staff of five lines.

"How?" Mac questioned.

"Well," Mr. Treble Clef slowly answered, as if this was very important, "if I put notes on the *bottom lines* or *spaces* on the staff, notes will sound **lower.** If I put notes on the *top lines* or *spaces*, notes will sound **higher.**

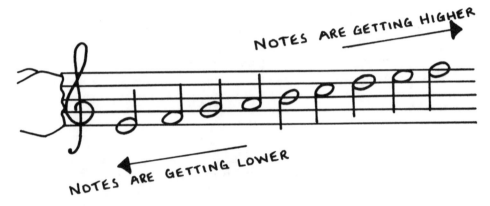

"Do the notes have names?" asked Christina.

"Gee, yes!" the old man sang proudly. "The *lines* are E G B D F and the *spaces* are FACE."

Point out EGBDF and FACE.

"That way we can read them!" shouted Christina. "We can play on our instruments or sing notes that we read on the staff!"

"Gee, you're right, young lady," crooned Mr. Treble Clef.

"Mr. Treble Clef, why do some people call you Mr. G Clef too?" asked Mac.

"Because my sign ends by curling around the *second line* from the bottom, which is called G! See?"

"When you know where G is you can find any note on a line or space because notes run alphabetically up the staff."

Make sure students
know notes move
alphabetically when
ascending.

Mr. Treble Clef then whispered to the children:

Lines and spaces are numbered from the bottom.
Think of apartment floors, and then you've got 'em!

Show the similarity
between line and space
numbering and
apartment floor
numbering.

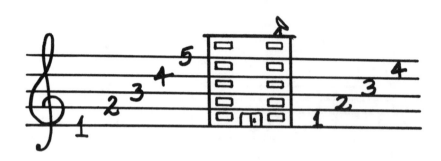

"Wow!" Mac and Christina shouted in unison, "We know
that music notes are always A B C D E F G. We know the
names of keys from A to G on our instruments, but how can
we possibly remember the names of the lines and spaces on
the staff?"

"Gee, by singing this magic song," warbled the old man. And Mr. Treble Clef taught Mac and Christina his magic song. They sang it over and over again. The more they sang it, the more they liked it. As a matter of fact, the kids liked it so much that they just had to dance too!

Together the three of them happily enjoyed their music.

As they sang their hearts out, Mr. Treble Clef raised his staff of five lines and four spaces and jingled, "The Pot of Musical Knowledge has been filled and so:

> E, G, B, D, F, lines
> and F, A, C, E, spaces—
> This you know,
> So away you go
> Back to reality places.

Poof! Mac and Christina found themselves singing in their new music class for the first time. They were still singing the magic song. The whole class immediately joined in. Soon, even the teacher was singing *Gee, Mr. Treble Clef.*

Ask:

1. What are the 5 lines called? (the staff)

2. Are lines and spaces named upwards or downwards? (upwards)

3. What's the treble clef's other name? (G clef)

4. Why? (it ends by curling around the line G)

Now, teach *Gee, Mr. Treble Clef.*

SUGGESTIONS FOR TEACHING THE SONG,
Gee, Mr. Treble Clef

1. Review the musical material by discussing the story events.
2. Play the tape of *Gee, Mr. Treble Clef* or perform it for your students. Then explain the words, making sure they understand what the words mean.
3. Let them hear the song again. (Students in Grades 2–6 can follow the words.)
4. Teach each line by rote, repeating each one several times successively. Maintain an unbroken, steady beat, retaining the lyric rhythms (with or without pitches as necessary).
5. Teach the hand motions while teaching the words.
6. Have all students *completely* memorize the song, through repetition over time.
7. Have students perform as soloists, in duets, and in other interesting combinations. Have the girls compete with the boys, or rows against each other for marks you announce. Kids love competitions.
8. Have a lot of fun!

THE HAND MOTIONS

bar:	
3	Point as if writing on each beat.
4	Hold up 5 fingers, pulsing on each beat.
5, 7, 9, 12	Draw a treble clef in the air, completing it over 4 beats.
6	On beats 1 and 2, point as if writing on each beat. Clap on beat 3 and hold arms apart on beat 4.
8	Salute on beat 1. Stretch arm out on beat 3.
10	Clap: ♫ ♫ ♩
11	Hands move upward on E, G, B, D, F.
13	Point to your face, ascending on each beat.
14	Stretch arms outward on beats 1 and 3.
15	Clap on beat 2.
15, 16	Stretch arms outward on beat 1.

GEE, MR. TREBLE CLEF

HOW MUCH CAN YOU REMEMBER ABOUT THE STORY YOU'VE JUST READ? GIVE YOUR BRAIN A WORKOUT BY FILLING IN THE BLANKS WITH THE CORRECT ANSWERS FOUND IN THE ANSWER BOX.

GOOD REMEMBERING!

Music notes are written on a (1) _____ which always has (2) _____ lines and (3) _____ spaces. Notes placed on the bottom lines and spaces will sound (4) _____ and notes placed on the upper lines and spaces will sound (5) _____. Only the letters (6) ___ ___ ___ ___ ___ ___ and ___ are used in music. Notes with letter names moving forwards $(_AB^{C)}$ in the alphabet are moving *higher* in sound. Notes with letter names $(^{C}B_{A)}$ are moving (7) _____ in sound. The (8) _____ (9) _____ which is also called the (10) _____ clef is written at the beginning of the staff and shows us where the (11) _____ _____ is. Now all lines and spaces can be named because their names are in the order of A B C D E F G. The bottom line on the staff is called (12) ___. The five lines are (13) ___ (14) ___ (15) ___ (16) ___ (17) ___ and the four spaces are (18) ___ (19) ___ (20) ___ (21) ___. When we name lines and spaces by number, we start at the (22) _____ and count (23) _____ just the same as we number (24) _____ in (25) _____ buildings.

ANSWER BOX

APARTMENT
UPWARDS
FIVE
E
LOW
TREBLE CLEF
BOTTOM
HIGH
G
STAFF
EGBDF
G CLEF
FACE
LINE G
FOUR
FLOORS
LOWER
ABCDEFG

FILL THE GOLDEN POT OF MUSICAL KNOWLEDGE WITH YOUR MARK!

25

DO YOU KNOW WHAT MAC AND CHRISTINA KNOW? TEST YOUR SKILL! PLACE A, B, OR C IN <u>EACH BOX</u> TO GIVE YOUR ANSWERS. GOOD LUCK!

1. Mr. Treble Clef says we write our music on a

   a. treble clef
   b. clef
   c. staff

2. How many lines do we write music on?

   a. 4
   b. 5
   c. 3

3. The five lines of music are called a

   a. staff
   b. lines
   c. music

(Mr. Treble Clef learned on one!)

4. The staff has how many lines?

   a. 4
   b. 3
   c. 5

5. Where do we start counting lines and spaces?

   a. from the bottom
   b. from the top
   c. from the middle

(Remember apartment buildings?)

6. The lowest line is

   a. line 3
   b. line 5
   c. line 1

7. The highest line is

   a. line 3
   b. line 5
   c. line 1

8. The middle line is

   a. line 3
   b. line 5
   c. line 1

9. What are the names of the lines with the treble clef?

   a. F D B G E
   b. E G B D F
   c. E G D F B

10. The first line on the staff is

   a. E
   b. G
   c. B

11. The second line on the staff is

   a. G
   b. B
   c. D

12. The third line on the staff is

   a. B
   b. D
   c. G

13. The fourth line on the staff is
    a. B
    b. D
    c. F
    [ ]

14. The fifth line on the staff is
    a. G
    b. D
    c. F
    [ ]

15. The staff has how many spaces?
    a. 3
    b. 5
    c. 4
    [ ]

16. The first space on the staff is
    a. F
    b. A
    c. C
    [ ]

17. The second space on the staff is
    a. F
    b. C
    c. A
    [ ]

18. The third space on the staff is
    a. E
    b. C
    c. F
    [ ]

19. The fourth space on the staff is
    a. A
    b. C
    c. E
    [ ]

20. Another name for the treble clef is the
    a. F clef
    b. G clef
    c. music clef
    [ ]

21. The treble clef is called a G clef because it ends
    by curling around the line
    a. F
    b. G
    c. B
    [ ]

22. The letters in the *spaces*, from the first to the
    fourth, spell the word
    a. MUSIC
    b. FACE
    c. SPACE
    [ ]

23. The letters of the *lines*, from the first to the fifth,
    spell the word
    a. FACE
    b. NO WORD
    c. SPACE
    [ ]

24. The *total* number of lines *and* spaces is
    a. 5
    b. 4
    c. 9
    [ ]

25. Music is
    a. fun
    b. easy
    c. both of these [C]

    A free mark!
    Gee!

FILL THE POT WITH YOUR MARK!

25

NAME _____

Quiz 1–3

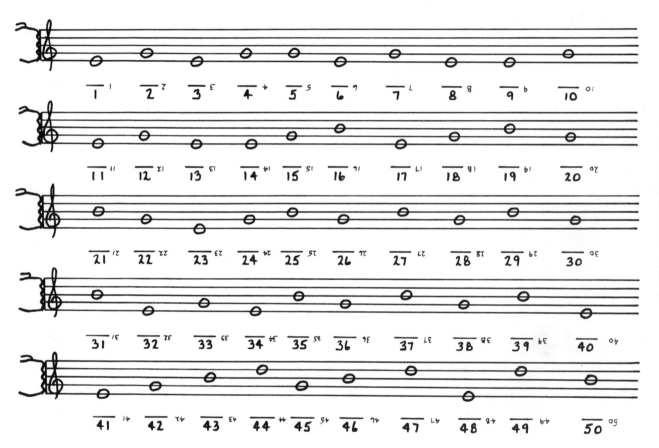

NAME _____

Quiz 1–4

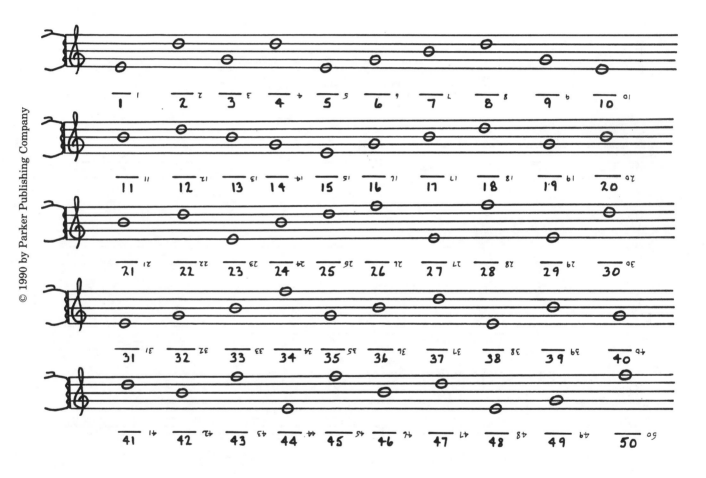

NAME _____

Quiz 1–5

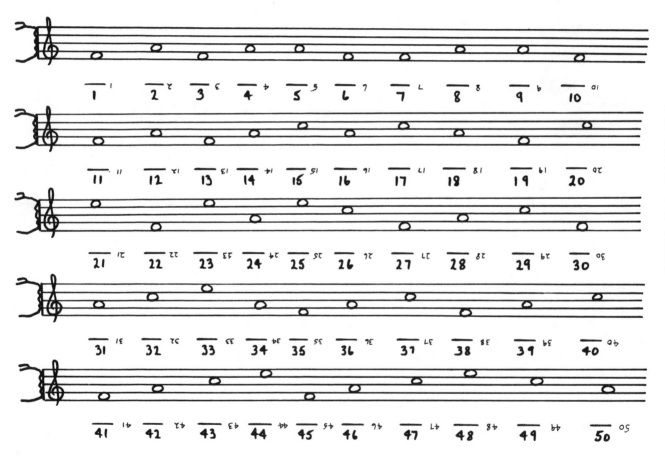

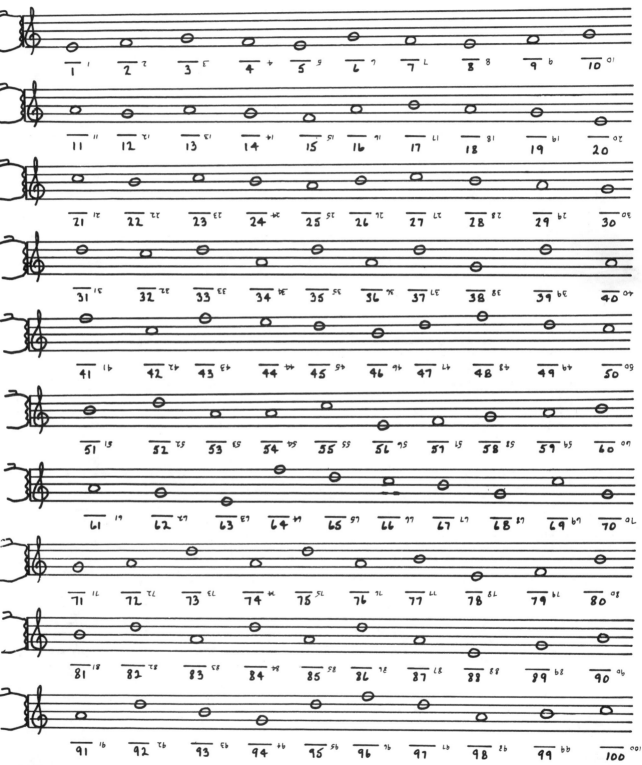

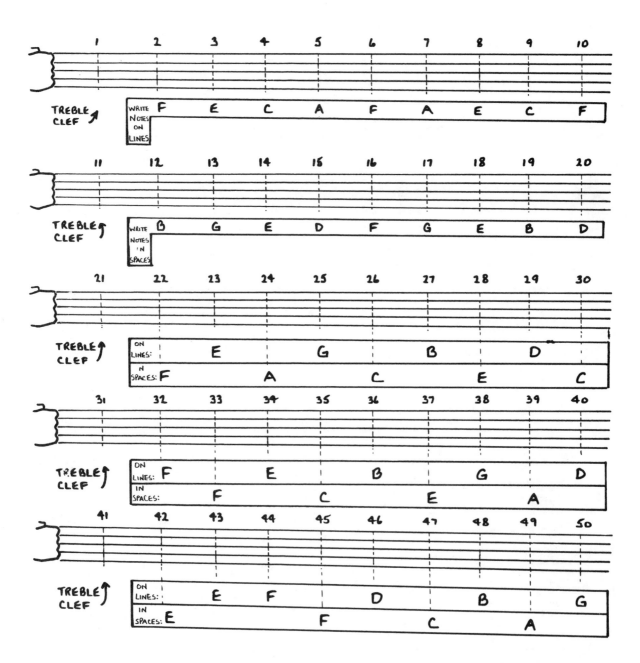

E G B D F,
ARE THE NAMES OF THE LINES
WITH THE TREBLE CLEF;
F A C E :
THE SPACES, ARE EASY!

NAME LINES AND SPACES BELOW.
PLACE YOUR ANSWERS IN THE FINGERNAILS.
USE YOUR OWN FINGERNAILS TO
COUNT UP YOUR ANSWERS, IF YOU WANT TO.

NAME THE FIRST LINE — 1

SECOND LINE? — 2

THIRD LINE? — 3

FOURTH LINE? — 4

FIFTH LINE? — 5

FIRST SPACE? — 6

SECOND SPACE? — 7

THIRD SPACE? — 8

FOURTH SPACE? — 9

FIRST LINE? — 10

SECOND LINE? — 11

FIRST SPACE? — 12

SECOND SPACE? — 13

THIRD LINE? — 14

THIRD SPACE? — 15

FOURTH LINE? — 16

FOURTH SPACE? — 17

FIFTH LINE? — 18

THIRD LINE? — 19

FOURTH SPACE? — 20

FIRST LINE? — 21

FOURTH LINE? — 22

THIRD SPACE? — 23

SECOND SPACE? — 24

FIRST SPACE? — 25

25

25

MY TREBLE CLEF SIGN
IS SURE FUN TO DRAW.
MAKE IT SO BEAUTIFUL,
IT HASN'T A FLAW.

1. Start below the staff.
2. Curve to the right and straight up and above the staff about one space.
3. Curve to the right and down so you touch your treble clef line at the fourth staff line (D).
4. Continue and curve your line until it touches the first staff line (E).
5. Continue your curve, circling the second staff line (G).
6. Cross over your first treble clef line.

TOUCH D

TOUCH E

START →

line 5
line 4
line 3
line 2
line 1

Trace the dotted lines and then make your own lines. You will draw 50 treble clef lines.

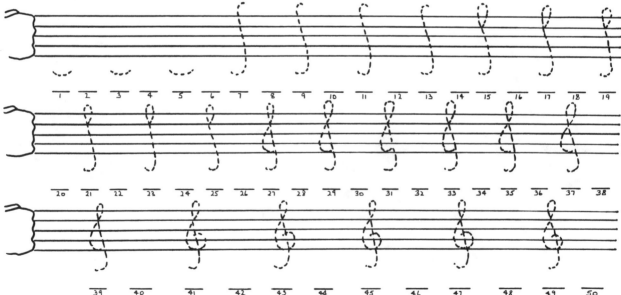

50

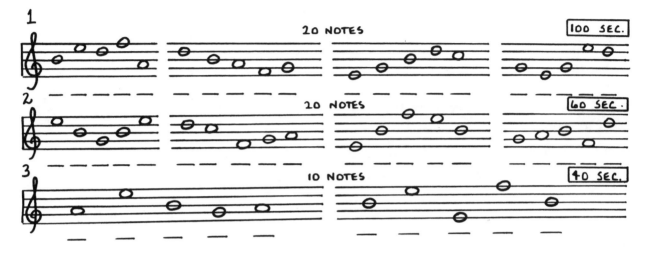

1 mark for each correct completed note

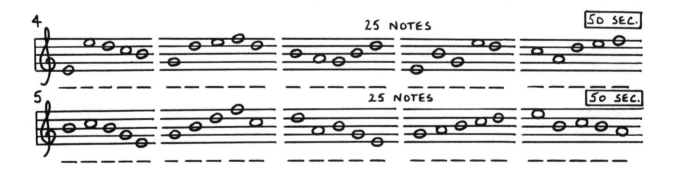

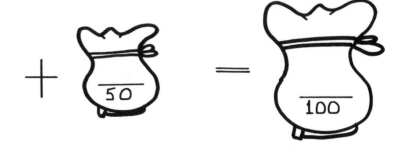

If you remember that *ledges* are outside buildings, you might remember that *ledger lines* are written outside the staff.

You can write notes on these lines or in between their spaces. See?

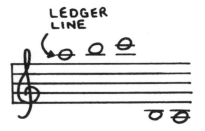

To find a note above the staff, start with the fifth line F and name notes alphabetically above F, until you arrive at the note name you want.

Try naming 25 notes using ledger lines.

If you remember that *ledges* are outside buildings, you might remember the *ledger lines* are written outside the staff.

You can write notes on these lines or in between their spaces. See?

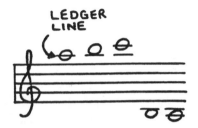

To find a note below the staff, start with the
first line E and name all the notes below E backwards
in the alphabet, until you arrive at the note you want.

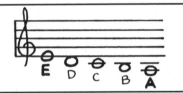

Try naming 25 notes using ledger lines.

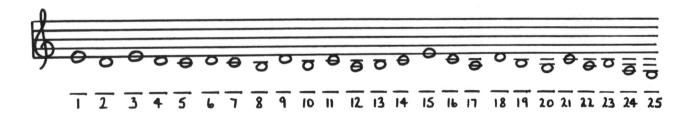

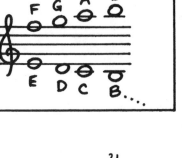

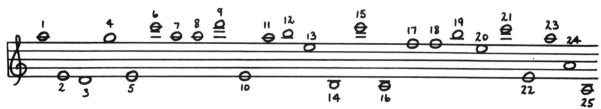

_ l___r lin_ is _lw_ys _in_
__ov_ or _elow th_ st___.
__ sur_ to know
Not_s _lw_ys go
_n _lph____ti__l p_th.
S__?

_ _ _ _ _ _ _

_ _ _ _ _ _ _

G__!

SEE HOW YOU DO—
WITH THIS SHORT
REVIEW!

1. DRAW A TREBLE CLEF

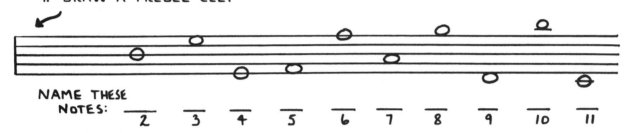

NAME THESE
NOTES: ‾2‾ ‾3‾ ‾4‾ ‾5‾ ‾6‾ ‾7‾ ‾8‾ ‾9‾ ‾10‾ ‾11‾

12. Are the notes ┃ F E D C B A ┃ going up or down? Check one: ✔

 up

down

Name the:

    13. fifth line ____
    14. second space ____
    15. fourth line ____
    16. third line ____

What number of line or space is C?
What number of line or space is B?

Write the following notes:

LINE OR SPACE?	NUMBER?
17.	
18.	

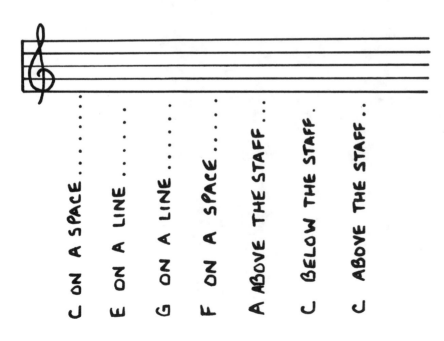

C ON A SPACE.........
E ON A LINE.........
G ON A LINE.........
F ON A SPACE.........
A ABOVE THE STAFF...
C BELOW THE STAFF..
C ABOVE THE STAFF..

25

BOREDOM BUSTER

Across

1. Staff lines and spaces are numbered _____.

4. Notes at the bottom of the staff sound _____.

5. The total number of lines and spaces in the staff is _____.

7. The seven letters used in music, from lowest to highest are _____.

8. Names of third line, first line, second line.

9. The spaces spell __ __ __ __.

12. There are _____ spaces in the staff.

14. Lines above or below the staff are _____ _____.

19. Are the lines FACE in the staff? Yes or no?

20. The five lines and four spaces for writing music is the _____.

21. The staff has five _____.

Down

2. The color of Mr. Treble Clef's tuxedo is _____.

3. Music is written on a _____ of five lines and four spaces.

4. Notes getting lower in sound have letter names that move _____ in the alphabet.

6. Names of the fourth space, second line, space above the staff.

10. C B A are notes that are moving _____. (Down or up?)

11. Mr. Treble Clef often says "_____" because the treble clef curls around G.

13. You can write notes above or below the staff on ledger _____.

15. __ __ __ __ __, are the names of the lines with the treble clef.

16. The treble clef's other name is the _____ _____.

17. Notes going higher in sound have names that move to the _____ in the alphabet.

18. The staff has four _____.

© 1990 by Parker Publishing Company

BOREDOM BUSTER

Write in the notes found in the staves below and then follow these letters around the hidden picture to the right. Always choose the closest letter you're asked for in the picture.

OK? Rock on!

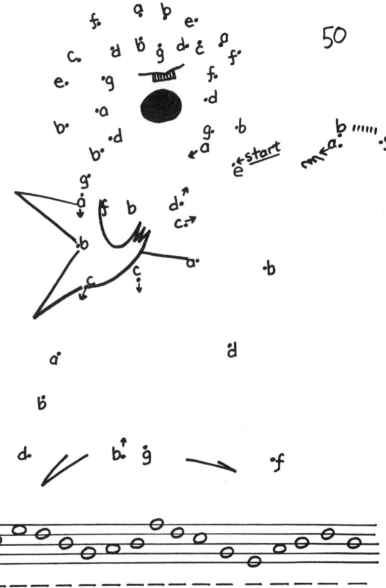

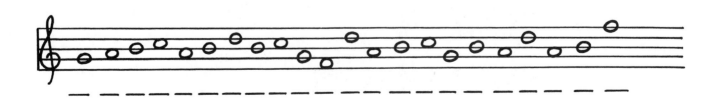

BOREDOM BUSTER

Answer the questions and fill in the correct spaces in the circle puzzle. Answers only move *clockwise* on the outside of the circle.

Clockwise

1. The names of the lines in the 𝄞 staff.
6. The "backwards S" at the beginning of the staff is called a _____ _____.
16. The name of the third space.
17. The treble clef's other name.
18. The name of the third space.
19. When notes are lower in sound, alphabet letter names move to the _____.
23. The 5 music lines are called the _____.
28. The name of the top line in the staff.
29. The name of the fourth line in the staff.
30. The name of the second space in the staff.

Towards the Center

1. Four notes moving in order down from F are E __ __ __.
4. Names of fourth line, second space, third space, fourth space.
7. When notes go higher
   If that's their goal
   To the *right* in the alphabet
   They will R __ __ L.
10. Soft music can L __ __ L you to sleep.
13. When notes go down in sound, their letter names move _____ in the alphabet.
16. E G B D F are the names of the lines with the treble _____.
19. You can write a note above or below the staff using the ledger _____.

When you've filled in all of the answer spaces, place the letters in the *pots* into the *secret circle*. Then rearrange these letters to discover what helps you to name notes in the staff.

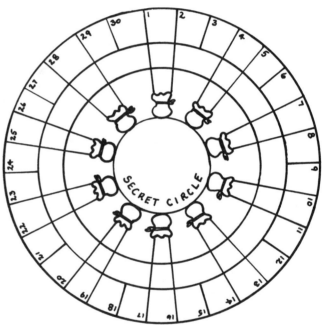

22. The story about Mr. Treble Clef in Musictown is a fairy _____ that teaches about music.
25. Names of second space, third line, second line, third space.
28. The staff has _____ spaces.

BOREDOM BUSTER

Start at the beginning and follow the word answers until you arrive at the Golden Pot of Musical Knowledge. Word answers can be across →

backwards ←

diagonal ↖ ↗ ↙ ↘

Trace your way to the Golden Pot of Musical Knowledge. There is only one way in. *Good luck!*

1. The names of the staff lines.
2. The G clef's other name.
3. Notes C, B, A are going higher or lower?
4. How many lines are in the staff?
5. The names of the spaces in the staff.
6. Notes C, F, G are going higher or lower?
7. The lowest line on the staff is _____.
8. Lines and spaces are named upwards or downwards?

9. The treble clef ends by curling around the line _____.
10. Lines above or below the staff are called _____ _____.
11. The name of line 4 is _____.
12. The name of space 2 is _____.
13. The name of line 5 is _____.
14. The name of line 1 is _____.
15. The name of line 3 is _____.
16. The name of space 1 is _____.
17. The space above the staff is _____.

E	G	B	D	F	A	C	E	D	C	A	L	C	A	P	O	R	E	P	E	A	T	Y	O	U	C	B	A
M	R	T	R	E	B	L	E	C	L	E	F	M	A	K	E	S	M	U	S	I	C	F	U	N	T	O	O
A	S	U	N	F	L	O	W	E	R	S	E	E	D	G	R	O	W	S	I	N	T	O	S	M	A	L	L
M	U	S	I	E	C	I	S	F	U	N	A	N	D	Y	O	U	C	N	A	A	M	K	E	I	T	E	V
S	E	E	Y	L	Y	O	I	R	F	R	I	S	D	A	F	E	B	E	N	D	S	M	R	B	A	S	S
L	O	U	D	C	D	V	D	C	A	L	C	A	E	P	O	A	N	F	D	S	A	L	C	O	D	A	T
A	B	C	D	E	E	F	G	H	I	J	K	L	M	N	O	P	Q	R	G	S	T	U	V	V	Y	Z	
F	I	N	D	L	S	F	O	M	E	G	R	E	A	T	I	E	X	C	I	T	I	N	G	M	O	M	
S	O	F	T	B	P	I	A	N	O	F	O	R	T	E	A	L	Q	U	I	E	T	T	I	M	E	S	S
S	O	N	A	E	T	E	A	C	S	O	N	A	T	E	A	R	R	F	O	R	M	C	R	E	S	C	E
B	E	A	T	R	B	E	A	T	E	B	E	A	T	L	E	S	T	E	S	A	X	O	P	H	O	N	E
R	O	C	K	T	I	M	E	S	A	H	M	E	T	R	O	N	O	M	G	E	A	F	T	E	R	W	E
B	A	C	H	F	M	O	Z	A	R	T	I	B	E	E	T	H	O	V	E	D	N	A	N	D	H	E	I
V	I	O	D	L	I	N	C	E	L	L	O	G	U	I	T	A	R	F	U	N	E	J	A	Z	Z	T	O
M	U	B	S	I	C	I	S	F	U	N	H	A	H	A	I	L	O	V	E	A	L	L	N	I	C	E	S
A	G	B	C	D	E	F	G	A	B	C	D	E	F	G	H	I	J	K	L	M	N	G	O	P	Q	R	
E	V	E	R	Y	S	I	N	G	E	R	N	I	C	E	R	E	U	P	W	A	R	D	S	T	O	T	O

START HERE

RULES TO "MUSIC 7-UP"

This is a variation of the "7-Up" game children like to play in class.

1. Seven children are chosen to come up to the front of the class. Each is given an Information Card.
2. Someone calls, "Heads down." Students in the class put their heads down and close their eyes.
3. The seven children with Information Cards each touch a seated person who then puts his thumb up, showing that he has been touched.
4. After seven students have been touched, someone calls, "Heads up. 7-Up!" The seven students who were chosen stand. One at a time, each of these students must identify who touched him and also identify that person's card correctly.
5. If the person is guessed correctly but not the Information Card the Cardholder turns the card over to reveal the correct answer, says "Right person, wrong answer" and remains a Cardholder. The guesser sits down. If the Information Card is guessed correctly but not the Cardholder, the Cardholder says, "Right answer, wrong person." The Cardholder stays at the front and the guesser sits down. If both the Information Card and the Cardholder are incorrectly guessed, the Cardholder reveals the card to show the correct answer and says, "Wrong person, wrong answer." The guesser sits down. **In all cases the correct answer should be given to students so everyone always experiences the correct information.**
6. After the seven guessers attempt to win a place as Cardholder, the new set of Cardholders have the seated students put "heads down" and the game begins again.

Make 30 laminated Information Cards (8½″ × 11″) for class
use in "Music 7-Up." Place answers (the letters shown below)
on backs of cards.

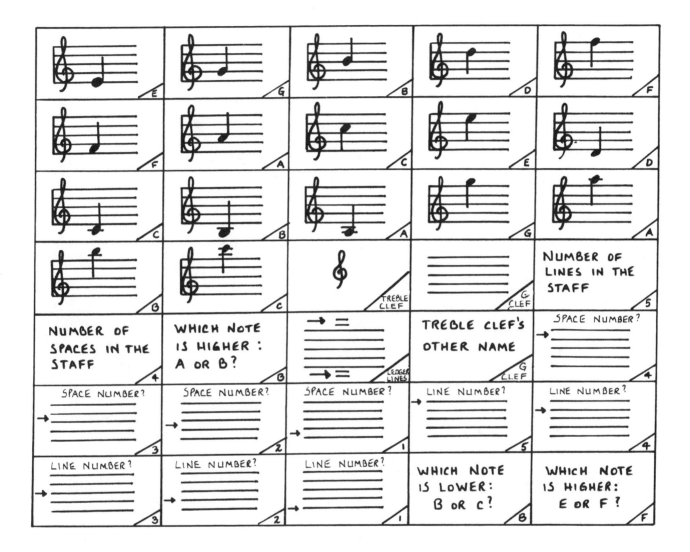

Student Evaluation Sheet

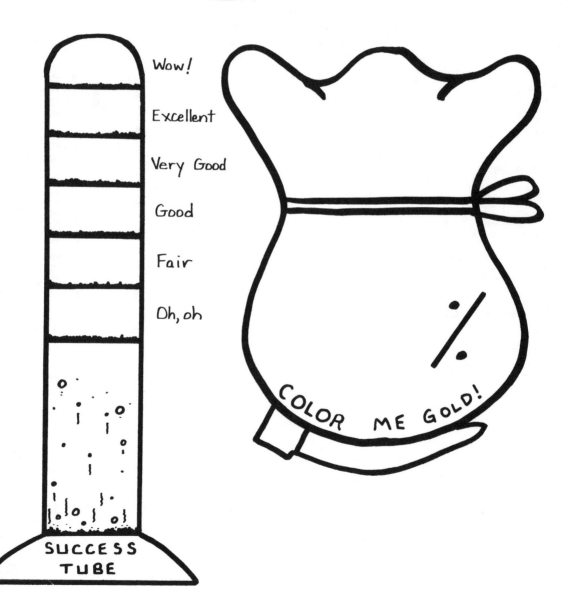

GEE, HOW DID YOU DO?
ASK YOUR TEACHER WHAT
MARK IS FOR YOU.

I HOPE ITS A LOT!
(YOUR PERCENT IN THE POT.)

NOW COLOR YOUR SUCCESS
IN THE TUBE!

Wow!

Excellent

Very Good

Good

Fair

Oh, oh

SUCCESS
TUBE

COLOR ME GOLD!

CHAPTER 1

CLASS RECORD SHEET

GRADE ☐ HOMEROOM TEACHER ☐ CLASS PERIOD/DAY ☐ YEAR ☐

Have students complete as many quizzes as necessary. All tests need not be completed. Write in students' names and fill in their marks in the squares below.

Column headers: SONG — UPSIDE DOWN

STUDENTS' NAMES | WORDS | MOTIONS | PITCHES | MUSICALITY | QUIZ 1-1 | QUIZ 1-2 | QUIZ 1-3 | QUIZ 1-4 | QUIZ 1-5 | QUIZ 1-6 | QUIZ 1-7 | QUIZ 1-8 | QUIZ 1-9 | QUIZ 1-10 | QUIZ 1-11 | QUIZ 1-12 | QUIZ 1-13 | QUIZ 1-14 | QUIZ 1-3 | QUIZ 1-4 | QUIZ 1-5 | QUIZ 1-6 | BB 1-1 | BB 1-2 | BB 1-3 | BB 1-4 | FINAL GRADE

PROGRESS OF CLASSES

A chart is given here to help you keep a record of the tasks your classes complete. After listing the class names in the top squares, indicate with a check mark (✔) or with the date that a task has been accomplished.

CHAPTER 1

LIST OF CLASSES									
= =			=	=	=	=	=	=	=
HAVE READ THE STORY									
HAVE STARTED THE SONG									
STUDENTS KNOW SONG									

HAVE COMPLETED QUIZ NO.	ACTIVITY	SKILL PRACTICED							
	1–1. Story review	naming staff, letter & no. names of notes, descending and ascending notes							
	1–2. Multiple choice	review of all Chapter 1 information							
	1–3. Name the lines	naming first 4 lines only							
	1–4. Name the lines	naming all 5 lines							
	1–5. Name the spaces	naming all spaces in the staff							
	1–6. Name lines and spaces	naming all lines and spaces in staff							
	1–7. Write in notes	writing in given notes in the staff							
	1–8. Identify numbered lines	given its number, identify lines and spaces							
	1–9. Draw treble clefs	practice 𝄞 step by step							
	1–10. Timed note-naming	lines-and-spaces naming							
	1–11. Notes on ledger lines	naming ledger line notes above staff							
	1–12. Notes on ledger lines	naming ledger line notes below staff							
	1–13. Ledger line notes	naming ledger line notes above and below the staff							
	1–14. Chapter review test	all chapter material plus ledger lines							
UPSIDE DOWN QUIZ NO.	1–3. Name the lines	naming first 4 lines only							
	1–4. Name the lines	naming all 5 lines							
	1–5. Name the spaces	naming all lines and spaces							
	1–6. Name the spaces	naming all lines and spaces							
BOREDOM BUSTER NO.	1–1. Crossword puzzle	review of all chapter material							
	1–2. Hidden picture	naming notes in the staff							
	1–3. Circle puzzle	review of all chapter material							
	1–4. Letter puzzle	review of all chapter material							
GAME: MUSIC 7-UP									

CHAPTER 1 ANSWER KEY

Quiz 1–1

1. staff	6. ABCDEFG	11. line G	16. D	21. E
2. five (lines)	7. lower	12. E	17. F	22. bottom
3. four (spaces)	8. treble	13. E	18. F	23. upwards
4. low	9. clef	14. G	19. A	24. floors
5. high	10. G (clef)	15. B	20. C	25. apartment buildings

Quiz 1–2

1. c	6. c	11. a	16. a	21. b
2. b	7. b	12. a	17. c	22. b
3. a	8. a	13. b	18. b	23. b
4. c	9. b	14. c	19. c	24. c
5. a	10. a	15. c	20. b	25. c

Quiz 1–3

1. E	11. E	21. B	31. B	41. E
2. G	12. G	22. G	32. E	42. G
3. E	13. E	23. E	33. G	43. B
4. G	14. E	24. G	34. E	44. D
5. G	15. G	25. B	35. B	45. G
6. E	16. B	26. G	36. G	46. B
7. G	17. E	27. B	37. B	47. D
8. E	18. G	28. G	38. G	48. E
9. E	19. B	29. B	39. B	49. D
10. G	20. G	30. G	40. E	50. B

Quiz 1–3 Upside Down

50. B	40. F	30. D	20. D	10. D
49. G	39. B	29. B	19. B	9. F
48. F	38. D	28. D	18. D	8. F
47. G	37. B	27. B	17. F	7. D
46. B	36. D	26. D	16. B	6. F
45. D	35. B	25. B	15. D	5. D
44. G	34. F	24. D	14. F	4. D
43. B	33. D	23. F	13. F	3. F
42. D	32. F	22. D	12. D	2. D
41. F	31. B	21. B	11. F	1. F

Quiz 1–4

1. E	11. B	21. B	31. E	41. D
2. D	12. D	22. D	32. G	42. B
3. G	13. B	23. E	33. B	43. F
4. D	14. G	24. B	34. F	44. E
5. E	15. E	25. D	35. G	45. F
6. G	16. G	26. F	36. B	46. B
7. B	17. B	27. E	37. D	47. D
8. D	18. D	28. F	38. E	48. E
9. G	19. G	29. E	39. B	49. G
10. E	20. B	30. D	40. G	50. F

Quiz 1–4 Upside Down

50. E	40. D	30. G	20. B	10. F
49. D	39. B	29. F	19. D	9. D
48. F	38. F	28. E	18. G	8. G
47. G	37. G	27. F	17. B	7. B
46. B	36. B	26. E	16. D	6. D
45. E	35. D	25. G	15. F	5. F
44. F	34. E	24. B	14. D	4. G
43. E	33. B	23. F	13. B	3. D
42. B	32. D	22. G	12. G	2. G
41. G	31. F	21. B	11. B	1. F

Quiz 1–5

1. F	11. F	21. E	31. A	41. F
2. A	12. A	22. F	32. C	42. A
3. F	13. F	23. E	33. E	43. C
4. A	14. A	24. A	34. A	44. E
5. A	15. C	25. E	35. F	45. F
6. F	16. A	26. C	36. A	46. A
7. F	17. C	27. F	37. C	47. C
8. A	18. A	28. A	38. F	48. E
9. A	19. F	29. C	39. A	49. C
10. F	20. C	30. F	40. C	50. A

Quiz 1–5 Upside Down

50. C	40. A	30. E	20. A	10. E
49. A	39. C	29. A	19. E	9. C
48. F	38. E	28. C	18. C	8. C
47. A	37. A	27. E	17. A	7. E
46. C	36. C	26. A	16. C	6. E
45. E	35. E	25. F	15. A	5. C
44. F	34. C	24. C	14. C	4. C
43. A	33. F	23. F	13. E	3. E
42. C	32. A	22. E	12. C	2. C
41. E	31. C	21. F	11. E	1. E

Quiz 1–6

1. E	21. C	41. F	61. A	81. B
2. F	22. B	42. C	62. G	82. D
3. G	23. C	43. F	63. E	83. A
4. F	24. B	44. E	64. F	84. D
5. E	25. A	45. D	65. D	85. A
6. G	26. B	46. B	66. C	86. D
7. F	27. C	47. D	67. B	87. A
8. E	28. B	48. F	68. G	88. E
9. F	29. A	49. D	69. C	89. G
10. G	30. G	50. C	70. G	90. B
11. A	31. D	51. B	71. G	91. A
12. G	32. C	52. D	72. A	92. D
13. A	33. D	53. A	73. D	93. B
14. G	34. A	54. A	74. A	94. G
15. F	35. D	55. C	75. D	95. D
16. A	36. A	56. E	76. A	96. F
17. B	37. D	57. F	77. B	97. D
18. A	38. G	58. G	78. E	98. A
19. G	39. D	59. A	79. F	99. B
20. E	40. A	60. B	80. B	100. C

Quiz 1–6 Upside Down

100. A	80. B	60. B	40. C	20. F
99. B	79. E	59. C	39. G	19. D
98. C	78. F	58. D	38. D	18. C
97. G	77. B	57. E	37. G	17. B
96. E	76. C	56. F	36. C	16. C
95. G	75. G	55. A	35. G	15. E
94. D	74. C	54. B	34. C	14. D
93. B	73. G	53. C	33. G	13. C
92. G	72. C	52. G	32. A	12. D
91. C	71. D	51. B	31. G	11. C
90. B	70. D	50. A	30. D	10. D
89. D	69. A	49. G	29. C	9. E
88. F	68. D	48. E	28. B	8. F
87. C	67. B	47. G	27. A	7. E
86. G	66. A	46. B	26. B	6. D
85. C	65. G	45. G	25. C	5. F
84. G	64. E	44. F	24. B	4. E
83. C	63. F	43. E	23. A	3. D
82. G	62. D	42. A	22. B	2. E
81. B	61. C	41. E	21. A	1. F

Quiz 1–7

1. 𝄞 correctly drawn	11. 𝄞 correctly drawn	21. 𝄞 correctly drawn	31. 𝄞 correctly drawn	41. 𝄞 correctly drawn
2. space 1	12. line 3	22. space 1	32. line 5	42. space 4
3. space 4	13. line 2	23. line 1	33. space 1	43. line 1
4. space 3	14. line 1	24. space 2	34. line 1	44. line 5
5. space 2	15. line 4	25. line 2	35. space 3	45. space 1
6. space 1	16. line 5	26. space 3	36. line 3	46. line 4
7. space 2	17. line 2	27. line 3	37. space 4	47. space 3
8. space 4	18. line 1	28. space 4	38. line 2	48. line 3
9. space 3	19. line 3	29. line 4	39. space 2	49. space 2
10. space 1	20. line 4	30. space 3	40. line 4	50. line 2

Quiz 1–8

1. E	6. F	11. F	16. D	21. E
2. G	7. A	12. G	17. E	22. D
3. B	8. C	13. A	18. F	23. C
4. D	9. E	14. B	19. B	24. A
5. F	10. E	15. C	20. E	25. F

Quiz 1–9

Quickly check through the student's sheet and give one mark for each correctly drawn line. Have students repeat the page to attain a higher mark if you wish.

Quiz 1–10

This is a timed notewriting test. Give one mark for each correct note written within the allotted time.

Staff 1: BEDFA, DBAFG, EGBDC, GEGED
Staff 2: EBGBE, DBFGA, EBFEB, GABFD
Staff 3: AEBGA, BEEFB
Staff 4: EEDCB, GDEFD, BAGBD, EBGED, CADEF
Staff 5: BDBGE, GBDFC, DABGE, GABCD, EBCBA

Quiz 1–11

1. F	6. G	11. G	16. A	21. C
2. G	7. A	12. B	17. C	22. B
3. F	8. G	13. G	18. G	23. A
4. G	9. A	14. C	19. B	24. G
5. A	10. B	15. F	20. D	25. B

Quiz 1–12

1. E	6. D	11. C	16. C	21. C
2. D	7. C	12. A	17. A	22. A
3. E	8. B	13. B	18. D	23. B
4. D	9. D	14. C	19. B	24. F
5. C	10. B	15. E	20. G	25. E

Quiz 1–13

1. A	11. A	21. E	31. A	41. G
2. E	12. B	22. E	32. A	42. A
3. D	13. E	23. A	33. E	43. B
4. G	14. B	24. A	34. E	44. C
5. E	15. E	25. A	35. A	45. D
6. E	16. A	26. A	36. B	46. E
7. A	17. F	27. A	37. C	47. F
8. A	18. F	28. B	38. D	48. G
9. F	19. B	29. E	39. E	49. E
10. E	20. E	30. C	40. F	50. E

Quiz 1–14

1. 𝄞 correctly drawn
2. B
3. E
4. E
5. F
6. F
7. A
8. G
9. D
10. B
11. C
12. down
13. F
14. A
15. D
16. B
17. third space
18. third line

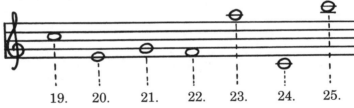

19.   20.   21.   22.   23.   24.   25.

Boredom Buster 1–1

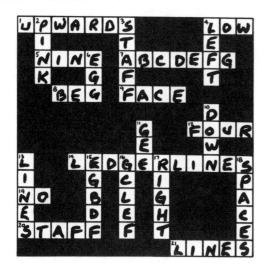

Boredom Buster 1–2

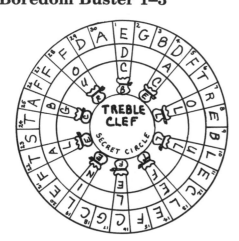

Boredom Buster 1–3

Boredom Buster 1–4

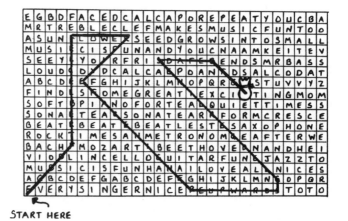

CHAPTER 2

Mac Discovers
Beat and Rhythm

One day, Mac hopped onto his bike to ride over to Christina's house. She lived four miles from him but she had asked him to come over for a special surprise. He didn't want to disappoint her. After all, they were very good friends.

On the way over, Mac began to feel a bit bored and so he kept himself occupied by singing to himself:

E G B D F
Are the names of the lines with the treble clef.
F A C E :
The spaces, are easy!

Before reading this story, review the events of the first story.
Then ask:
What are the lines? (EGBDF)
What are the spaces? (FACE)
How are lines and spaces numbered? (upwards)
What is BEAT? (a steady pulse)
What is RHYTHM? (changing note values)

He was feeling pretty tired from watching a TV special the night before and so about half way to Christina's house, he stopped to rest on a lawn next to the sidewalk.

"I'm bushed!" he said to himself and lay down under a small tree that had berries hanging from it. He squinted up at the tree and thought to himself that the berries looked like music notes. He felt something in his shirt pocket. As he felt what it was with his hand he drifted off to sleep.

"Hi!" chimed a familiar voice and there in front of Mac was old Mr. Treble Clef perched right on top of a tree!

"I see you are admiring my notes!" bellowed Mr. Treble Clef.

"Those are actually notes up there on that tree, Mr. Treble Clef?" asked Mac.

"Gee, but of course they're notes," sang the old man and then he threw himself off the tree with such force that a bunch of notes fell off the tree with him.

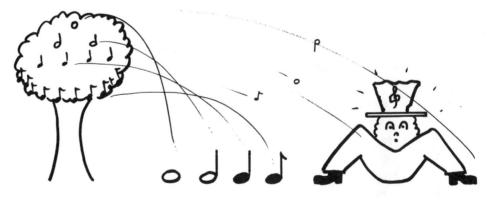

Point out each type of note on the tree or draw them on the board.

Some notes were like circles; some were like circles with stems. Other notes were like black circles with stems and some of these had tails too!

"Watch!" said Mr. Treble Clef with a big smile on his face and he began to clap an *even beat*. Soon Mac joined in with enthusiasm. Just then the notes came to life.

40

"Look at my notes," crooned Mr. Treble Clef and then he sang:

> The "circle" is the *whole note*
> In the staff it will sit.
> Sing or play or tap away
> But *play four beats to it.*

Point out the whole note here or draw it on the board.

And as soon as the old man said we should *"play four beats"* of sound when we see a whole note, a nicely shaped whole note jumped up and onto Mr. Treble Clef's staff and the old gentleman immediately sang a beautiful note for four beats.

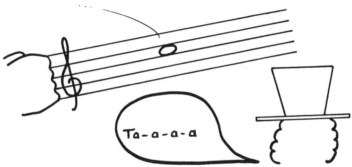

Point out this whole note and show it has four beats.

Mac giggled.

Then Mr. Treble Clef started to rhyme again:

> A "circle" with a stem is a *half note*
> Found on a space or a line
> Tap or sing,
> Do anything.
> But play *two beats* this time.

Show a half note.

And before you could say, "A half note gets two beats," a half note bounced onto Mr. Treble Clef's staff. Right away, Mac and Mr. Treble Clef sang the most beautiful E for two beats.

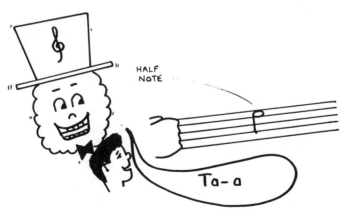

Demonstrate that half notes are two beats long.

Show the quarter note, telling them it gets one beat.

And then, faster than you could say "A whole note gets *four* beats and a half note gets *two* beats," a jet black *quarter note* screamed over and settled itself right on the middle line B, on the staff. It went "zoop" as it landed.

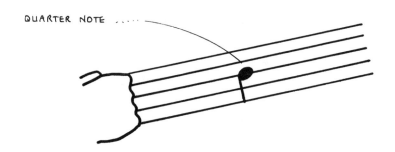

Mr. Treble Clef sang:

> Quarter notes, black with a stem
> They do get one beat
> Tap your foot but just one time
> And play!—a simple feat.

And so Mac began to sing too. Mr. Treble Clef and Mac sang any notes they found on the staff. With whole notes they sang for *four* beats and with half notes, they sang for *two* beats. Whenever they found a quarter note they sang for *one* beat.

Mr. Treble Clef sang for joy:

> Quarter notes get *one* beat,
>   Tah, tah, tah, tah!
> Half notes they get *two* beats,
>   Ta-ah! Ta-ah!
> Four beats for the whole note:
>   Ta-a-a-ah, Ta-a-a-ah, Ta-a-a-ah, 1-2-3-4!

"What about these, Mr. Treble Clef?" asked Mac.

Show eighth notes here or on the board.

Mac was pointing at the bunch of black notes with stems *and* tails that were moving toward him.

"These are *eighth notes* and you play *two* of these in *one beat*," said Mr. Treble Clef. "Every time you tap a quarter note beat with your foot, you sing or play two eighth notes. In other words, *two* eighth notes take up the same time as *one* quarter note."

Right away two quarter notes and four eighth notes hopped up onto the staff.

Demonstrate eighth notes played against quarter notes.

Point out the eighths and quarters. Show that two eighth notes take up the same time as one quarter note.

Mr. Treble Clef sang the two quarter notes found at the bottom of the staff. He gave each one beat, singing "Tah, tah." Mac sang the eighth notes, singing "Ti-ti-ti-ti." Each time Mr. Treble Clef sang one quarter note, Mac sang two evenly spaced eighth notes.

"Mr. Treble Clef, eighth notes are heard twice as often as quarter notes. Quarter notes get one beat. Do eighth notes get *one-half a beat*?" asked Mac.

"That's correct!" bellowed the old man, and then he continued:

> The eighth note gets one half a beat;
> Two eighths in a *quarter*! (Really neat!)

"When all the different notes sing their sounds at the same time, it sounds fantastic!" exclaimed Mac "And, they do it to a *steady beat*!"

Write ♩♩♩♩♩♩ on the board and say this is *beat*—then write ♩♩♪♪♩ on the board and say this is *rhythm*.

"Right," sang Mr. Treble Clef and then he sang:

> *Rhythm* is the *changing value* of the notes you hear in song.
> The *beat* is the pulse that stays the same.
> How can you go wrong?

And so Mac learned that notes can be long or short. Some notes are played for several beats and some are played for just one beat, or even less, like the eighth note. And altogether the short and long notes sounding at different times together make a *rhythm*.

"Music is wonderful!" exclaimed Mac. He clapped and danced to the steady beat and the changing rhythm and then began to feel a bit tired. He let out a big sigh.

"I'm bushed," he said and lay down under the shade of the note tree. He was feeling quite sleepy. His head felt like a huge golden pot just stuffed with musical knowledge. He was starting to doze off when . . . "Bonk!" One of the quarter notes fell out of the tree and onto his head. He quickly looked up with a start. Gazing up at the tree, he noticed that the notes were now black berries hanging from long stems and that he was lying on a lawn next to the sidewalk.

"I fell asleep!" he said. "I was dreaming . . . but it sure seemed like I was actually in Musictown. But that's crazy! I don't have the coin with me. Oh well, I'd better get over to Christina's house. I must be very late."

Mac scrambled onto his bike and raced to Christina's house as fast as he could. When he arrived, he knocked on the door and Christina greeted him.

"You're late, Mac. What happened?" she asked.

"I fell asleep and dreamt that I was in Musictown with Mr. Treble Clef. It sure seemed real, though. But I don't have the coin," he puzzled.

"You were tired from staying up late last night. You probably dreamt it all when you slept," she said.

Just then, Mac felt something pressing against his chest and he automatically reached for his shirt pocket.

"Hey!" Mac exclaimed, "What's this?" He put his hand into his shirt pocket and there was the coin.

Mac and Christina looked up at each other and after a short, thoughtful silence, Christina uttered, "Gee, Mr. Treble Clef. . . ."

Ask students to name and tell how many beats are in:
1. o (Whole note −4 beats)
2. ρ (Half note −2 beats)
3. ♩ (Quarter note −1 beat)
4. ♪ (Eighth note −½ beat)
Ask: What is *beat*? (A steady pulse)
What is *rhythm*? (Changing note values being heard)

SUGGESTIONS FOR TEACHING THE SONG,
The Rhythm Song

1. Perform *The Rhythm Song* for your class or play the tape at least twice.
2. Go through the words with your students, making sure that they understand the meaning of the words.
3. Teach line 1 by rote with a steady tempo, using correct word rhythms. Teach the body motions at the same time. This helps students to learn note values because they can "feel" them. Now teach line 2. Put lines 1 and 2 together and so on. After learning one verse well, have students learn another verse, until all are memorized.
4. When teaching *The Rhythm Song* as a *round*, begin with two parts only. After this is done successfully, teach 3 parts and afterwards, 4 parts.
5. Teach by rote *with* or *without* pitches as necessary at first. Add pitches at an appropriate time.
6. Have a ball!

THE BODY MOTIONS

bar: 3, 4	Clap or tap the rhythm of the words.
5, 6	Clap quarter note beats.
7, 8	Point your index finger, on each beat.
9	Form half notes with two hands on every second beat.
10	With two fingers, count 1-2, 1-2 on the beat.
11	Form a whole note with two hands and pulse it for 4 beats.
12–14	Count 1-2-3-4 with fingers on each beat, in each bar.
15–18	Tap quarter notes with one foot and clap eighth notes at the same time. (If too difficult, only perform *one* task.)
19	Count 1-2-3-4 with fingers on each beat.
20	Count 1-2, 1-2 with fingers on each beat.
21	Point your index finger on each beat.
22	Tap 3 quarter notes with one foot and clap 6 eighth notes at the same time. (If too difficult, only perform *one* task.)

THE RHYTHM SONG

1. A steady even pulse is called a   a. heartbeat
      b. note
      c. beat

2. Short notes and long notes played at different times together make   a. beats
      b. rhythms
      c. notes

3. When you tap your foot evenly to a song, you tap the   a. rhythm
      b. beat
      c. notes

4. "Tah-tah, tah-tah," sung evenly are   a. beats
      b. rhythms
      c. "thank-you's"

5. o is a   a. half note
      b. whole note
      c. quarter note

6. ρ is a   a. whole note
      b. half note
      c. quarter note

7. ρ is a   a. half note
      b. quarter note
      c. eighth note

8. ρ is a   a. half note
      b. whole note
      c. eighth note

9. How many *beats* are in o?   a. 4
      b. 2
      c. 1

10. How many *beats* are in ♩?   a. 4
      b. 2
      c. 1

11. How many *beats* are in ♩?   a. 4
      b. 2
      c. 1

12. How many *beats* are in ♪?   a. 2
      b. 1
      c. ½

13. Is this a *beat* or a *rhythm?* ρ ρ ρ ρ   a. beat
      b. rhythm
      c. neither

14. Is this a *beat* or a *rhythm*? ♩♩♩
    a. beat
    b. rhythm
    c. both *a* and *b*
    ☐

15. How many *beats* does ♩ + ♩ add up to?
    a. 3
    b. 2
    c. 1
    ☐

16. How many *beats* does ♩ + ♩ add up to?
    a. 2
    b. 4
    c. 6
    ☐

17. How many *beats* does ♩ + ♩ add up to?
    a. 4
    b. 8
    c. 2
    ☐

18. How many *eighth* notes (♪) can you play during a quarter note (♩)?
    a. 2
    b. 1
    c. 4
    ☐

19. One "tah" would be one
    a. quarter note
    b. half note
    c. eighth note
    ☐

20. One "ti" would be one
    a. quarter note
    b. eighth note
    c. whole note
    ☐

21. "Tah-ah-ah-ah" would be one
    a. half note
    b. whole note
    c. quarter note
    ☐

22. "Tah-ah" would be one
    a. half note
    b. whole note
    c. quarter note
    ☐

23. What are these? o ♩
    a. half note and then a whole note
    b. whole note and then a half note
    c. quarter note and then a whole note
    ☐

24. How many *beats* in this? o + ♩ + ♩ =
    a. 6
    b. 7
    c. 5
    ☐

25. Rhythm and beat make music
    a. exciting
    b. fun
    c. both of these
    ☐ C

A free mark!
Gee!

Time is measured in seconds and minutes, highways are measured in miles or kilometers, but the length of music notes is measured in 1. _____. A steady quarter note pulse can be called the 2. _____. Notes played having changing lengths result in 3. _____. A whole note usually is given 4. _____ beats of sound but half notes are given 5. _____ beats. Quarter notes get 6. _____ beat and eighth notes get 7. _____ - _____ of a beat. When you sing a quarter note you can call it 8. _____. Half notes can be sung 9. _____ and whole notes can be sung 10. _____. Eighth notes, getting one half of a beat each, are sung with the syllable 11. _____. Since $\quarternote$ is given one beat, $\quarternote\ \quarternote\ \quarternote$ must take up 12. _____ beats of musical time. Since $\halfnote$ gets two beats, $\halfnote\ \halfnote\ \halfnote$ must get 13. _____ beats of musical time. The $\wholenote$ gets four beats, so $\wholenote\ \wholenote$ must receive 14. _____ beats of musical time. I wonder if I can add up the number of beats in these notes:

15. $\wholenote + \quarternote$? _____   18. $\quarternote + \eighthnote$? _____

16. $\halfnote + \halfnote + \halfnote + \quarternote$? _____   19. $\wholenote + \wholenote + \quarternote$? _____

17. $\wholenote + \wholenote + \quarternote$? _____   20. $\wholenote + \wholenote + \wholenote$? _____

So, rhythm is the 21. _____ _____ of the 22. _____ you hear in songs and the beat is the 23. _____ that stays the 24. _____. How can you go 25. _____?

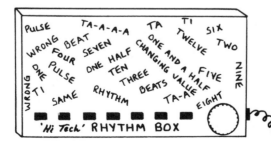

PULSE TA-A-A-A TA TI SIX
WRONG BEAT SEVEN ONE AND TWELVE TWO
ONE FOUR PULSE ONE HALF CHANGING A HALF FIVE
WRONG TI TEN THREE VALUE NINE
SAME RHYTHM BEATS TA-AE EIGHT

'Hi Tech' RHYTHM BOX

25

NAME _____

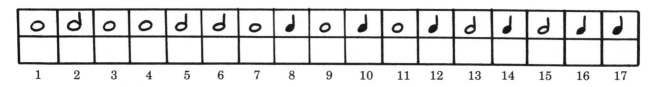

NAME _____

Quiz 2–4

I WONDER HOW MANY QUESTIONS
OF THESE YOU CAN DO!
WRITE IN THE SQUARES
IF THEY'RE <u>FALSE</u> OR THEY'RE <u>TRUE</u>.

© 1990 by Parker Publishing Company

1. ♩ is a *quarter* note.

2. o is a *whole* note.

3. ♩ is a *half* note.

4. ♪ is an *eighth* note.

5. ♩ has 1 beat.

6. ♩ has 2 beats.

7. o has 4 beats.

8. ♪ has ½ beat.

9. ♩ + ♩ = 3 beats.

10. ♩ + ♩ = 3 beats.

11. ♩ + ♩ = 3 beats.

12. o + ♩ = 6 beats.

13. ♩ + ♩ + ♩ = 4 beats.

14. o + ♩ = 6 beats.

15. ♩ + ♩ + ♩ = 5 beats.

16. ♩ + o = 6 beats.

17. ♩ + ♩ + ♩ = 5 beats.

18. o + ♩ = 5 beats.

19. ♩ + ♩ + ♩ = 5 beats.

20. ♩ + ♩ + ♩ + ♩ = 6 beats.

21. ♪ = ½ beat.

22. ♪ + ♪ = 1 beat.

23. o + ♪ = 4½ beats.

24. ♩ + o = 4 beats.

25. o + ♩ − ♩ = 6 beats.

25

WELL MY DEAR FRIEND
JUST HOW DID YOU DO?
PLACE YOUR MARK IN THE POT!
IT DOES BELONG TO YOU!

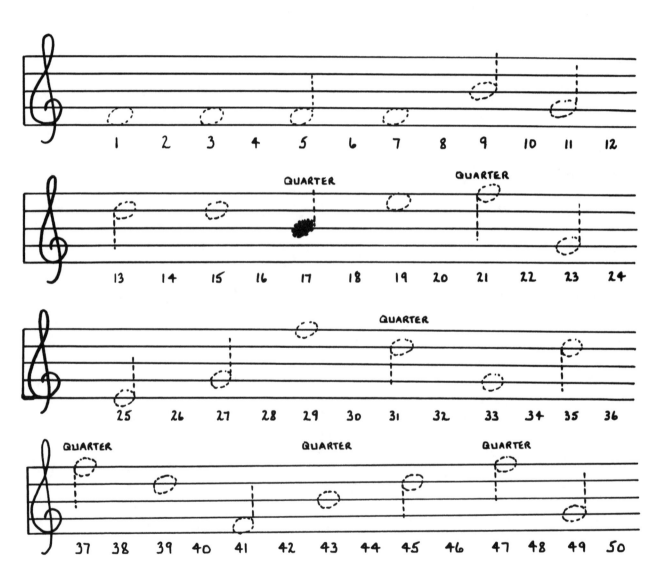

o = whole note
ρ = half note
• = quarter note
♪ = eighth note

A. HEADS AND STEMS

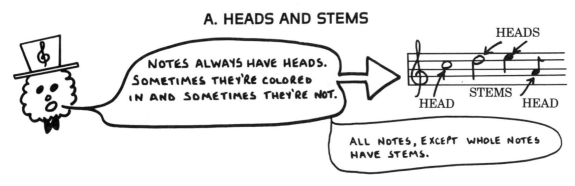

When note heads are on the third line, stems go up and to the right of note heads *or* down and to the left of note heads.

Note heads below the third line have stems that go up, and to the right.	Note heads above the third line have stems that go down, and to the left.

Place stems on these note heads, making half notes or quarter notes.

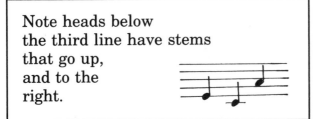

B. TAILS AND BEAMS

Notes with tails can be joined with a beam. Beams follow the same rules as tails.

When you beam a group of notes together that are both above and below the third line, stems should be in the direction determined by the majority of note heads.

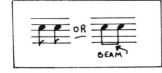

Place tails or beams correctly in the staff to make the notes indicated.

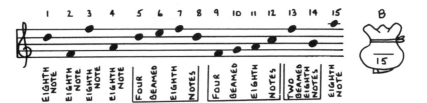

HEADS AND STEMS

NOTES ARE HIGH, NOTES ARE LOW.
NOTES ARE SHORT AND LONG.
DRAW THE NOTES I SAY BELOW,
TO MAKE A CATCHY SONG!

(All notes will be in the staff.)
Do not beam notes.

HOW MANY DID YOU GET RIGHT?
I HOPE THAT NONE WERE WRONG!
CONGRATULATIONS FOR DOING YOUR BEST
TO WRITE THIS SECRET SONG.

Look at each of the boxes below. If numbered boxes have correct information in them, place a check (✔) in the right boxes. If information is incorrect, place an ✖ in the right boxes.

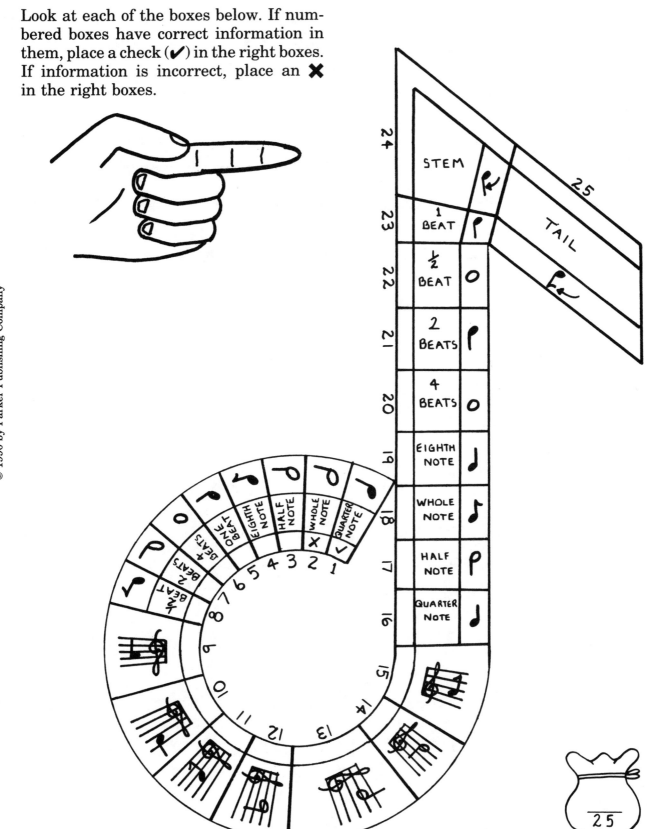

© 1990 by Parker Publishing Company

1. ♪ + ♪ =

2. ♪ + ♪ =

3. ♩ + ♩ =

4. ♪ + ♪ + ♪ + ♪ =

5. o + o =

6. ♩ + ♩ + ♩ + ♩ =

7. ♪ + ♪ + ♪ + ♪ + ♪ + ♪ + ♪ + ♪ =

8. ♪ + ♪ + ♪ + ♪ + ♪ + ♪ =

9. ♩ + ♩ + ♩ + ♩ =

10. ♪ + ♪ =

11. ♪ + ♪ + ♪ =

12. ♪ + ♪ =

13. ♪ + ♪ + ♪ =

14. ♩ + ♩ + ♩ =

15. ♩ + ♩ =

ANSWER WHAT I WROTE!
(ALL ANSWERS ARE 1 NOTE.)

16. ♩ + ♩ =

17. ♪ + ♪ =

18. ♪ + ♪ + ♪ + ♪ =

19. ♪ + ♪ =

20. o − ♩ =

21. ♩ − ♪ =

22. ♪ − ♪ =

23. o + ♩ − ♩ =

24. o − ♩ − ♩ =

25. ♩ + ♩ − ♩ =

2

25

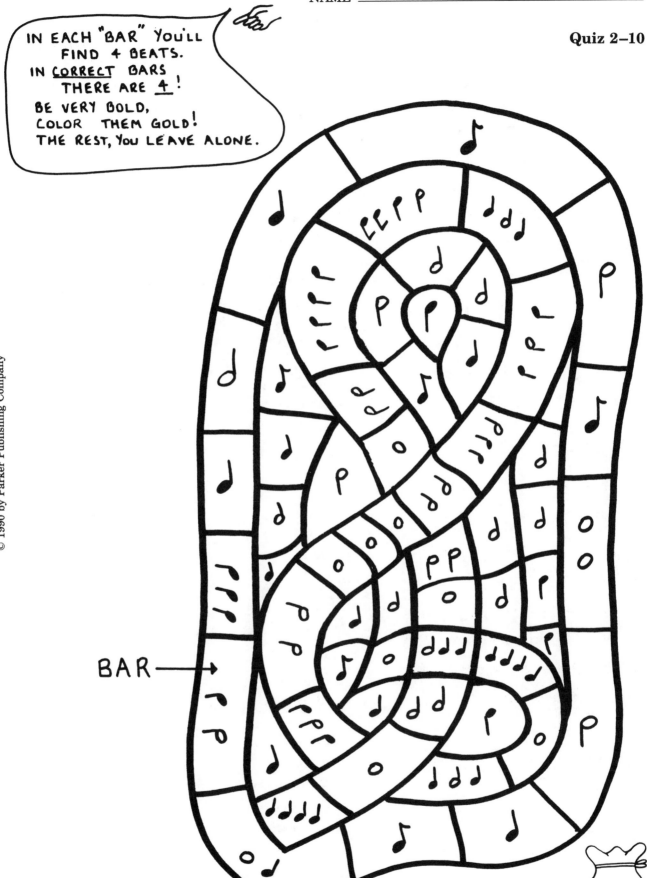

BAR →

SEE HOW MANY QUESTIONS YOU KNOW
FROM CHAPTERS ONE AND TWO.
SCRATCH YOUR BRAIN,
AND THINK AGAIN.
LET'S SEE HOW YOU DO!

Name the following:

1.
   a. treble clef
   b. staff
   c. music

2.
   a. treble clef
   b. staff
   c. music

3. The lines of the staff
   a. A B C D E
   b. E G B D F
   c. F A C E

4. The spaces of the staff
   a. C D E F G
   b. E G B D F
   c. F A C E

5.
   a. A
   b. G
   c. B

6.
   a. G
   b. E
   c. F

7.
   a. D
   b. C
   c. E

8.
   a. E F
   b. E G
   c. F G

9.
   a. F A C
   b. A B C
   c. C B A

10.
    a. line 1
    b. line 2
    c. clothesline

11.
    a. space ship
    b. space 3
    c. space 2

12.
    a. treble clef
    b. G clef
    c. both of these

13. 𝅝
    a. whole note
    b. half note
    c. quarter note
☐

14. 𝅗𝅥
    a. whole note
    b. half note
    c. quarter note
☐

15. ♩
    a. whole note
    b. half note
    c. quarter note
☐

16. ♪
    a. eighth note
    b. quarter note
    c. whole note
☐

17. 𝅝
    a. 4 beats
    b. 2 beats
    c. 1 beat
☐

18. 𝅗𝅥
    a. 4 beats
    b. 2 beats
    c. 1 beat
☐

19. ♩
    a. 1 beat
    b. 2 beats
    c. 4 beats
☐

20. ♪
    a. 2 beats
    b. 4 beats
    c. one half beat
☐

21. Changing value of notes
    a. rhythm
    b. beat
    c. music
☐

22. Steady, even pulse
    a. rhythm
    b. beat
    c. music
☐

23. Middle line stems always go
    a. upwards
    b. downwards
    c. both *a* and *b*
☐

24. Stems go
    a. up
    b. down
    c. sideways
☐

25. Stems go
    a. up
    b. down
    c. any direction
☐

BOREDOM BUSTER

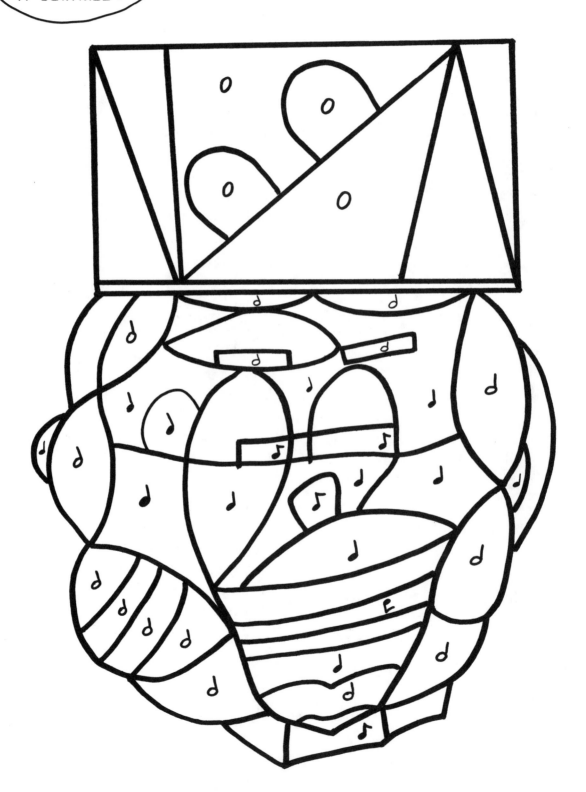

BOREDOM BUSTER

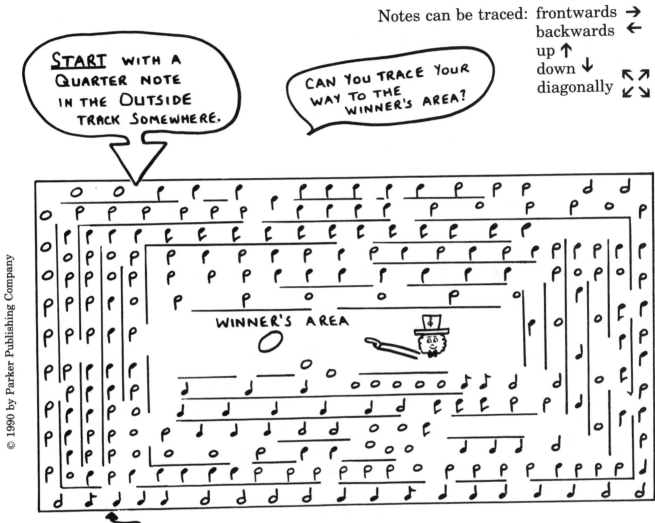

6 quarter notes
6 half notes
6 whole notes
6 eighth notes
8 whole notes

NAME _____

BB 2–3

BOREDOM BUSTER

MATCH UP THE ANSWERS OF THE TOP 37 QUESTIONS WITH THE BLANKS IN THE STORY BELOW.

1. 🎵 NOTE NAME? 2. ♩ ____ NOTE 3. 🎵 NOTE NAME? 4. ♩ ____ NOTE 5. 𝆶 ____ NOTE

6. ♪ ____ NOTE 7. STAFF LINES ARE NUMBERED 8. 🎵 9. 𝆶 ____ NOTE

10. ♩ ____ NOTE 11. 🎵 12. ♩ HOW MANY BEATS? 13. 𝅘𝅥 A NOTE ____

14. 𝄚 ← THE ____ LINE 15. ♪ NOTE ____ 16. 🎵 +T 17. ♪ NOTE ____ 18. ♪ ← NOTE ____

19. ♪ NOTE ____ 20. ♩ NO. OF BEATS? 21. 🎵 22. 🎵 23. ♪ 24. 𝆏𝆏𝆏𝆏 MAKES A STEADY ____

25. ♩♩♩♩ IS A ____ 26. 🎵 STEMS GO ____ 27. 🎵 ____ LINE 28. ____ CLEF 29. NOTE TAILS GO ____

30. ♩ HAS ____ BEATS 31. 𝄞 TREBLE ____ 32. OTHER NAME IS THE ____ CLEF 33. ♩ IS ____ BEAT

34. ♩ IS ____ BEATS 35. ♩♩ IS ____ BEATS 36. 🎵 +S 37. 𝄚 IS THE ____ .

1. _____ 2. _____ of 3. _____ million

years ago. 4. _____ of the people in the world wouldn't eat

their 5. _____ supper. They could only handle eating an

6. _____ of their feasts because dinosaur steaks were

so huge (7. _____ of a zillion pounds!) Most people couldn't

8. _____ eating a 9. _____ dinosaur!

Even 10. _____ of a dinosaur 11. _____ was

12. _____ much for breakfast. The father, the

13. _____ of the family might be able to eat a

14. _____ of a dinosaur 15. _____ at best. The

mother would never 16. _____ some 17. _____. This

probably 18. _____ med from the fact that 19. _____s

were usually 20. _____ tough because microwave ovens weren't in-

vented yet! Sometimes 21. _____ would 22. _____

the 23. _____ and 24. _____ it. Sometimes with a

musical 25. _____. That made it easier to eat. Moms would often

hang the meat 26. _____ over a 27. _____ perhaps

take the 28. _____ to hang-dry it just 29. _____ by

fastening it between 30. _____ 31. _____s. All in all,

something was usually done so that the family had a nice meal. Usually mom and

daddy would simply say 32. _____ to their 33. _____

or 34. _____ or 35. _____ children:

Numbers one, two, and three —

Let's take 36. _____'s 37. _____ and go
And munch some buttered popcorn
At the prehistoric show!

BOREDOM BUSTER

1. o = _____ beats.
4. Eighth note tails go _____.
8. F is the _____ line on the staff.
11. Staff lines.
15. First space.
16. _____ clef (𝄞).
21. ♪ is an _____ note.
26. There are two beats in a _____ note.
29. Fifth line.
30. Stems on notes below the third line point _____.
38. ♩← is a _____.
39. A beat needs a steady _____.

43. The staff has _____ 4 spaces.
46. Is the fourth line D?
48. What are F-A-C-E?
54. Lines above or below the staff are _____.
65. ♩ has _____ beat.
68. ♩ has _____ beats.
70. ♪ has _____ _____ of a beat.
77. ♩♩♪ is a _____.
83. Music uses _____ letters in the alphabet.
87. ♩♩♩♩ is a _____ a rhythm.

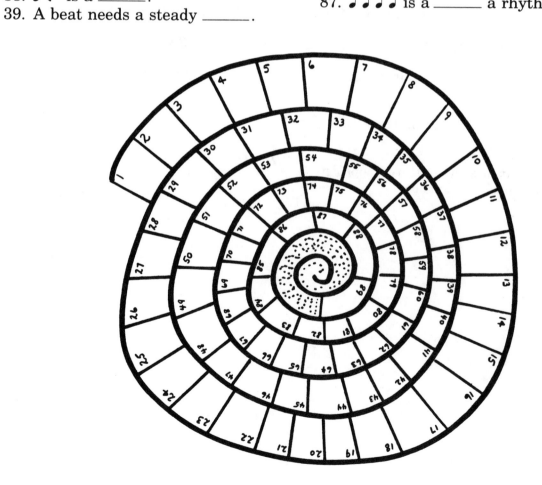

RULES TO "MUSIC HOPSCOTCH"

1. Two or more teams of equal numbers are formed.
2. Information Cards are laid on the floor, forming two hopscotch boards. The cards are question-side-up.
3. Each team lines up in front of one of the hopscotch boards and will play the game independently of the other team. One student referee is chosen for each team.

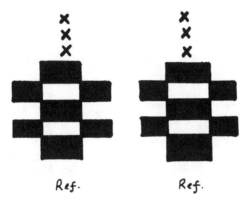

4. Each member from a team takes a turn at the hopscotch board. A player hops on one foot to the *side* of the first card, identifies it and if he is correct, he turns the card over, while standing on one foot. He is then allowed to try another card. As he guesses correctly, he continues to complete as many cards as possible. When a player is finished, he returns the cards to their original position.

    His cards are continually checked by the team referee who gives one point for each correct guess.
5. When the first student has finished guessing as many cards correctly as he can, the next student in the team takes his turn.
6. Points are added up by the referees after everyone has taken a turn. The winning team is determined by the higher score.

Note: Students are disqualified if they touch a card with their feet at any time. While "hopscotching," students hop on one foot only. A foot must land in front of the card to be picked and within the boundaries set by the cards.

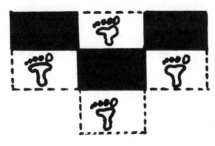

Touching the floor with hands also disqualifies the player. Marks acquired prior to disqualification are kept by the player. Make 30 cardboard laminated Information Cards (8½″ × 11″).

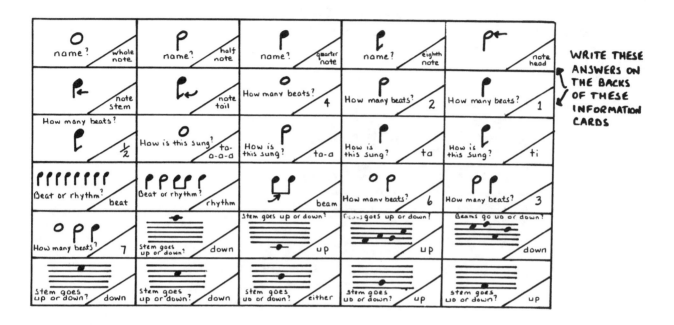

These cards can also be used with "Music 7-Up," if you wish.

Student Evaluation Sheet

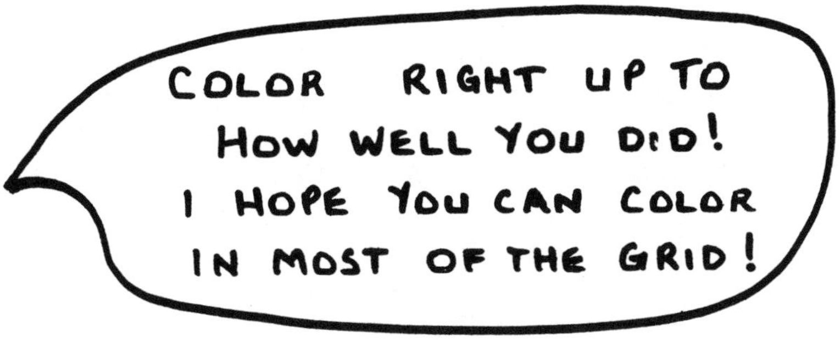

COLOR RIGHT UP TO
HOW WELL YOU DID!
I HOPE YOU CAN COLOR
IN MOST OF THE GRID!

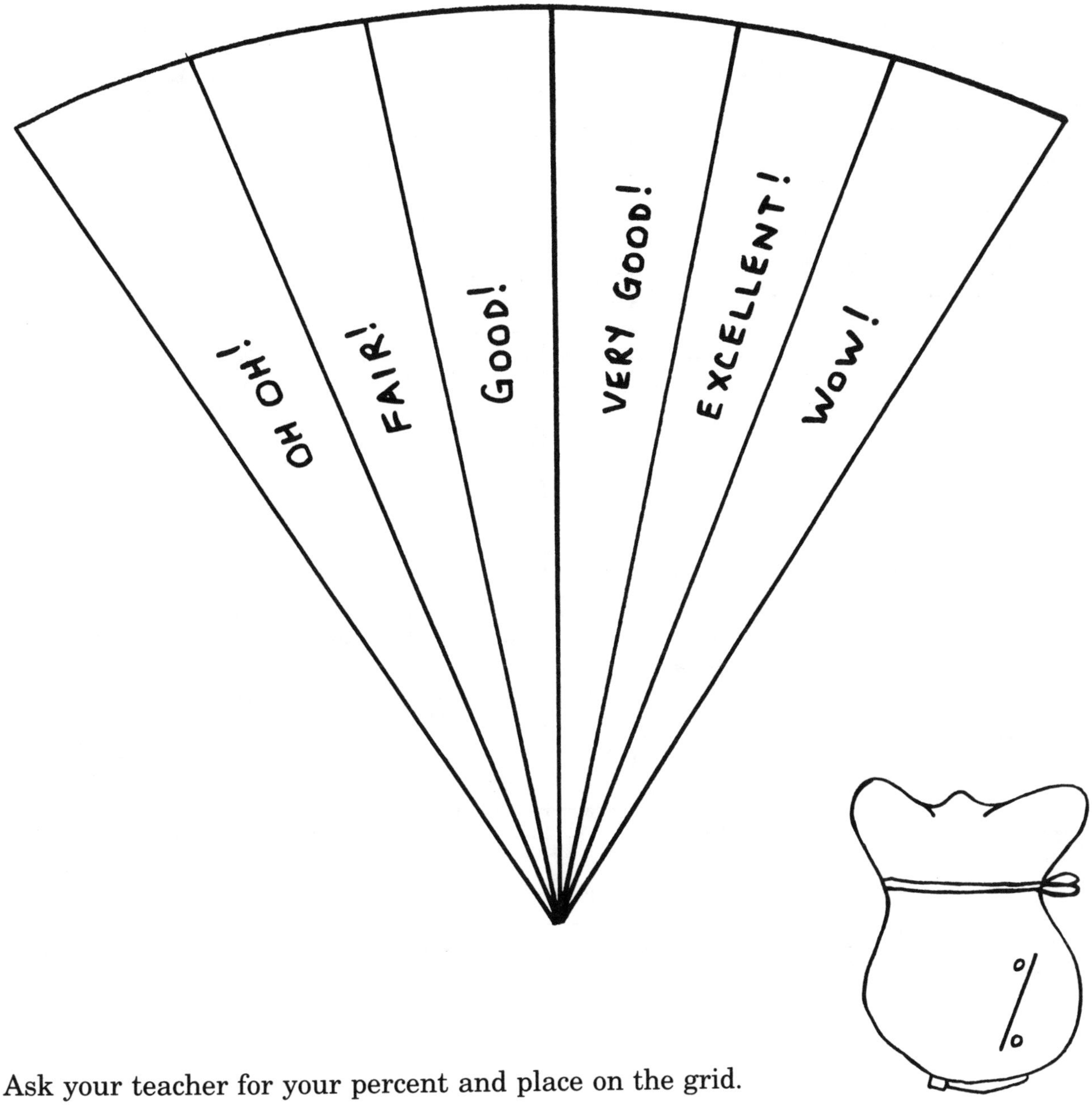

OH OH!

FAIR!

GOOD!

VERY GOOD!

EXCELLENT!

WOW!

%
%

Ask your teacher for your percent and place on the grid.

CHAPTER 2
CLASS RECORD SHEET

GRADE

HOMEROOM TEACHER

CLASS PERIOD/DAY

YEAR

Have students complete as many quizzes as necessary. All tests need not be completed. Write in students' names and fill in their marks in the squares below.

STUDENTS' NAMES	SONG				QUIZ 2-1	QUIZ 2-2	QUIZ 2-3	QUIZ 2-4	QUIZ 2-5	QUIZ 2-6	QUIZ 2-7	QUIZ 2-8	QUIZ 2-9	QUIZ 2-10	QUIZ 2-11	BB 2-1	BB 2-2	BB 2-3	BB 2-4	FINAL MARK
	WORDS	MOTIONS	PITCHES	MUSICALITY																

PROGRESS OF CLASSES

A chart is given here to help you keep a record of the tasks your classes complete. After listing the class names in the top squares, indicate with a check mark (✔) or with the date that a task has been accomplished.

CHAPTER 2

LIST OF CLASSES													
HAVE READ THE STORY													
HAVE STARTED THE SONG													
STUDENTS KNOW SONG													

HAVE COMPLETED QUIZ NO.	ACTIVITY	SKILL PRACTICED							
	2–1. Multiple choice	beat, rhythm							
	2–2. Word search	beat, rhythm, adding note values							
	2–3. Length of notes	naming values of 𝅝 𝅗𝅥 ♩ ♪							
	2–4. Adding note lengths	adding combinations of 𝅝 𝅗𝅥 ♩ ♪							
	2–5. Drawing notes	drawing 𝅝 𝅗𝅥 ♩							
	2–6. (a) Stems	drawing correct stems on notes							
	2–6. (b) Tails and beams	drawing correct tails and beams							
	2–7. Writing notes	writing given notes to the *Rhythm Song*							
	2–8. Answer finding	identify notes for beats, stem direction, and tails							
	2–9. Note math	adding and subtracting note values							
	2–10. 4-Beat puzzle	find "bars" having 4 beats							
	2–11. Multiple choice	review of all Chapter 2 material							
BOREDOM BUSTER NO.	2–1. Hidden face	identify 𝅝 𝅗𝅥 ♩ ♪							
	2–2. Note value puzzle	identify 𝅝 𝅗𝅥 ♩ ♪							
	2–3. Dinosaur dittie	review of Chapter 2 material							
	2–4. Spiral puzzle	review of Chapter 2 material							
GAME: MUSIC HOPSCOTCH									

CHAPTER 2 ANSWER KEY

Quiz 2–1

1. c	6. b	11. c	16. a	21. b
2. b	7. b	12. c	17. a	22. a
3. b	8. c	13. a	18. a	23. b
4. a	9. a	14. b	19. a	24. b
5. b	10. b	15. a	20. b	25. c

Quiz 2–2

1. beats	6. one	11. Ti	16. seven	21. changing
2. beat	7. one half	12. three	17. nine	value
3. rhythm	8. Ta	13. six	18. one and one	22. notes
4. four	9. Ta-a	14. eight	half	23. pulse
5. two	10. Ta-a-a-a	15. five	19. ten	24. same
			20. twelve	25. wrong

Quiz 2–3

1. 4	11. 4	21. 4	31. ½	41. ½
2. 2	12. 1	22. ½	32. 2	42. 1
3. 4	13. 2	23. 1	33. 1	43. 2
4. 4	14. 1	24. 4	34. ½	44. 4
5. 2	15. 2	25. 2	35. ½	45. 4
6. 2	16. 1	26. ½	36. ½	46. ½
7. 4	17. 1	27. 4	37. 1	47. 1
8. 1	18. 2	28. 4	38. 2	48. 4
9. 4	19. 4	29. 2	39. 4	49. 2
10. 1	20. 1	30. 1	40. 1	50. 1

Quiz 2–4

1. T	6. T	11. T	16. F	21. T
2. T	7. T	12. T	17. T	22. T
3. T	8. T	13. T	18. T	23. T
4. T	9. F	14. F	19. T	24. F
5. T	10. F	15. T	20. T	25. F

Quiz 2–5

Check to see that students have copied the appropriate notes on the staves.

Quiz 2–6

Quiz 2–7

Quiz 2–8

1. ✔	6. ✔	11. ✔	16. ✔	21. ✘
2. ✘	7. ✔	12. ✘	17. ✔	22. ✘
3. ✔	8. ✔	13. ✘	18. ✘	23. ✔
4. ✔	9. ✘	14. ✔	19. ✘	24. ✔
5. ✔	10. ✘	15. ✘	20. ✔	25. ✔

Quiz 2–9

1. 2	6. 8	11. 3	16. 𝅝	21. ♩
2. 2	7. 8	12. 1	17. ♩	22. ♩
3. 4	8. 6	13. 2	18. 𝅝	23. 𝅗𝅥
4. 4	9. 6	14. 4	19. ♩	24. 𝅗𝅥
5. 8	10. 2	15. 1½	20. ♩	25. 𝅗𝅥

Quiz 2–10

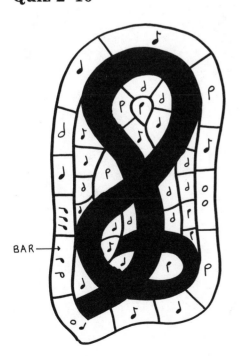

Quiz 2–11

1. b	6. b	11. b	16. a	21. a
2. a	7. b	12. c	17. a	22. b
3. b	8. a	13. a	18. b	23. c
4. c	9. b	14. b	19. a	24. b
5. b	10. a	15. c	20. c	25. a

Boredom Buster 2–1

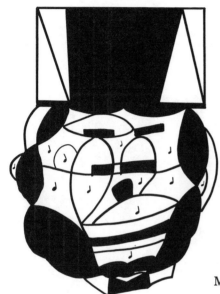

MR. TREBLE CLEF!

Boredom Buster 2–2

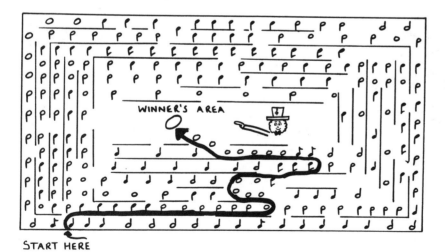

Boredom Buster 2–3

1. A
2. quarter
3. a
4. half
5. whole
6. eighth
7. upwards
8. face
9. whole
10. half
11. egg
12. two (too)
13. head
14. third
15. tail
16. eat
17. tail
18. stemmed
19. tails
20. two (too)
21. dad
22. age
23. tail
24. beat
25. rhythm
26. downwards
27. ledger
28. treble
29. right
30. two (too)
31. clefs
32. G (Gee)
33. one
34. two
35. three
36. dad's
37. staff

Boredom Buster 2–4

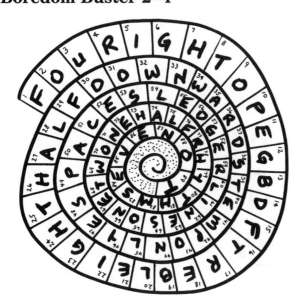

CHAPTER 3
The Kids Discover
Silence in Music

76

Mac and Christina were still thinking about Mac's last trip to Musictown when Mac broke the silence:

"Hey Christina, you said you had a surprise for me. What is it?" Secrets always drove Mac crazy.

"Look, I'll show you," Christina answered while lifting up a cover on the sofa, revealing a big pink top hat!

"Mr. Treble Clef's hat!" shouted Mac, ". . . but what's it doing here?"

"I don't know," said Christina, "but there's something funny about this hat. Watch! I'll show you. If I say anything in front of the hat, you can't hear my voice. It's as if the hat can *make silence.*"

"That's very strange," Mac said. "It seems like it's a magic hat and I'll bet that Mr. Treble Clef needs it. I wish we could give it back to him."

"You've got the coin," replied Christina. "Try rubbing it. Maybe Mr. Treble Clef will show up and we can give him his hat back."

"OK!" said Mac and he started to rub the coin. Immediately smoke began to pour out of the hat. The billowing clouds became thicker and thicker. Suddenly two old hands, dressed in pink cuffs pulled the children right into the hat, and then . . .

Poof! The children, the hat, and the smoke completely disappeared from sight.

"Gee, thanks for my hat!" rang a familiar voice. Mac and Christina gasped upon realizing they were back in Musictown.

"Hi, Mr. Treble Clef," shouted the children. "Your hat must be magic," added Christina. "When your hat's around, it makes *silence!*"

"That's right! I use my hat to make silences in music," the old man said.

"How?" Mac was getting very curious.

"Well," the old gentleman explained, "music isn't always just sound. Sometimes music has moments of *silence* in it and if you write musical signs in the staff, performers will be silent when they see these signs! Understand?"

"Sure," answered Mac. "What are the musical signs that make the silences in music?"

"Rests," sang Mr. Treble Clef. "*Rests are the silences in music.* If you see a rest in the staff that looks like my hat upside down, it tells you to be silent for *four* beats. It hangs below the fourth line and is called a *whole rest.*"

Before reading ask:
1. What happened in the last story?
2. What is

o? (whole note)

o? (half note)

o? (quarter note)

o? (eighth note)

3. How many beats in

o? (4)

o? (1)

o? (2)

o? (½)

4. How are these sung?

o (ta-a-a-a)

o (ta-a)

o (ta)

o (ti)

5. Clap a steady beat and ask if it's *rhythm* or *beat.* (beat) Why? (it's steady)
6. Clap changing note values and ask if it's *rhythm* or *beat.* Why? (it changes)

Show the whole rest.

"I see," said Mac. "What about shorter silences? What do they look like?"

"If you want to write *two* beats of silence, place a rest in the staff that looks like my hat sitting upright. This is a *half rest* and it sits on the middle line."

Show the half rest.

Now Christina was getting a bit worried and piped up, "How can we remember if the hat should be upright or upside down?"

Mr. Treble Clef knew somebody would ask this question and he answered, "Remember that the whole rest is *four beats* "big" and is so heavy with all of its beats, that it has to hang *below* the fourth line. The half rest is *two beats* "light" and can hold itself up, *above* the third line."

Show that the whole rest hangs down from line 4 and that the half rest sits on the third line.

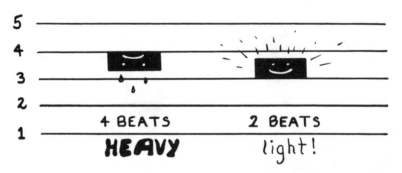

"A rest having one beat looks like a squiggle (𝄾). To draw a simple one, write a seven on top of another seven, like this:

Show the quarter rest.

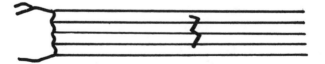

This is called a *quarter rest*."

"A shorter rest is an *eighth rest*. It's one-half of a beat long, and it looks like a '7.' Usually it's forwards. Sometimes it's backwards.

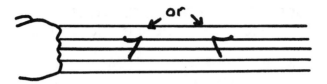

Show the eighth rest.

"You can make a silence any number of beats you want," bellowed Mr. Treble Clef, and then he burst into song, singing:

Say this *with* the class or sing it to them.

A *whole rest*, it gets *four* beats.
It's an upside-down hat.
Remember it hangs below the fourth line,
Because it's four beats fat!

A *half rest*, it gets *two* beats:
A hat that sits upright!
Sitting right above the third line,
Because it's two beats light.

A *quarter rest* gets *one* beat—
Seven-over seven! Correct!
Tap your shoe; one tap will do
One beat, quarter rest—perfect!

An *eighth rest* gets *one-half beat*—
Looks like a seven in the staff,
Backwards, forwards—ah, who cares?
The eighth rest is a laugh!

"That's neat!" exclaimed Mac and then he burst into song, singing:

Music is silence and sound,

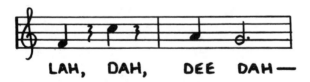

LAH, DAH, DEE DAH —

Say this with the class or sing it to them.

The sounds are *notes* and the silences—*rests*!
With sound and silence; music's the best!

The song Mr. Treble Clef and Mac sang was so catchy that Christina started to join in. To a steady beat they sang about *whole, half, quarter,* and *eighth rests*. They were so happy. They thought they could sing this song forever. . . .

Ask:
1. What is
➖? (whole rest)
➖? (half rest)
𝄽? (quarter rest)
𝄾? (eighth rest)
2. How many beats in
➖? (4 beats of silence)
➖? (2 beats of silence)
𝄽? (1 beat of silence)
𝄾? (½ beat of silence)

SUGGESTIONS FOR TEACHING THE SONG,
Music Needs Silence and Sound

1. Review the story material. Make sure that students know (a) notes make sounds and rests make silences, and (b) ▬ = 4 beats, ▬ = 2 beats, ♩ = 1 beat, ๆ = ½ beat of silence.
2. Play the tape of *Music Needs Silence and Sound* or perform it for your students. Make sure students know what the lyrics mean.
3. Let students hear the song again. (Students in grades 2–6 can follow the words.)
4. Teach each line by rote, including the body motions. Repeat each line successively, until students have memorized each line. Try to maintain an unbroken, steady beat while retaining the lyric rhythms. Eliminate pitches wherever necessary while teaching correct rhythms.
5. Have students completely memorize the song (with body motions, if possible). Move on to the quiz section after this is accomplished.
6. Enjoy!

THE BODY MOTIONS

bar: 5   Index finger covers mouth, as if saying "sh."
        6   Arm outstretched, palm up.
        7   Alternate between open mouth and "sh"-ing.
        8   Head rocks from side to side to side.
        9   On "sounds," hand cups ear.
             On "notes," make a whole note.
        10   "Sh" and pretend sleeping.
        11   Arms outstretched, and "sh."
        12   Cheering motion with arm.

Verse 1
bar: 14–29 Make whole, half rests and point 4 or 2 singers.
        21   Put hand over "fat" tummy.

Verse 2
bar: 15   Point one finger.
        16   Draw parts of ♮, each on a beat.
     18–19   Tap foot on each beat.
        20   Point index finger and pretend sleeping.
        21   Thumb up signifying "perfect."
        22   Draw an eighth rest in the air.
        23   Point bent (half of a) finger in the air.
     24–25   Stretch the drawing of ꓶ over 5 beats.
        26   Draw ꓶ backwards and forwards.
        27   Shoulders up, arms bent, palms up, then arms completely
             outstretched.
        28   Draw a ꓶ.
        29   Hand over tummy as if "belly-laughing."
        30   Arms bent, palms up.
             "Sh."
             Arms bent, palms up.
        32   Arms outstretched dramatically.

MUSIC NEEDS SILENCE AND SOUND

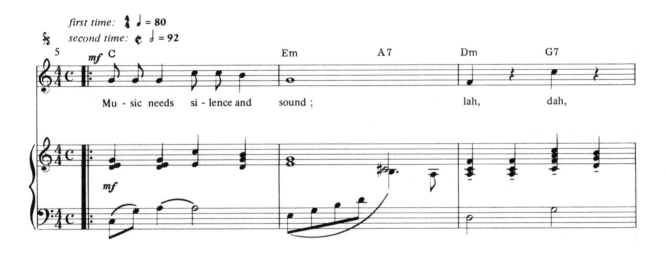

sound and si - lence mu-sic's the best!

1. A
2. A

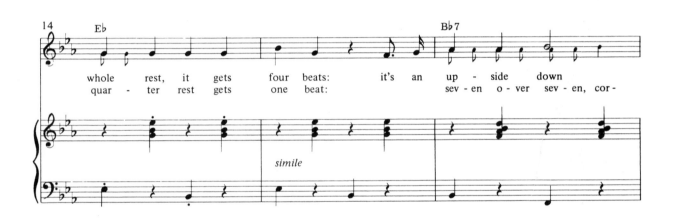

whole rest, it gets four beats: it's an up - side down
quar - ter rest gets one beat: sev - en o - ver sev - en, cor -

simile

hat! Re - mem - ber it hangs be - low the fourth line, be -
rect! Tap your shoe: one tap wil do— One

cause   it's   four   beats   fat.   Heav - y!   A   half   rest,   it   gets
beat   quar - ter   rest,   per - fect.   An   eighth rest it gets one

two   beats: a   hat   that   sits   up - right...
half beat: looks like sev - en in the staff...

Sit - ting   right   a - bove   the   third   line,   be - cause   it's   two   beats   light!
Back - wards, for - wards, ah   who cares?   The eighth   rest   is   a   laugh!

Sound and si - lence, mu - sic sounds the   best!

AND NOW MY FRIEND, PUT YOUR SKILLS TO THE TEST! SEE WHAT YOU REMEMBER WHAT YOU LEARNED ABOUT RESTS.

1. Music can be sound and
   a. paint
   b. more sound
   c. silence

2. In music, silences are made with
   a. notes
   b. rests
   c. treble clefs

3. The length of rests is measured in
   a. inches
   b. seconds
   c. beats

4. ___ is a
   a. half rest
   b. whole rest
   c. quarter rest

5. ___ is a
   a. half rest
   b. whole rest
   c. quarter rest

6. Whole rests have
   a. 1 beat
   b. 4 beats
   c. 2 beats

7. Quarter rests have
   a. 1 beat
   b. 4 beats
   c. 2 beats

8. ___ is a
   a. whole rest
   b. eighth rest
   c. a seven rest

9. ___ is a
   a. half rest
   b. whole rest
   c. eighth rest

10. Quarter rests have
    a. 1 beat
    b. 2 beats
    c. one-half of one beat

11. Eighth rests have
    a. one-half of one beat
    b. 2 beats
    c. 4 beats

12. Whole rests are written
    a. below the fourth line
    b. above the third line
    c. any way you want

13. Half rests are written
    a. below the fourth line
    b. above the third line
    c. any way you want

14. Rests are written   a. in the staff
                                   b. above the staff
                                   c. below the staff   ☐

15. Sounds are written with notes.   a. soft notes
     Silences are written with   b. rests
                                   c. silences   ☐

How many beats are in the following?

16. 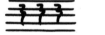   ☐

17.   ☐

18.   ☐

19. ☐

20. ☐

21.   ☐

22. ☐

23. ☐

24.   ☐

25. ☐

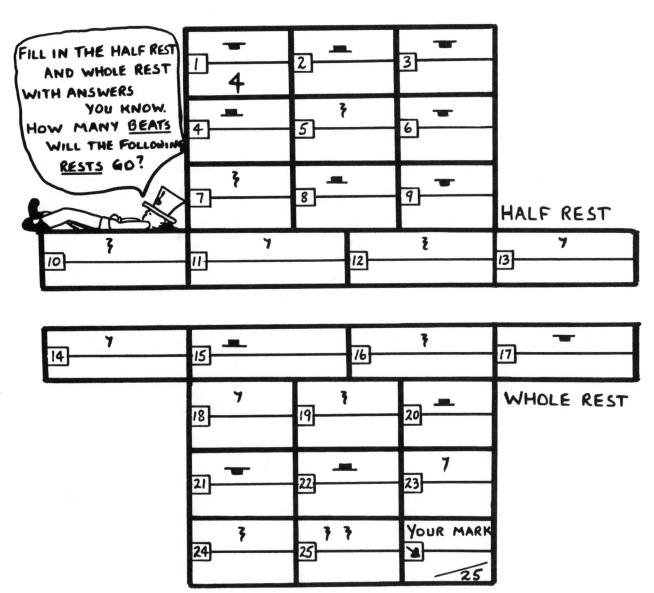

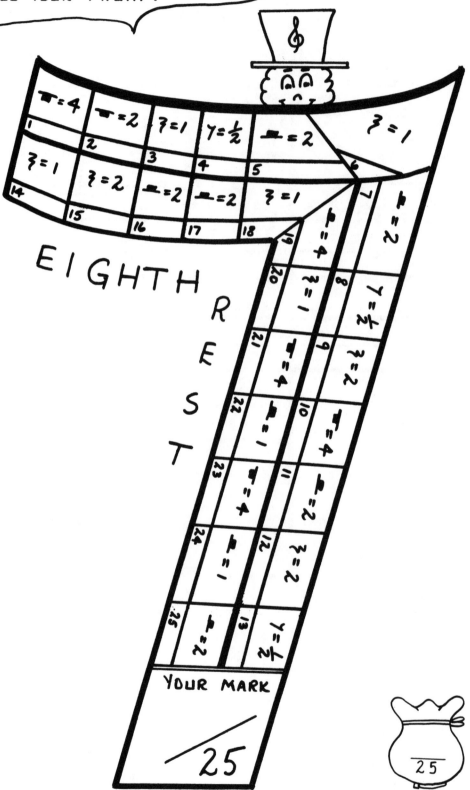

NAME _____

NAME _____

Quiz 3-4

HERE'S ONE OF YOUR FEATS :
TO COUNT UP ALL THE BEATS!

1. 𝄾 + 𝄾 = ☐ beats   17. 𝄾 𝄿 = ☐ beats

2. ♩ + ♩ = ☐ beats   18. ♩ 𝄿 = ☐ beats

3. 𝄼 + 𝄼 = ☐ beats   19. ♩ 𝄾 = ☐ beats

4. ♩ + 𝄼 = ☐ beats   20. 𝄾 𝄾 𝄿 = ☐ beats

5. ♩ + 𝄾 = ☐ beats   21. 𝄾 𝄾 𝄾 𝄿 = ☐ beats

6. 𝄾 + 𝄾 + 𝄾 = ☐ beats   22. 𝄼 𝄼 ♩ = ☐ beats

7. ♩ + ♩ + 𝄾 = ☐ beats   23. ♩ 𝄾 𝄿 = ☐ beats

8. 𝄿 + 𝄿 = ☐ beats   24. 𝄾 𝄾 𝄾 𝄿 = ☐ beats

9. 𝄼 + 𝄼 + 𝄼 = ☐ beats   25. 𝄼 ♩ 𝄾 𝄿 = ☐ beats

10. 𝄾 + 𝄾 + 𝄾 + 𝄾 = ☐ beats

11. 𝄾 𝄾 𝄾 𝄾 = ☐ beats

12. 𝄾 𝄾 = ☐ beats

13. ♩ 𝄾 = ☐ beats

14. 𝄼 𝄾 = ☐ beats

15. 𝄿 𝄿 = ☐ beats

16. 𝄿 𝄿 𝄿 = ☐ beats

PRACTICE YOUR QUARTER RESTS.
THEY'RE TRICKY! (OH BROTHER!)
START WITH TWO SEVENS.
(SIT ONE OVER THE OTHER.)

KEEP DRAWING THESE QUARTER RESTS
BELOW AND YOU'LL SEE,
HOW THE SEVENS BECOME RESTS!
(HOW BEAUTIFUL THEY'LL BE.)

After tracing each dotted rest, draw your own.

WRITE WHATEVER RESTS
HAVE THE FOLLOWING NUMBER OF BEATS.
PLACE THEM ON CORRECT LINES.
BE CAREFUL AND NEAT!

1	2	3	4	5	6	7
4 BEATS	2 BEATS	1 BEAT	½ BEAT	2 BEATS	4 BEATS	1 BEAT

8	9	10	11	12	13	14
1 BEAT	2 BEATS	4 BEATS	½ BEAT	2 BEATS	1 BEAT	1 BEAT

15	16	17	18	19	20	21
2 RESTS 2 BEATS	2 RESTS 4 BEATS	2 RESTS 1 BEAT	2 RESTS 8 BEATS	3 RESTS 3 BEATS	1 REST 1 BEAT	2 BEATS

22	23	24	25
4 BEATS	2 BEATS	½ BEAT	1 BEAT

25

WRITE WHAT THE NOTES AND THE
RESTS ARE BELOW.
TWENTY-FIVE QUESTIONS!
HOW MANY DO YOU KNOW?
          YOU HAVE _____ MINUTES.

1.
HALF REST

2.
WHOLE
NOTE

3.

4.

5.

6.

7.

8.

9.

10.

11.

12.

13.

14.

15.

16.

17.

18.

19.

20.

21.

22.

23.

24.

25.

25

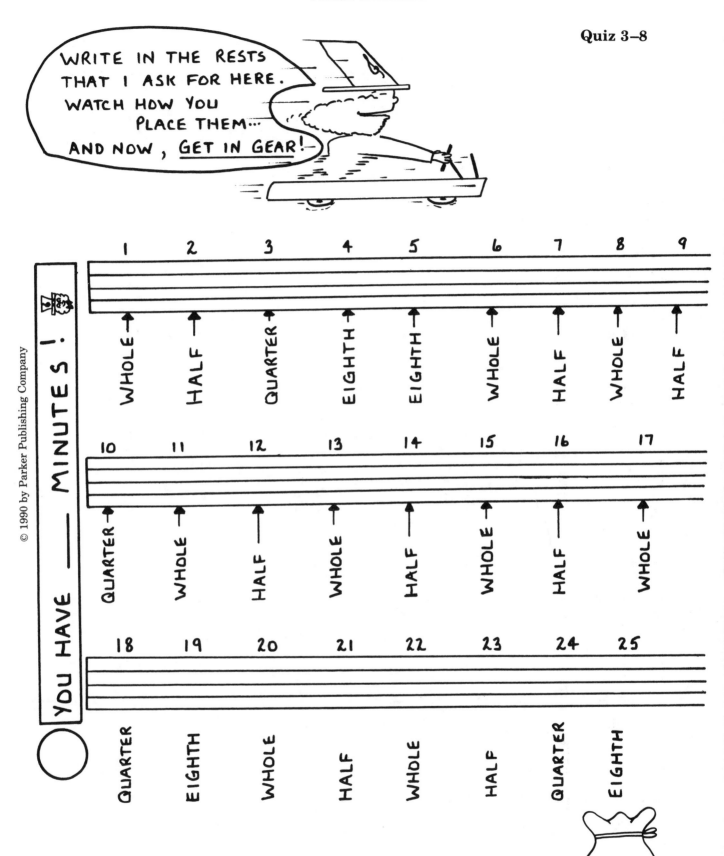

All notes will be in the staff unless you're told they're not.

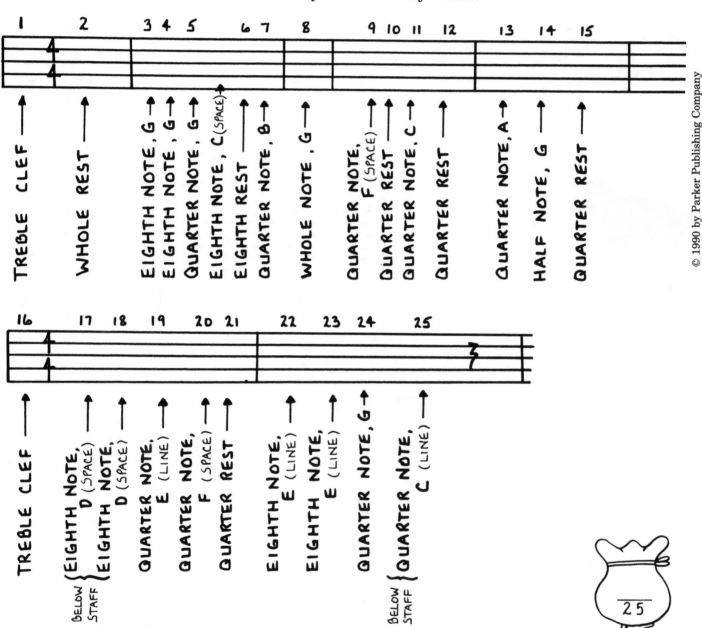

25

THE GREAT
CHAPTER THREE
. . . SUPERQUIZ . . .

1. The backwards "S" at the beginning of the staff is the _____ _____.

2. 𝄞 is called the _____ _____.

3. The staff lines are _____ _____ _____ _____ _____.

4. The staff spaces are _____ _____ _____ _____.

5. The treble clef's other name is the _____ _____.

6. The steady even pulse in music is called the _____.

7. The changing values of notes make _____.

8. Rest and note values are measured in _____.

9. Four-beat notes are called _____ _____.

10. Two-beat notes are called _____ _____.

11. One-beat notes are called _____ _____.

12. Notes having ½ beat are called _____ _____.

13. ▬ is a _____ _____.

14. 𝅝 is a _____ _____.

15. ▬ is a _____ _____.

16. 𝄽 is a _____ _____.

17. 𝅘𝅥 is a _____ _____.

18. 𝄾 is a _____ _____.

19. 𝅘𝅥 is a _____ _____.

20. 𝅘𝅥𝅮 is a _____ _____.

21. 𝄽 gets _____ beat.

22. 𝅘𝅥 gets _____ beats.

23. ▬ gets _____ beats.

24. ▬ gets _____ beats.

25. o gets _____ beats.

26. ♩♩♩ gets _____ beats.

27. ≣≣≣← is the _____ line.

28. ≣≣≣← is the _____ line.

29. ≣≣≣← is the _____ space.

30. Eighth note tails go left or right? _____ .

31. 𝄞 This note is _____ .

32. 𝄞 This note is _____ .

33. 𝄞 This note is _____ .

34. 𝄞 This note is _____ .

35. 𝄞 This note is _____ .

36. 𝄞 This note is _____ .

37. 𝄞 This note is _____ .

38. _____ make silences in music.

39. _____ make sounds in music.

40. o♩ adds up to _____ beats.

41. ♩♩ is _____ beats.

42. ♩♩♩ is _____ beats.

43. ♩♩ is _____ beats.

44. ♩ ⅘ ♩ is _____ beats.

45. ▬♩ is _____ beats.

46. ⅔⅔♩ is _____ beats.

47. ▬ ⅘ ♩ is _____ beats.

48. ▬ ⅘ ♩ is _____ beats.

49. ♩← The arrow points to a
_____ _____ .

50. ♩← The arrow points to a
_____ _____ .

50

BOREDOM BUSTER

Begin at the "Start here" sign and follow the rests and notes through the following pattern:

Sound: ½ beat, 1 beat, 2 beats, 4 beats, then—
Silence: ½ beat, 1 beat, 2 beats, 4 beats.

Keep repeating through this pattern until you discover a grand surprise!

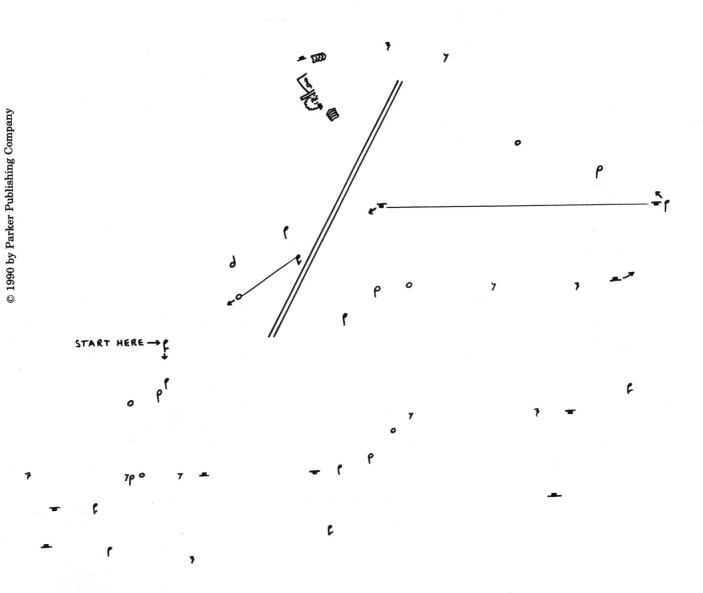

START HERE →

BOREDOM BUSTER

Add up and subtract the following rows of *notes* and *rests*. Each *total* number will represent a letter in the alphabet. For example, a total of 1 would mean A; a total of 2 would mean B; and a total of 26 would mean Z. When you write in the letters in the boxes, *you will find out something wonderful about yourself.*

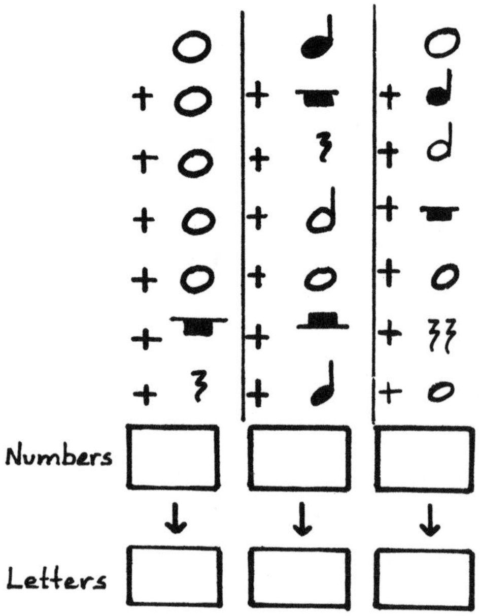

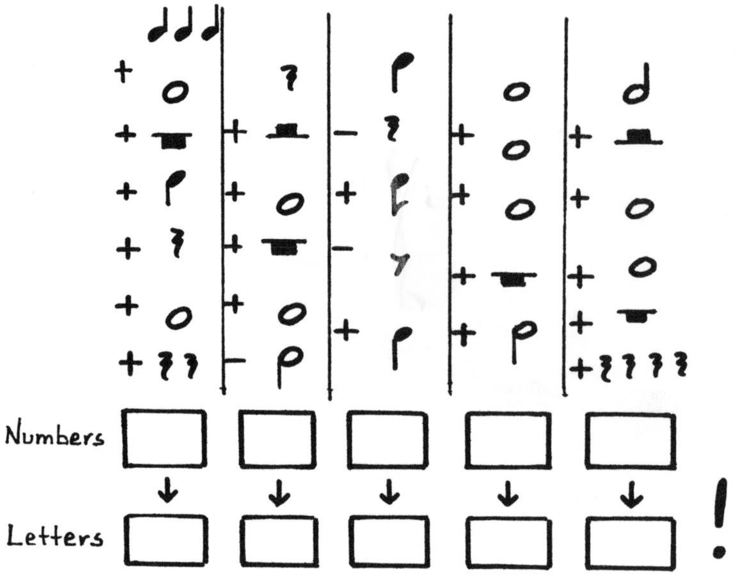

Numbers

Letters

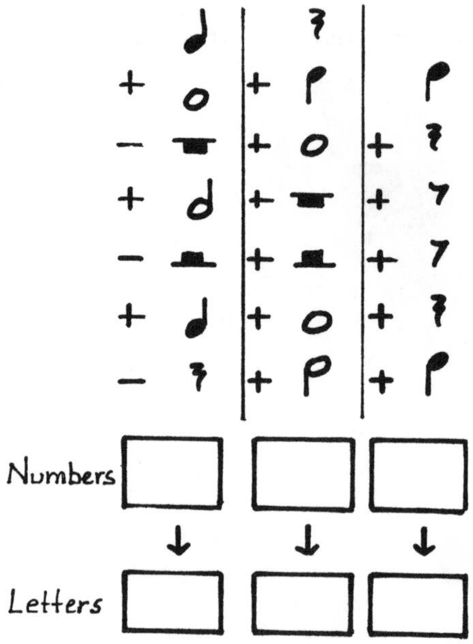

A	B	C	D	E	F	G	H	I	J	K	L	M	N	O	P	Q	R	S	T	U	V	W	X	Y	Z
1	2	3	4	5	6	7	8	9	10	11	12	13	14	15	16	17	18	19	20	21	22	23	24	25	26

NAME _____

BOREDOM BUSTER

Follow the directions below and you will draw a music maker!

Draw a big half rest between numbers 1 and 2.

Draw quarter rests between numbers 3, 4, 5, and 6. Then between 7, 8, 9, and 10, and between 18 and 23, and 19 and 23.

Draw whole notes below 12 and 13 then quarter notes (stems down) at 14 and 15.

Draw a treble clef at 16 and a staff at 17.

Draw a quarter note (stem up) at 18 and a quarter note (stem down) at 19.

Draw quarter notes (stems down) at 20, 21.

Draw a bigger half note (stem down) at 23.

Draw whole rests at 24 and 25.

Draw a staff from line 26 to the 18–23 quarter rest, and from line 27 to the 19–23 quarter rest.

Draw whole notes at 28 and 29.

Draw a staff from line 31–32–33 upwards, stopping when lines meet other lines, ignoring whole rests.

Draw a staff from 30, 31 down to 33, 35 and from 31, 32 to 34, 36.

Draw quarter notes (stems up) at 35 and 36.

Draw a treble clef at 37!

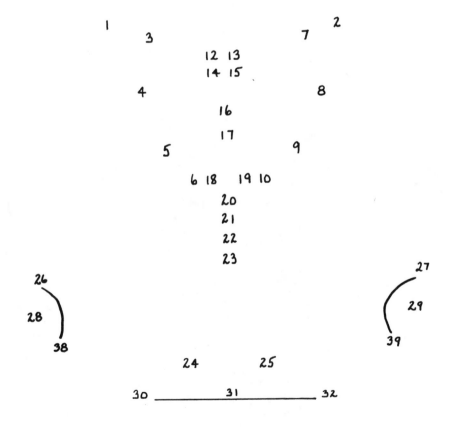

BOREDOM BUSTER

Directions for "Amazing Maze":

1. Staff
2. Treble clef
3. Fourth line on the staff
4. First space on the staff
5. Fifth line on the staff
6. The lines of the treble clef staff
7. The spaces of the treble clef staff
8. Extra lines for notes above and below the staff
9. Two beats of sound

10. A whole note
11. Four quarter rests
12. Three half notes
13. Three eighth rests
14. The letters used in music
15. Three half notes
16. A steady pulse
17. The number of beats in ♪ ♪
18. What the changing value of notes makes

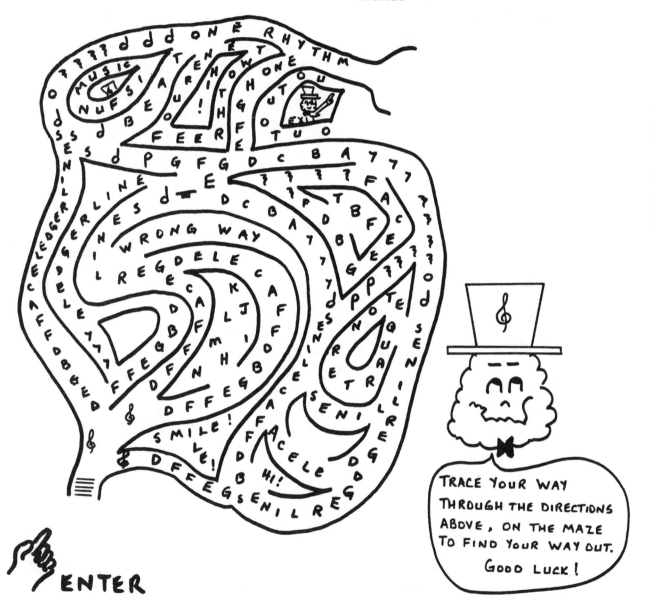

ENTER

RULES TO "EYESHOT SCRAMBLE"

1. The class sits in a circle, around a single student.
2. The students sitting in the circle hold Music Information Cards so that the center person can see the question sides only.
3. The center person attempts to identify *two* Information Cards correctly. When cards are correctly guessed, the Cardholders stand, place their cards in front of them on the floor, and run in opposite directions around the outside of the circle.
4. The center person now sits at one of the vacant places. Each student running around the circle attempts to sit at the remaining place. The runner left without a place to sit, becomes the center person and the game begins again.

Note: If the center person guesses Information Cards incorrectly, the answer is shown to the class. In subsequent guesses, different cards must be selected. The guesser is allowed three consecutive errors after which he must return to the circle and a new guesser is chosen.

To vary the game, students may use a maraca or a bottle to spin, in order to select what cards to guess.

Make laminated cardboard cards with questions on the front and answers on the back. Make 2 of each.

FRONT								
BACK	REST REST REST REST	REST REST	REST	REST REST TA TA	TA REST TA REST	REST TA TA TA	TA-A REST TA	REST REST TA REST

FRONT								
BACK	TA TI-TI REST REST	TA TI-TI REST TA	REST TA TI-TI REST	REST TA REST TA	TI-TI REST TI-TI REST	TA-A REST TI-TI	TI-TI TA REST REST	TI-TI REST TA REST

NAME _____

Student Evaluation Sheet

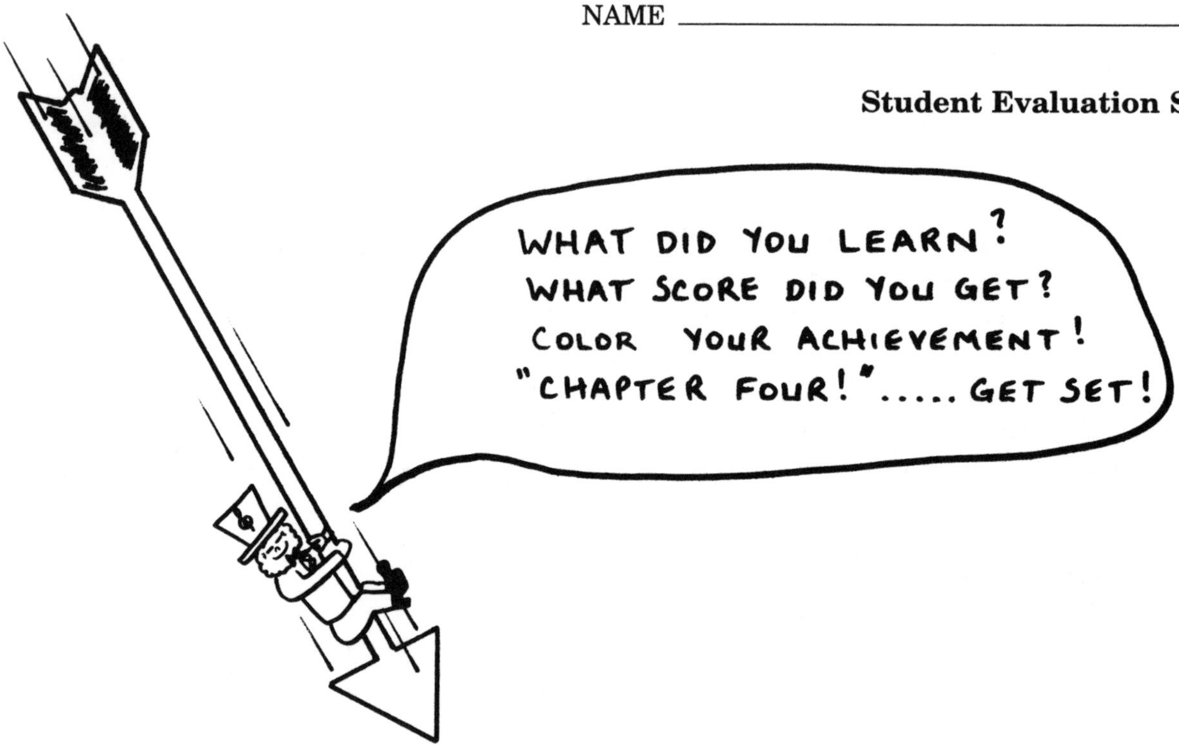

WHAT DID YOU LEARN?
WHAT SCORE DID YOU GET?
COLOR YOUR ACHIEVEMENT!
"CHAPTER FOUR!"..... GET SET!

EXCELLENT!
VERY GOOD!
GOOD!
FAIR!
OH, OH!

%

Ask your teacher what circle to color in the target.

© 1990 by Parker Publishing Company

CHAPTER 3
CLASS RECORD SHEET

GRADE	HOMEROOM TEACHER	CLASS PERIOD/DAY	YEAR

Have students complete as many quizzes as necessary. All tests need not be completed. Write in students' names and fill in their marks in the squares below.

STUDENTS' NAMES	WORDS	MOTIONS	PITCHES	MUSICALITY	QUIZ 3-1	QUIZ 3-2	QUIZ 3-3	QUIZ 3-4	QUIZ 3-5	QUIZ 3-6	QUIZ 3-7	QUIZ 3-8	QUIZ 3-9	QUIZ 3-10	BB 3-1	BB 3-2	BB 3-3	BB 3-4	FINAL MARK

(SONG: WORDS, MOTIONS, PITCHES, MUSICALITY)

PROGRESS OF CLASSES

A chart is given here to help you keep a record of the tasks your classes complete. After listing the class names in the top squares, indicate with a check mark (✔) or with the date that a task has been accomplished.

CHAPTER 3

LIST OF CLASSES										
= =										
HAVE READ THE STORY										
HAVE STARTED THE SONG										
STUDENTS KNOW SONG										

HAVE COMPLETED QUIZ NO.	ACTIVITY	SKILL PRACTICED							
	3–1. Multiple choice	values of rests ▬ ▬ 𝄽 𝄾							
	3–2. Fill in the answer	identifying beats in rests							
	3–3. Write in ✔ or ✖	identifying correct number of beats in rests							
	3–4. Write in numbers	adding beats in rests							
	3–5. Practicing hand control	drawing quarter notes							
	3–6. Drawing the staff	drawing rests correctly							
	3–7. Identifying notes and rests	identifying ○ ♩ ♩ ♩ ▬ ▬ 𝄽 𝄾							
	3–8. Writing rests	writing ▬ ▬ 𝄽 𝄾							
	3–9. Writing notes and rests	writing 𝄞 ○ 𝅗𝅥 ♩ ♩ ♫ ▬ ▬ 𝄽 𝄾							
	3–10. Fill in the blanks	review of Chapters 1–3							
BOREDOM BUSTER NO.	3–1. Tracing a hidden picture	finding values of ○ ♩ ♩ ♩ ▬ ▬ 𝄽 𝄾							
	3–2. Discovering the secret message	adding and subtracting note and rest values							
	3–3. Drawing the hidden picture	drawing ▬ ▬ 𝄽 𝄾 ○ ♩ ♩ ♩							
	3–4. Traveling through a maze	identifying staff, 𝄞, staff lines and spaces, music letters, ledger lines, notes, and results							
GAME: "EYESHOT SCRAMBLE"										

CHAPTER 3 ANSWER KEY

Quiz 3–1

1. c	6. b	11. a	16. 2	21. 1
2. b	7. a	12. a	17. 2	22. 1
3. c	8. b	13. b	18. ½	23. 4
4. b	9. a	14. a	19. 3	24. 1½
5. c	10. a	15. b	20. 3	25. 6

Quiz 3–2

1. 4	6. 4	11. ½	16. 1	21. 4
2. 2	7. 1	12. 1	17. 4	22. 2
3. 4	8. 2	13. ½	18. ½	23. ½
4. 2	9. 4	14. ½	19. 1	24. 1
5. 1	10. 1	15. 2	20. 2	25. 2

Quiz 3–3

1. ✔	6. ✔	11. ✔	16. ✔	21. ✔
2. ✘	7. ✔	12. ✘	17. ✘	22. ✘
3. ✔	8. ✔	13. ✔	18. ✔	23. ✔
4. ✔	9. ✘	14. ✔	19. ✔	24. ✘
5. ✔	10. ✔	15. ✘	20. ✔	25. ✔

Quiz 3–4

1. 2	6. 3	11. 4	16. 2	21. 3½
2. 4	7. 5	12. 2	17. 1½	22. 10
3. 8	8. 1	13. 3	18. 2½	23. 3½
4. 6	9. 12	14. 5	19. 3	24. 3½
5. 3	10. 4	15. 1	20. 2½	25. 7½

Quiz 3–5

Check to see that students have correctly drawn 50 quarter rests.

Quiz 3–6

Quiz 3–7

1. half rest	6. whole note	11. half note	16. eighth note	21. eighth note
2. whole note	7. half rest	12. quarter rest	17. quarter note	22. quarter note
3. whole rest	8. half note	13. eighth rest	18. whole rest	23. quarter rest
4. half note	9. quarter rest	14. eighth note	19. quarter note	24. half note
5. whole rest	10. quarter note	15. eighth rest	20. half rest	25. quarter note

Quiz 3–8

Quiz 3–9

Quiz 3–10

1. treble clef	11. quarter notes	21. 1 beat	31. C	41. 3 beats
2. staff	12. eighth notes	22. 2 beats	32. F	42. 5 beats
3. E G B D F	13. half rest	23. 4 beats	33. B	43. 2 beats
4. F A C E	14. whole note	24. 2 beats	34. E	44. 4 beats
5. G clef	15. whole rest	25. 4 beats	35. G	45. 6 beats
6. beat	16. quarter rest	26. 3 beats	36. D	46. 3 beats
7. rhythm	17. half note	27. first line	37. E	47. 4 beats
8. beats	18. eighth rest	28. fourth line	38. rests	48. 6 beats
9. whole notes	19. quarter note	29. fourth space	39. notes	49. note head
10. half notes	20. eighth note	30. right	40. 6 beats	50. note stem

Boredom Buster 3–1

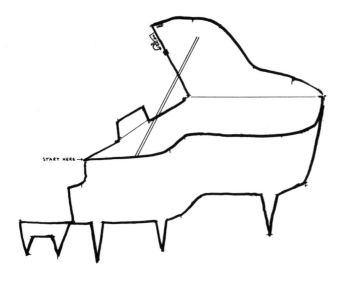

Boredom Buster 3–3

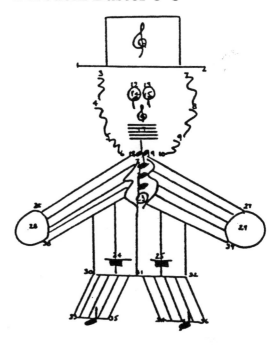

Boredom Buster 3–2

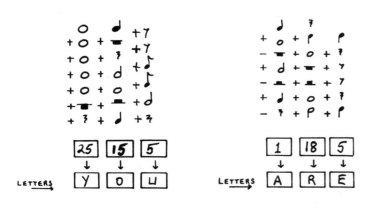

Boredom Buster 3–4

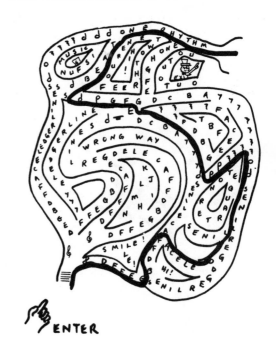

Mr. Treble Clef Stretches Sounds and Silences

Mac, Christina, and Mr. Treble Clef had been singing about rests for what seemed to be forever. The catchy, changing rhythms of the song made them tap and clap a steady even beat until their hands and feet ached and now they were feeling a bit tired.

Mac thought for a second. "Mr. Treble Clef," he asked slowly, "I was just thinking. I know a whole note or whole rest is four beats, a half note or half rest is two beats, a quarter note or quarter rest is one beat, and an eighth note or eighth rest gets one-half of one beat. Can notes or rests have other numbers of beats?"

"Gee, of course," warbled Mr. Treble Clef, "you can stretch notes and rests to make them longer."

"How?" Christina piped up.

"Well, for one thing, you can add a dot to a note or rest," said Mr. Treble Clef.

"What does that do?" asked Mac.

"If you add a dot the note or rest will be worth one-half more," answered Mr. Treble Clef.

"Huh?" Mac seemed confused.

Just then Mr. Treble Clef grinned, opened the palm of his hand and said, "Look!" A perfectly round black dot suddenly appeared in his hand. It flew up and wavered over his head. "Watch what happens when my magic dot appears to the right of anything!"

Before reading ask:
1. What is
𝄻 ? (whole rest)
𝄼 ? (half rest)
𝄽 ? (quarter rest)
𝄾 ? (eighth rest)
2. How many beats in:
𝄻 ? (4 beats of silence)
𝄼 ? (2 beats of silence)
𝄽 ? (1 beat of silence)
𝄾 ? (½ beat of silence)

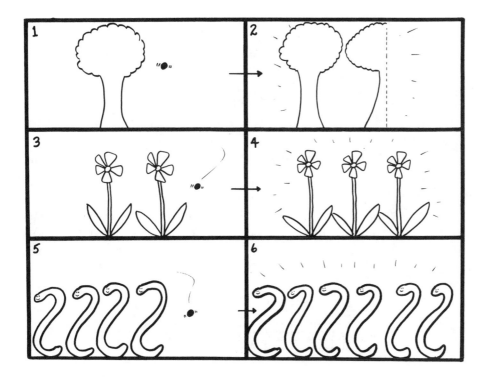

Show picture to demonstrate the following points.

And everything with a dot had one-half more added to it. "Wow!" exclaimed Mac and Christina.

Mr. Treble Clef laughed and then said, "The dot will do the same to the lengths of notes and rests. Watch now."

And sure enough, the magic dot began to place itself after notes and rests, adding one-half more to each.

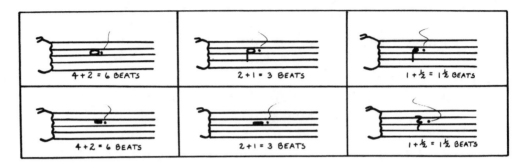

And then, Mr. Treble Clef sang:

Have class say or sing together:

A dot with a whole note or whole rest
Gets *six* beats always;
The whole if *four*; the dot is *two*,
six beats is what you play.

A dot with a half note or half rest
Three beats is what it's got.
The half is *two*, the dot is *one*—
What a clever dot!

A dot with a quarter note or rest
Gets one and one-half beats.
One and a half beats for this note:
The dot makes life easy!

"That's easy!" boomed the children.

"Mr. Treble Clef, you said there was another way to make notes longer. How do we do it?" asked Mac.

"Just tie notes together with a tie," answered the old man. "Any two notes with *exactly* the same letter name can be joined with a tie. See?"

Mr. Treble Clef blinked three times. Immediately three curved lines came out of nowhere and landed over the notes that were sitting on his staff. The ties formed new notes that were longer.

And then Mr. Treble Clef sang in a full voice:

> Ties are small curved lines
> Two notes together they tie.
> Notes with same names
> Are joined as one, for life.

Have students say or
sing together:

"That's simple," Mac and Christina exclaimed, and they all sang:

> Dots or ties
> Make notes extend;
> Use both ways,
> So notes will end
> (Just when you want them to!)

Have students say or
sing together:

"This is so much fun, Mr. Treble Clef," said Christina, "but I think we should be getting back home now."

"You'll have to go back by the Magic Keyboard," Mr. Treble Clef explained.

"What's that?" the children asked.

Right away, the old man chanted:

> The Magic Keyboard
> Is of keys, white and black.
> Let's whisk you right to it
> So you can get back!

And *"whoosh"*—the three of them landed in a very unusual place indeed . . . .

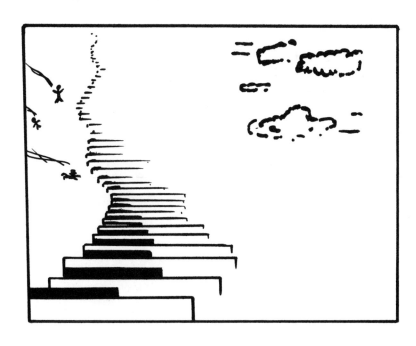

Ask Students:
1. What do dots and ties do? (make notes longer)
2. How does the dot do this? (it adds ½ more to notes and rests)
3. How do ties make notes longer? (by joining two notes together to become one note)
4. Can notes E and F be tied together? (no)
5. Why? (tied notes have to have the same name)

SUGGESTIONS FOR TEACHING THE SONG,
Dots or Ties

1. Review the story material by discussing the story events.
2. Play the tape of *Dots or Ties* or perform it for your students. Then make sure they understand all of the words in the song.
3. Let them hear the song again. (Students in grades 2–6 might want to follow the words in the written music.)
4. Teach the song by rote as with the previous songs. Include the body motions.
5. Have your students learn the song completely before working on the quiz section.
6. Have students perform the song as soloists, in duets, or in any other interesting combinations. Have groups compete against each other for marks.

THE BODY MOTIONS

Verse 1
bar: 8   On "dot," point as if writing one. Make whole and half notes and rests.
  9   Point 6 fingers.
10–11   Point 4,2,6 fingers. "Write" a dot.

Verses 2–3
bar: 8   "Write" dots; make half notes and rests, quarter notes with two hands. Draw quarter rests in the air.
  11   (Verse 2) "Thumbs up."
  12   Draw a dot and a tie in the air.
  14   "Write" a dot *and* draw a tie in the air.
  15   Perform a "cutting off" motion.
16–17   Look at your "watch."
18–19   Draw a tie one way, then in the opposite direction.
  21   Fists together, as if bound.

DOTS OR TIES

1. A dot with a whole note or whole rest gets six beats al - ways._____ The
2. dot with a half note or half rest: three beats is what it's got._____ The
3. dot with a quar - ter note or rest gets one and one half beats._____

whole is four; the dot is two. Six beats is what you play.__
half is two; the dot is one. What a clev - er dot.__
Ond and a half beats for this note: the dot makes life eas -y! ——

1. *Notes* and *rests* are made longer by writing

    a. dots
    b. ties
    c. both of these

2. Dots add how much to notes or rests?

    a. half more
    b. nothing
    c. a little bit

3. 𝅝· is how many beats?

    a. 4
    b. 6
    c. 8

4. 𝅗𝅥· is how many beats?

    a. 3
    b. 4
    c. 5

5. 𝅘𝅥· is how many beats?

    a. 1½
    b. 2
    c. 3

6. 𝅗𝅥‿𝅝 is how many beats?

    a. 4
    b. 6
    c. 8

7. 𝅘𝅥‿𝅘𝅥 is how many beats?

    a. 3
    b. 4
    c. 5

8. 𝅘𝅥‿𝅘𝅥 is how many beats?

    a. 1½
    b. 2
    c. 3

9. 𝅘𝅥·‿𝅘𝅥· is how many beats altogether?

    a. 5
    b. 6

10. 𝅘𝅥·‿𝅘𝅥·‿𝅘𝅥· is how many beats altogether?

    a. 8
    b. 9
    c. 10

11. 𝅘𝅥‿𝅝 is how many beats altogether?

    a. 7
    b. 8
    c. 6

12. 𝅘𝅥· is how many beats?

    a. 2
    b. 3
    c. 4

13. 𝅘𝅥‿𝅘𝅥 is how many beats altogether?

    a. 2
    b. 3
    c. 4

NAME _____

Quiz 4-1, *continued*

14. ♩. ♩ is how many beats?

     a. 3
     b. 4
     c. 6

15. ♩. ♩. is how many beats?

     a. 5
     b. 8
     c. 6

16. 𝅗𝅥. is how many beats?

     a. 5
     b. 6
     c. 8

17. 𝅗𝅥. ♩ is how many beats of sound?

     a. 5
     b. 6
     c. 7

18. ▬ ▬ is how many beats of silence?

     a. 5
     b. 6
     c. 7

19. is two E's with a _____.

     a. line
     b. tie

20. is two notes that are tied together.

     a. True
     b. False

21. is two notes that are tied together.

     a. True
     b. False

22. is two notes that are tied together.

     a. True
     b. False

23. is two notes that are tied together.

     a. True
     b. False

24. How many beats long is this note A?

     a. 4
     b. 7
     c. 3

25. How many beats of music is this?

     a. 5
     b. 6
     c. 7

25

NAME _____

Quiz 4–2

THE DOT ADDS ONE HALF
TO WHATEVER YOU SEE;
LOOK AT THESE BELOW,
AND ADD UP ALL THE BEATS.

25   ♭ ♩· o 𝅘· 𝄼· 𝅗𝅥· =

1   o· =

2   𝅗𝅥· =

3   𝅘𝅥· =

4   o· o· =

5   𝅗𝅥· 𝅗𝅥 =

6   𝅘𝅥· 𝅘𝅥· =

7   o· 𝅗𝅥· =

8   𝅗𝅥· 𝅘𝅥· =

9   𝅗𝅥· 𝅗𝅥· =

10   𝄼· =

11   𝄼· =

12   𝄽· =

13   𝄼· 𝄼· =

14   𝄼· 𝄼· =

15   𝄼· 𝄼· =

16   𝄼· 𝄽· =

24   𝅗𝅥· 𝅗𝅥· 𝄼· =

23   o· 𝅗𝅥· 𝄼 =

22   𝅘𝅥· 𝄽· =

21   𝅗𝅥· 𝄽· =

20   𝅗𝅥· 𝄼· =

19   o· 𝄼· =

18   𝄽· 𝄽· =

17   𝄼· 𝄽· =

25

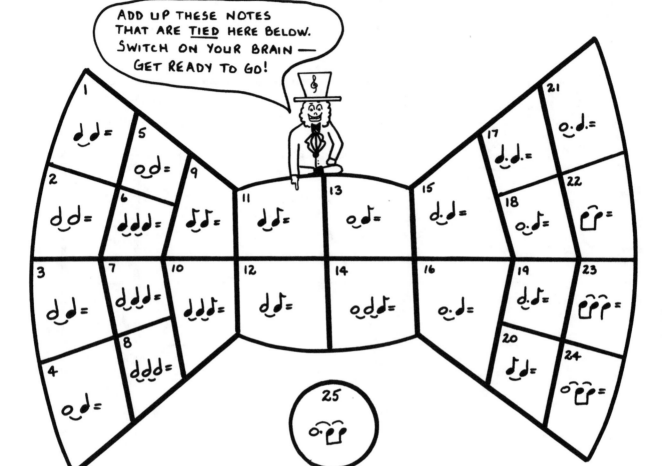

HERE'S SOME MATH!
(MADE FROM MUSIC, YOU SEE.)
ADD AND SUBTRACT, AND
GIVE ANSWERS IN BEATS!

1. 　＋　＝ 4

2. 　＋　＝

3. 　＋　＝

4. 　−　＝

5. 　−　＝

6. 　−　＝

7. 　＋　＝

8. 　＋　＝

9. 　＋　＝

10. 　＋　＝

11. 　＋　＝

12. 　＋　＝

13. 　＋　＝

14. 　−　＝

15. 　−　＝

16. 　−　＝

17. 　−　＝

18. 　−　＝

19. 　−　＝

20. 　＋　＝

21. 　＋　＝

22. 　＋　＝

23. 　−　＝

24. 　−　＝

25. 　−　＝

25

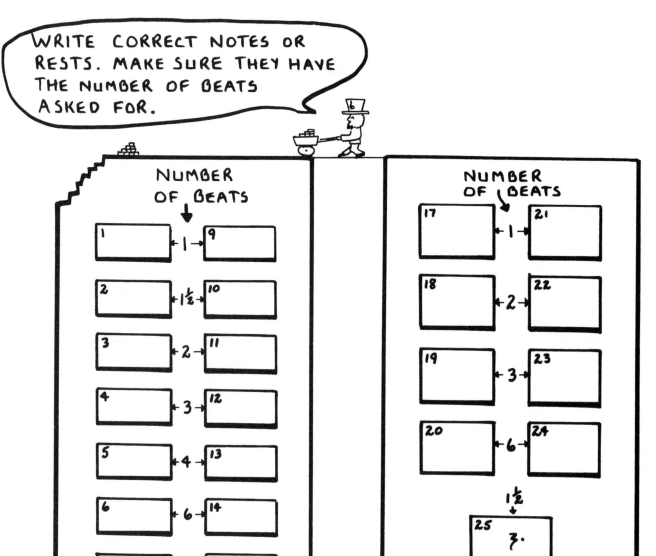

Note: For numbers 1–8, use *two notes* with a *tie*. 9–16, use *one note* with a *dot*, or *one note* alone. 17–20, use *two rests*. 21–24, use *one rest* with a *dot*, or *one rest* alone.

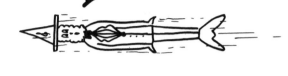

IDENTIFY THE ARROWS
(JUST LIKE BEFORE)
PLACE ANSWERS IN BOXES
AND GET A GREAT SCORE!

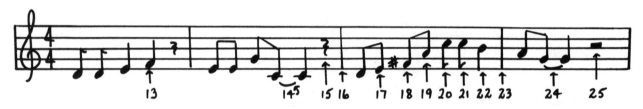

1. Name?	10. Name?	18. Note letter name? ___ #
2. Note letter name?	11. How many beats?	19. Note letter name?
3. How many beats?	12. Name?	20. Note letter name?
4. Note letter name?	13. Note letter name?	21. How many beats?
5. How many beats?	14. Name?	22. Note letter name?
6. How many beats?	15. Type of rest?	23. Name?
7. Name?	16. Name	24. Name?
8. Note letter name?	17. Note letter name?	25. Number of beats?
9. Name?		

25

MUSIC NEEDS SILENCE AND SOUND!
SO... GO AHEAD AND FOLLOW THE DIRECTIONS BELOW AND WRITE PART OF THE SONG, "MUSIC NEEDS SILENCE AND SOUND."

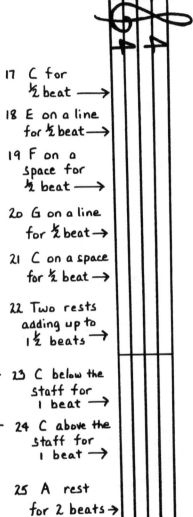

17 C for ½ beat →

18 E on a line for ½ beat →

19 F on a space for ½ beat →

20 G on a line for ½ beat →

21 C on a space for ½ beat →

22 Two rests adding up to 1½ beats →

USE LEDGER LINES
23 C below the staff for 1 beat →

24 C above the staff for 1 beat →

25 A rest for 2 beats →

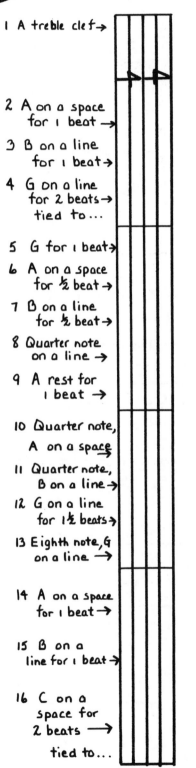

1 A treble clef →

2 A on a space for 1 beat →

3 B on a line for 1 beat →

4 G on a line for 2 beats → tied to...

5 G for 1 beat →

6 A on a space for ½ beat →

7 B on a line for ½ beat →

8 Quarter note on a line →

9 A rest for 1 beat →

10 Quarter note, A on a space →

11 Quarter note, B on a line →

12 G on a line for 1½ beats →

13 Eighth note, G on a line →

14 A on a space for 1 beat →

15 B on a line for 1 beat →

16 C on a space for 2 beats → tied to...

25

SOMETHING NEW

You've probably been noticing that straight lines are drawn in the staff from *top* to *bottom* in between some notes.

These are called *bar lines*.

All of the music between two bar lines is called a *bar* or a *measure*.

Normally in a piece of music, each bar (or measure) has the same number of beats as in the above example. Can you see that notes and rests in each bar add up to 4 beats?

In the staves below, place bar lines between notes so that the bars each have the correct number of beats in them.

> A double bar line at the end of a piece of music tells us the music is finished.
>
> Questions 1–5 would need double bar lines, wouldn't they?

Two Beats in Each Bar

1

Three Beats in Each Bar

2

Four Beats in Each Bar

3

Five Beats in Each Bar

4

Seven Beats in Each Bar

5

FIVE MARKS FOR EACH OF QUESTIONS 1-5!

25

NAME _____

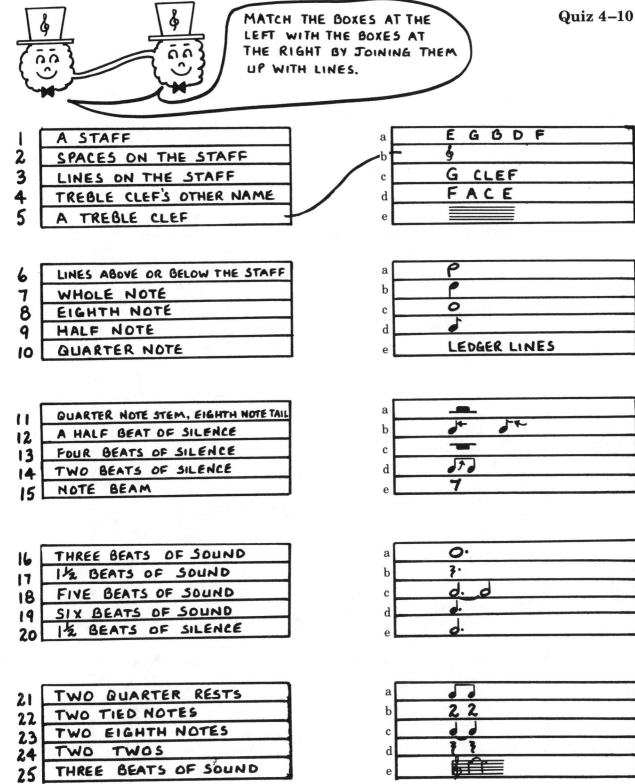

BOREDOM BUSTER

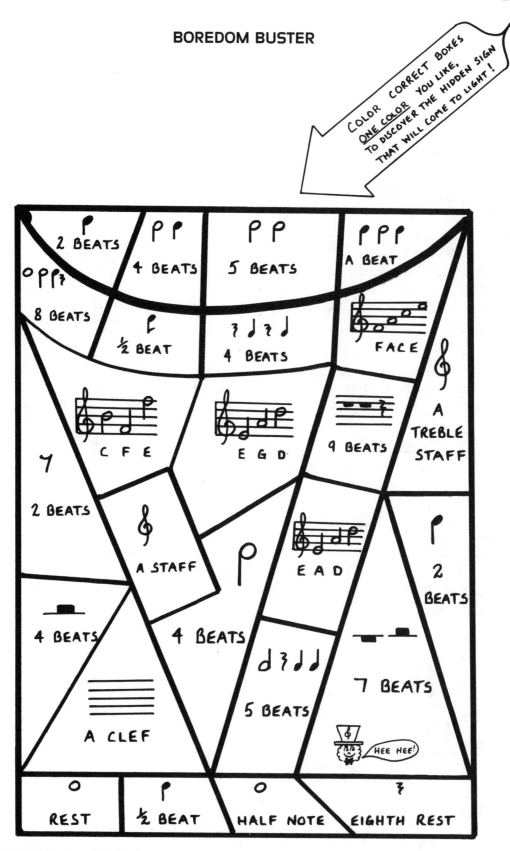

THE HIDDEN SIGN IS AN _____ _____!

BOREDOM BUSTER

Across

1. ♪ is an _____ _____.

4. Lines in the 𝄞 staff are _____.

6. ♩ is a _____ note.

10. 𝅝 ♩ adds up to _____ beats.

11. 𝅝 is a _____ _____.

13. ▰ is a _____.

15. ♩ is a _____ _____.

19. spells _____.

21. spells _____.

22. ▰ is a _____ rest.

24. ♩ is the same _____ ♩ ♩.

26. ♩. has _____ _____ of sound.

30. are _____ _____.

33. 𝄼 is _____ beat of silence.

34. ♩ ♩ is _____ beats of sound.

35. ♩ ♩ is a _____.

36. is _____.

Down

2. ♩ is a _____ note.

3. ♩ is a quarter _____.

5. spells _____.

7. ▬ ♩ has _____ beats.

8. 𝄞 is a treble _____.

9. ♫ has _____ beat of sound.

12. is a note _____.

14. The 𝄞 spaces spell _____.

16. 𝄾 is an _____ _____.

17. 𝄿𝄿 is _____ beat of silence.

18. spells _____.

20. are note _____.

25. is a note _____.

27. G is line _____ on the 𝄞 staff.

32. ♩. is the _____ as ♩ ♩.

LET'S GET STARTED.
DON'T GET OUTSMARTED!

BOREDOM BUSTER

NAME _____

Trace your way to the "Magic Bar" by following these 16 questions:

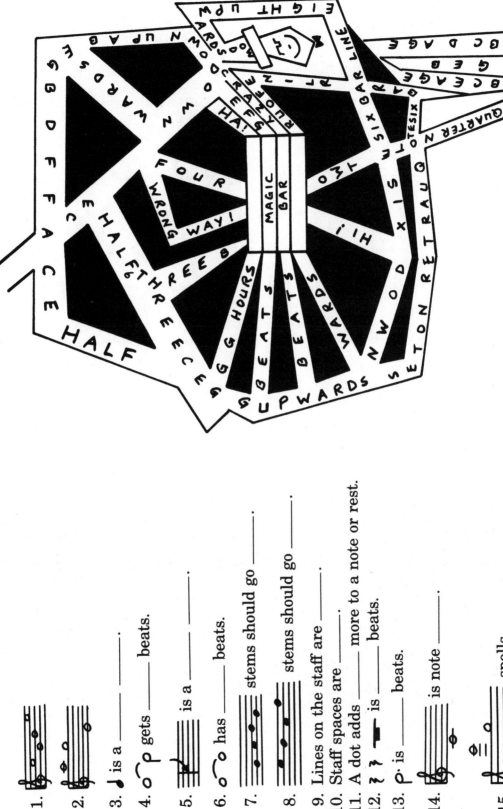

1. [staff with notes] _____

2. [staff with notes] _____

3. ♪ is a _____.

4. ♪ gets _____ beats.

5. [staff] is a _____.

6. ♪ has _____ beats.

7. [notes on staff] stems should go _____.

8. [notes on staff] stems should go _____.

9. Lines on the staff are _____.

10. Staff spaces are _____.

11. A dot adds _____ more to a note or rest.

12. [rests] is _____ beats.

13. ♪. is _____ beats.

14. [staff] is note _____.

15. [staff] spells _____.

16. Music lengths are measured in _____.

BOREDOM BUSTER

Compose your very own song! Just follow the directions. Write in:

1. A treble clef
2. A whole note E, G, or C
3. Quarter notes B, A, G, and F in any order
4. Half note F, A, or C and another half note G, B, or D
5. A dotted half note C, E, or G, and a quarter rest
6. Quarter notes F and G in any order
7. Quarter notes E and G in any order
8. Quarter notes D, E, F, and G in any order
9. A treble clef
10. A half note A, C, or E followed by a half rest

11. Quarter notes G, A, B, and C in any order
12. Quarter notes G, A, and B in any order
13. Quarter notes F, G, A, and B in any order
14. A whole note C, E, or G
15. Quarter note D
16. Three quarter notes of E and one quarter rest
17. A treble clef
18. One half note and two quarter notes of F in any order
19. A dotted half note of G, B, or D followed by a quarter rest

_____

(your song's title)

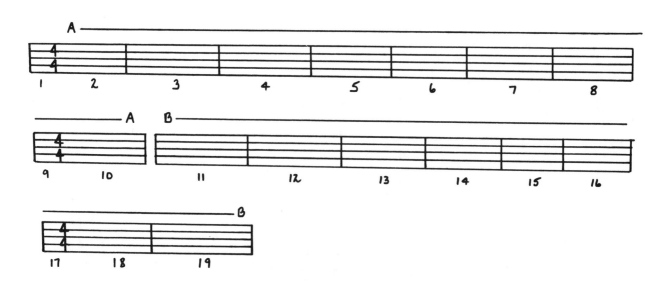

After you've written your piece, have your teacher play it with you. Your teacher or a friend can play the piano accompaniment. Play bars in the order of A A B A.

RULES TO "BLIND MAN'S CARDS"

1. Students sit in a circle. A small number of cards (about half the number of students) are selected and distributed among the seated students. These cards will be passed from one student to another around the circle. Half of the cards are to travel in one direction; half are to travel in the opposite direction.
2. One student sits in the middle of the circle and is blind-folded.
3. The teacher says, "Go!" and the cards are passed. The idea is for students to *pass* the cards as quickly as possible to the next person. They do not want to be caught holding a card.
4. The teacher says "Stop!" and the students freeze. The blindfolded person spins around and then moves toward the circle and touches a person. If the person he touches has a card and it is guessed correctly the guesser gets 1 point. A second card held by a student is worth 5 points if guessed correctly. Any other cards in his possession at one time are worth 10 points each. *Now a new person is in the middle.*
5. If a student in the circle is not holding any cards at all and is picked by the blindfolded person, the *student in the circle* may choose any two cards and try to identify them. In this case, each card is worth 5 points.
6. To add excitement, finish the game by having correctly picked cards be worth 20 points each to the blindfolded person. If a person with no cards is picked, allow him to pick and identify as many cards as he wishes, having each correct card be worth 10 points.

Note: Make up several pieces of paper and place numbers 1, 5, 10, and 20 on them. These will be points that students keep as they accumulate them during the game.

Make laminated cardboard cards with questions on the front and answers on the back.

O·	ρ	ρ·	▬·.	▬·.	₹·	ℓ	7·	o⌢ρ	ρ⌢ρ
6 BEATS	3 BEATS	1½ BEATS	3 BEATS	6 BEATS	1½ BEATS	½ BEAT	¾ BEAT	6 BEATS	3 BEATS

ρ⌢ℓ	ρ⌢ρ·	ρ⌢ρ·	o⌢ρ	ρ⌢ρ·	o⌢ρ⌢ρ	ρ⌢ρ⌢ρ·
1½ BEATS	6 BEATS	3½ BEATS	5 BEATS	3 BEATS	7 BEATS	5½ BEATS

NAME _____

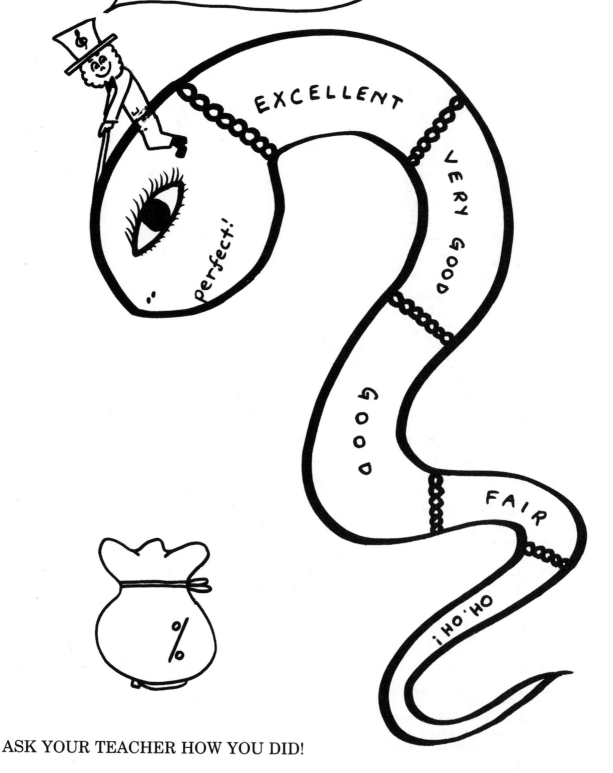

ASK YOUR TEACHER HOW YOU DID!

CHAPTER 4
CLASS RECORD SHEET

GRADE

HOMEROOM TEACHER

CLASS PERIOD/DAY

YEAR

Have students complete as many quizzes as necessary. All tests need not be completed. Write in students' names and fill in their marks in the squares below.

STUDENTS' NAMES	SONG				QUIZ 4–1	QUIZ 4–2	QUIZ 4–3	QUIZ 4–4	QUIZ 4–5	QUIZ 4–6	QUIZ 4–7	QUIZ 4–8	QUIZ 4–9	QUIZ 4–10	BB 4–1	BB 4–2	BB 4–3	BB 4–4	FINAL MARK
	WORDS	MOTIONS	PITCHES	MUSICALITY															

PROGRESS OF CLASSES

A chart is given here to help you keep a record of the tasks your classes complete. After listing the class names in the top squares, indicate with a check mark (✔) or with the date that a task has been accomplished.

CHAPTER 4

LIST OF CLASSES										
= =										
HAVE READ THE STORY										
HAVE STARTED THE SONG										
STUDENTS KNOW SONG										

HAVE COMPLETED QUIZ NO.	ACTIVITY	SKILL PRACTICED								
	4–1. Multiple choice	Chapter 4 review								
	4–2. Studying the dot	adding notes and rests having dots								
	4–3. Studying the tie	adding notes and dotted notes using ties								
	4–4. Note/rest math	adding and subtracting note and rest values								
	4–5. Note/rest writing	writing note and rest values with and without dots and ties								
	4–6. Note/rest balancing	examining rest and note values								
	4–7. Identifying music nomenclature	identifying note and rest names and values								
	4–8. Writing music	writing notes and rests								
	4–9. Learning about bar lines and bars	placing bar lines in their correct places								
	4–10. Matching	review of Chapters 1–4								
BOREDOM BUSTER NO.	4–1. Discovering the hidden picture	review of Chapters 1–4								
	4–2. Crossword puzzle	review of Chapters 1–4								
	4–3. Tracing the maze	review of Chapters 1–4								
	4–4. Composing your own song	writing correct notes, rests, and number of beats in each measure								
GAME: BLIND MAN'S CARDS										

CHAPTER 4 ANSWER KEY

Quiz 4–1

1. c	6. b	11. c	16. b	21. a
2. a	7. a	12. b	17. c	22. a
3. b	8. a	13. b	18. c	23. b
4. a	9. b	14. b	19. b	24. b
5. a	10. b	15. c	20. b	25. c

Quiz 4–2

1. 6	6. 3	11. 3	16. 4½	21. 4½
2. 3	7. 9	12. 1½	17. 4½	22. 3
3. 1½	8. 4½	13. 12	18. 3	23. 11
4. 12	9. 6	14. 6	19. 9	24. 12
5. 6	10. 6	15. 9	20. 6	25. 21

Quiz 4–3

1. 2	6. 3	11. 1½	16. 7	21. 7½
2. 4	7. 4	12. 2½	17. 3	22. 1
3. 3	8. 6	13. 4½	18. 6½	23. 2
4. 5	9. 1	14. 6½	19. 3½	24. 5
5. 6	10. 2½	15. 4	20. 1½	25. 7

Quiz 4–4

1. 4	6. 3	11. 9	16. 1	21. 2
2. 3	7. 2	12. 5	17. 0	22. 5
3. 6	8. 4	13. 2	18. 1	23. 1
4. 2	9. 5	14. 0	19. 2	24. ½
5. 2	10. 4	15. 2	20. 4	25. ½

Quiz 4–5

Quiz 4–6

1. ✔	6. ✘	11. ✘	16. ✘	21. ✘
2. ✔	7. ✔	12. ✔	17. ✘	22. ✔
3. ✔	8. ✘	13. ✘	18. ✔	23. ✘
4. ✔	9. ✘	14. ✘	19. ✘	24. ✔
5. ✔	10. ✘	15. ✔	20. ✔	25. ✘

Quiz 4–7

1. treble clef	6. 1	11. 2	16. bar line	21. ½
2. G	7. bar line	12. bar line	17. E	22. B
3. ½	8. B	13. F	18. F♯	23. bar line
4. C	9. bar line	14. tie	19. A	24. tie
5. 3	10. tie	15. quarter rest	20. C	25. 2

Quiz 4–8

Quiz 4–9

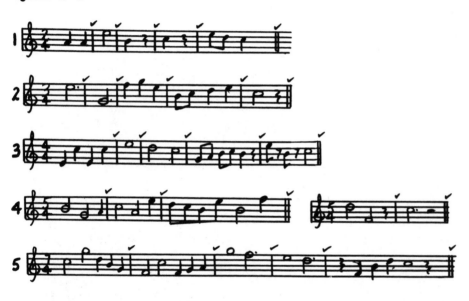

Quiz 4–10

1. e	6. e	11. b	16. e	21. d
2. d	7. c	12. e	17. d	22. c
3. a	8. d	13. c	18. c	23. a
4. c	9. a	14. a	19. a	24. b
5. b	10. b	15. d	20. b	25. e

Boredom Buster 4–1

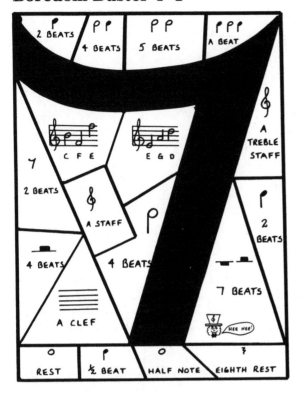

The hidden sign is an eighth rest.

Boredom Buster 4–2

Boredom Buster 4–3

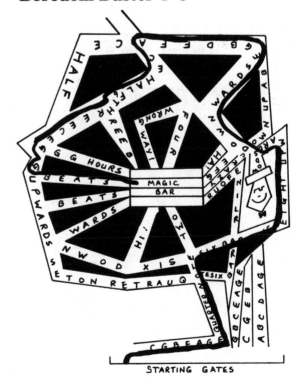

Boredom Buster 4–4

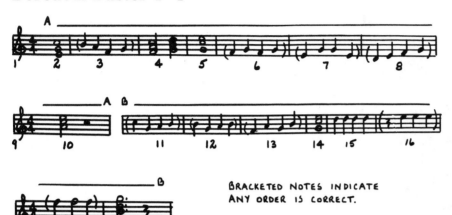

BRACKETED NOTES INDICATE
ANY ORDER IS CORRECT.

Piano accompaniment:

CHAPTER 5
The Magic
Keyboard

139

Before reading ask:
1. What happened in the last story?
2. What does a dot after notes and rests do? (adds ½ more)
3. How many beats in
o·? (6) ♩·? (3) ♪·? (1½)
4. What does a tie do? (joins two notes of same pitch)
5. How many beats in
o ♩·? (7) ♩ ♩·? (3) ♪ ♪·? (1½)

Whoosh! Whoosh! Whoosh! Mac, Christina, and Mr. Treble Clef soared all over Musictown until they flew to the very edge of it. There the children saw what appeared to be a long black and white bridge stretching right out of sight. And it was a very strange looking bridge indeed!

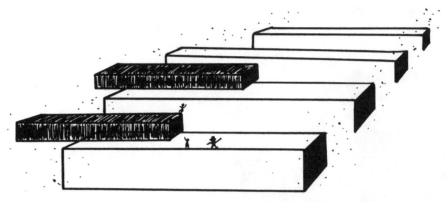

"Wow! What's that?" shouted Mac, as he flew high in the air over the bridge.

"That is the *piano keyboard*!" answered Mr. Treble Clef. "All musical things can be understood with the piano keyboard . . . and, the piano keyboard can send you home!"

"How does the piano keyboard work?" asked Christina.

"Well," said Mr. Treble Clef, "it has white keys and black keys. Each one makes a different sound. As you play keys to the right, sounds go higher. As you play to the left, sounds go lower.

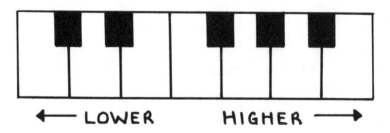

"Why are some keys white and some keys black?" asked Mac.

"So you can see and find notes more easily," answered the old man, and he continued by saying, "The white notes are all in a row but the black notes are grouped in two's and three's. See?"

Demonstrate this on a real piano keyboard.

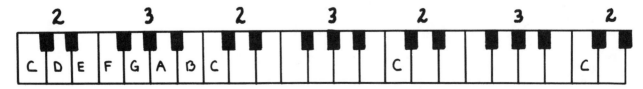

"The note *to the left* of any group of *two* black notes is *C*. From *C*, just play white notes to the right, and you'll have D E F G A B!"

"That's easy!" squealed Christina. "As notes go to the right on the keyboard, they go higher and move to the right in the alphabet, playing A B C D E F G, A B C D E F G. Going left on the keyboard makes notes go lower, and backwards in the alphabet."

Demonstrate on a real piano keyboard.

"Kee-rect," shouted Mr. Treble Clef, and then he started to sing:

Class reads together:

> There are twenty-six letters in the alphabet.
> Music, it has seven:
> A B C D E F G
> And then you start again.
>
> Read to the right in the alphabet
> When the notes go higher;
> Read to the left, when the notes go down—
> Both in band and choir.

Mac and Christina were giggling as they clapped along to Mr. Treble Clef's song. Mac was starting to act silly. Christina became annoyed because Mac was acting silly and so she started to clap on Mac's head. And pretty hard too!

"Ow! Cut it out Christina," cried Mac.

"Well, quit fooling around!" said Christina.

"I can do what I want to do! I know all of the names of notes on the piano keyboard anyway," said Mac indignantly.

"Well then, smarty, what are the names of the black keys?" asked Christina.

Mac was looking a bit uneasy and was starting to scratch his head when Mr. Treble Clef piped up to save Mac.

"The black keys have *sharp* or *flat* names," said Mr. Treble Clef. "Black keys to the *right* of white keys have the white key's name with a *sharp* added to it. Adding a sharp to a note name makes it sound higher."

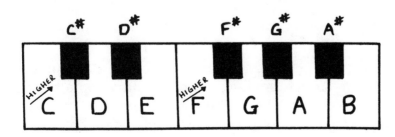

Show the black keys on a real piano keyboard.

"Black keys to the *left* of white keys have white key's names, with a *flat* added to it. Adding a flat to a note name makes it sound lower."

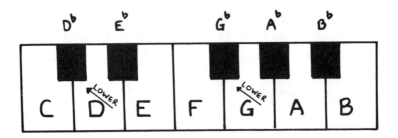

Then Mr. Treble Clef burst into song while walking away, singing:

> A B C D E F G
> Are the piano white keys.
> Black notes are the sharps or flats,
> Grouped in two's or three's.

"Wait!" Mac shouted, "How do we know when notes are in the staff, if they are sharp, flat, or just *natural* notes?"

Mr. Treble Clef hesitated, turned, and said, "Natural notes, which are the white notes on the piano, can have a ♮ sign in front of them. Sharp notes have a ♯ sign in front and flat notes have a ♭ sign in front of them. See?"

Point out sharp (♯), flat (♭), and natural (♮) signs.

You may want to stop here, and continue in a later class.

"Sure!" Mac and Christina answered in unison.

Christina piped up. "Learning about the piano keyboard has been fun and I can't wait until I play some music back home . . ." There was a bit of uneasiness in her voice. " . . . But how can this piano keyboard get us home?"

"Don't worry, Christina," said Mr. Treble Clef. "Your understanding of the piano keyboard will help you to play music and get you home. Now, just start at the bottom of the keyboard, and travel *upwards* moving C, C♯, D, D♯, E, F, F♯, G, G♯, A, A♯, B. Don't leave any notes out and you'll get home."

So, the children said their goodbyes and hopped up onto the giant keyboard note C, just left of two giant black notes. Then they climbed up onto C♯, jumped to D, scrambled up to D♯, and so on, making sure they always went higher by moving to the right on the keyboard. They never missed a key. Key by key, faster and faster they traveled from one neighboring note to another . . .

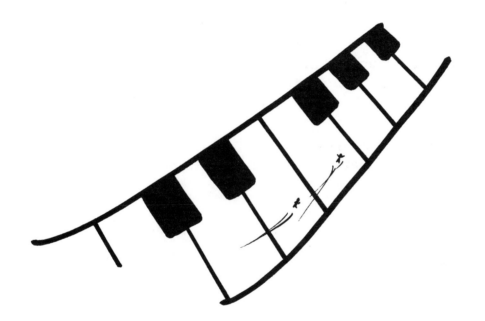

Ask:
1. What is ♯? (sharp) ♭? (flat) ♮? (natural)
2. What are the black notes? (sharps and flats)
3. What is the musical space between any two neighboring notes? (a semitone)
4. What are the sharps or flats at the start of staves called? (key signatures)

. . . until all they could see was a blur. Then they suddenly found themselves in a very dark place. In this place a very strange sound rang out as if it would ring forever. . . .

SUGGESTIONS FOR TEACHING THE SONG, *Sharp, Flat, and Natural Notes*

1. Perform *sharp, flat, and natural notes* for your class or play the tape.
2. Go through the words with your students, making sure they understand the words.
3. Teach each line by rote, maintaining a steady, unbroken tempo. Maintain the correct rhythms of the lyrics. Teach the body motions at the same time.

4. Remove the pitches to learn the rhythms of the lyrics whenever necessary. After lines are learned in this manner, put the pitches back in.
5. Have fun!

THE BODY MOTIONS

Verse 1:
bar: 3–4   Point a finger on each beat.
          6   Hold up 7 fingers on "seven."
        7–8   A hand moves higher and higher on each note sung.

Verse 2:
bar: 3–4   Beat 1—Head to the left then move from left to right during these bars.
        5–6   A hand moves higher and higher on each beat.
          7   Beat 1—head forward. Beat 3—head turns left.
          8   Point downwards on the third beat.

Verse 3:
bar: 3–4   Point a finger on each beat.
        5–6   Play an imaginary piano through these bars.
          8   Point up on "sharp" and down on "flat."
         10   Point two fingers.
         11   Point three fingers.

Chorus:
bar: 12   Point finger up on "notes."
         13   Point finger upwards on "up."
         15   Point finger downwards on "down."
      16–17   Draw a line of a natural sign on each beat.

SHARP, FLAT, AND NATURAL NOTES

146

The Magic Keyboard

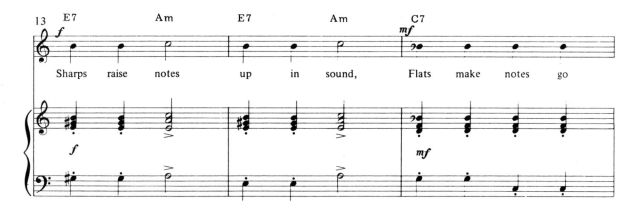

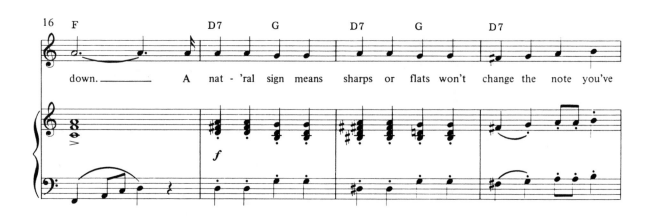

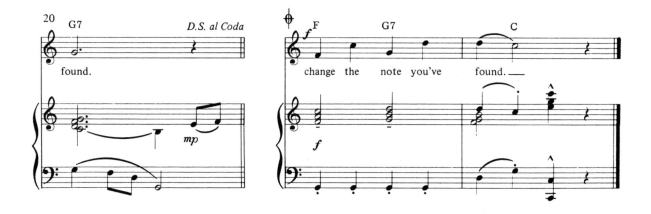

NAME _____

Quiz 5–1

WHAT DO YOU REMEMBER ABOUT THE KEYBOARD ?

© 1990 by Parker Publishing Company

1. ▮▮▮▮▮▮▮▮▮▮ is a
    a. white key
    b. piano keyboard
    c. staff
    ☐

2. The piano keyboard has
    a. white keys
    b. black keys
    c. both of these
    ☐

3. Each key
    a. makes the same sound
    b. makes no sound
    c. makes different sounds
    ☐

4. As you play to the right on the keyboard, notes
    a. stay the same
    b. go higher
    c. go lower
    ☐

5. As you play to the left on the keyboard, notes
    a. go lower
    b. go higher
    c. stay the same
    ☐

6. Keys are black and white, so you can
    a. see notes more easily
    b. find notes more easily
    c. both A and B
    ☐

7. White keys are grouped
    a. in a row
    b. in two's and three's
    c. upside down
    ☐

8. Black keys are grouped
    a. in a row
    b. in two's or three's
    c. upside down
    ☐

9. The note C is found
    a. to the left of a group of two black notes
    b. anywhere
    c. on top of the piano
    ☐

10. White notes *following C*, going higher, are
    a. D E F G A B C
    b. B A G F A
    c. A B C D E
    ☐

11. Notes A B C D E F G are
    a. going lower
    b. going higher
    c. going nowhere
    ☐

12. Notes G F E D C B A are
    a. going lower
    b. going higher
    c. going nowhere

13. Music uses how many different letters?
    a. 26
    b. 7
    c. 9

14. Black keys are
    a. sharp notes
    b. flat notes
    c. both a and b

15. The black key to the right of C is
    a. C♯
    b. C♭
    c. C♮

16. The black key to the left of D is
    a. D♯
    b. D♭
    c. D♮

17. The black key to the right of G is
    a. G♮
    b. G♭
    c. G♯

18. The black key to the left of B is
    a. B♭
    b. B♮
    c. B♯

19. Another name for the white note G is
    a. G♯
    b. G♭
    c. G♮

20. Sharps make notes go
    a. crazy
    b. lower
    c. higher

21. Flats make notes go
    a. lower
    b. go away
    c. higher

22. Natural signs before notes tell us notes are
    a. white notes
    b. black notes
    c. where nature is

23. A natural sign in front of a note means the note
    a. has a sharp
    b. has a flat
    c. has no sharp or flat

24. D♯ is higher than D
    a. True
    b. False

25. B♭ is lower than B
    a. True
    b. False

© 1990 by Parker Publishing Company

25

Name *each* note on the two keyboards.

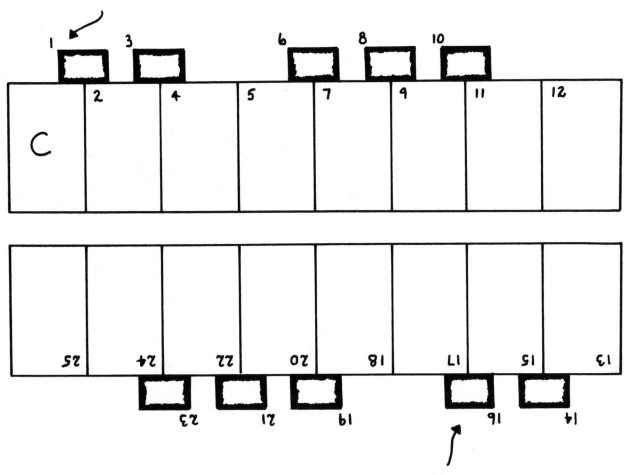

GIVE SHARP NAMES TO THE BLACK KEYS
ON THE UPPER KEYBOARD AND...

1   3   6   8   10

2   4   5   7   9   11   12

C

25   24   22   20   18   17   15   13

23   21   19   16   14

... GIVE FLAT NAMES TO THE BLACK KEYS
ON THE LOWER KEYBOARD.

WOO!
FUN, EH?

25

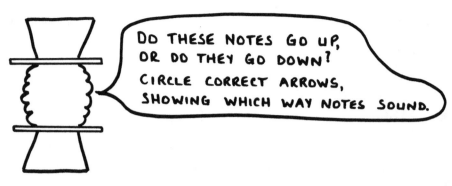

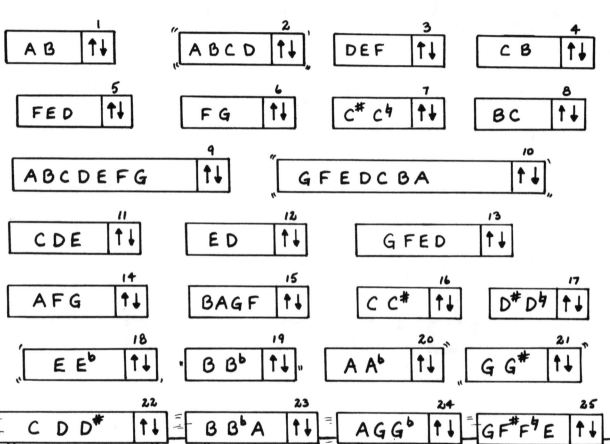

NAME _____

Quiz 5–4

© 1990 by Parker Publishing Company

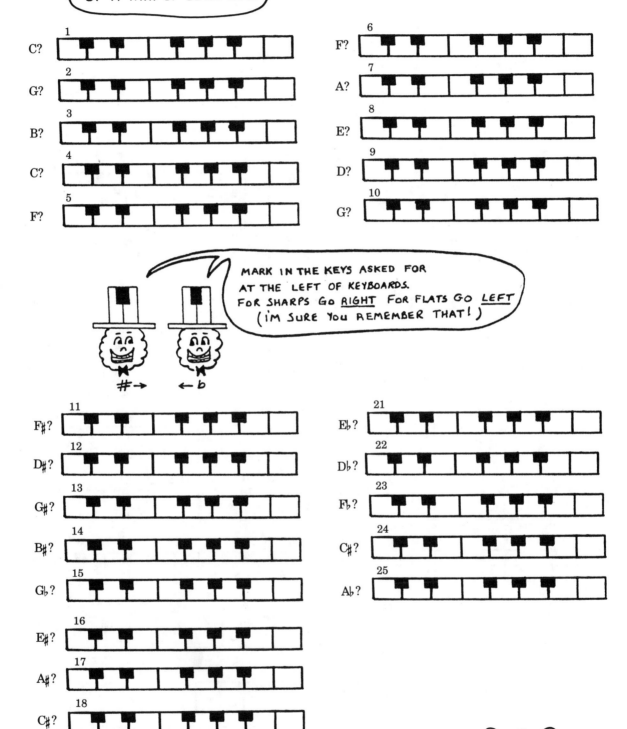

NAME _____

Quiz 5–5

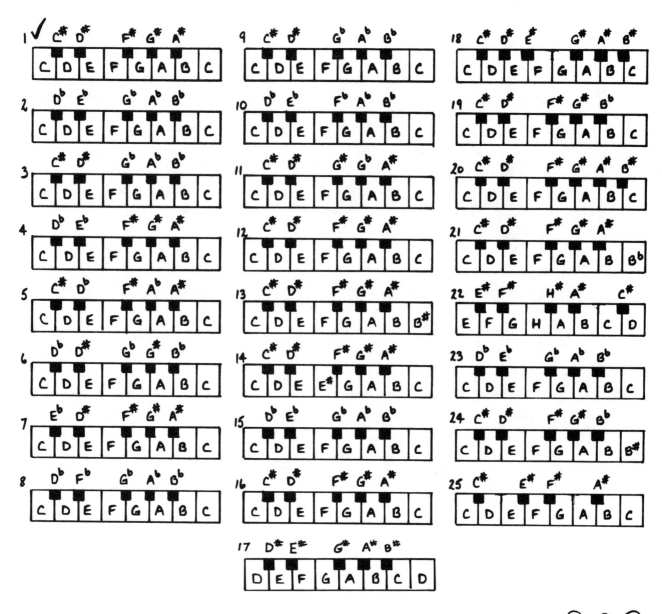

© 1990 by Parker Publishing Company

25

SOMETHING NEW

When you write sharps, flats, or natural signs in the staff, *you always place them in front of the note.*

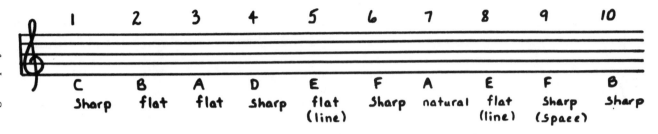

Write the following notes *in the staff.*

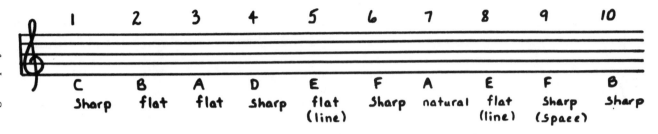

1	2	3	4	5	6	7	8	9	10
C sharp	B flat	A flat	D sharp	E flat (line)	F sharp	A natural	E flat (line)	F sharp (space)	B sharp

When you write notes with sharps, flats, or natural signs *that are not in the staff,* you always place them after the note name. ("Yesterday, I played a C♯, B♭, and an E♮.")

Write the full names of the following notes *below the staff.*

1   2   3   4   5   6   7   8   9   10

Fill in what you find is missing below.

EXAMPLE: D♯   E♭   1   2   3   4   5
                         G♯   A♭ F♯ C

25

HAVE YOU NOTICED . . .

. . . that a note can have two different names?

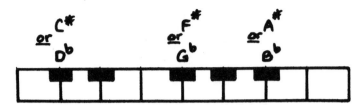

Any time you move *upwards one note* from a white note, you can add a sharp
(♯) to the white note name.

C–C♯, E–E♯, F–F♯

Any time you move *downwards one note* from a white note, you can add a flat
(♭) to the white note name.

D–D♭, C–C♭, F–F♭

Use the keyboard below and give a new, correct name to each given note, in the
boxes below.

EXAMPLE
↓

Eᵇ	C♯	D♯	F♯	G♯	A♯	B♯	E♯	Eᵇ	Dᵇ	Bᵇ	Aᵇ	Gᵇ	Fᵇ	Cᵇ	F
→D♯	1	2	3	4	5	6	7	8	9	10	11	12	13	14	15

C	Dᵇ	C♯	B	A♯	D♯	E♯	F	G♯	C
16	17	18	19	20	21	22	23	24	25

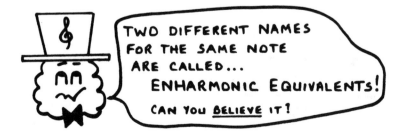

TWO DIFFERENT NAMES
FOR THE SAME NOTE
ARE CALLED...
ENHARMONIC EQUIVALENTS!
CAN YOU BELIEVE IT!

PLAY THE PAPER PIANO

You can see numbers below a staff on this page. You can find these same numbers on the keys of the keyboard.

Look for each number (you find below a staff) *on the keyboard* and then place the note the number means, *in the staff*.

All notes will be quarter notes.

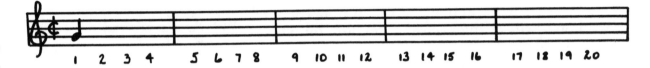

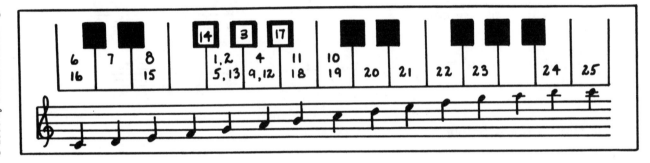

25

NOTES INSIDE BARS

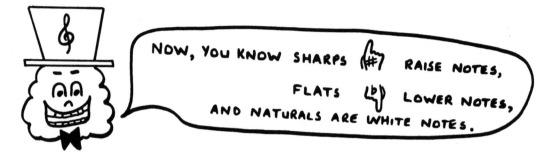

© 1990 by Parker Publishing Company

New Rules:

1. Sharps, flats, and natural signs in front of notes will change these notes for the whole bar.

2. After the bar line these sharps, flats, and natural signs are canceled.

3. A natural sign always makes a note a natural note.

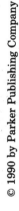

Name the 25 notes below:

THE OCTAVE

Words with "oct" in them have 8 of something:

8 LEGS

OCTAGON
8 SIDES

8 PLAYERS

Octave in music means 8 notes.

IF YOU START ON ANY NOTE CALL IT **1** AND COUNT UP TO THE EIGHTH NOTE. THE EIGHTH NOTE IS <u>ONE OCTAVE</u> HIGHER THAN NOTE **1**. NOTES **1** AND **8** WILL HAVE THE SAME NAME!

ONE OCTAVE (8 NOTES) → C D E F G A B C

ONE OCTAVE (8 NOTES) → D E F# G A B C# D

ONE OCTAVE (8 NOTES) → F G A B♭ C D E F

Write notes one octave higher than those in the staff below.

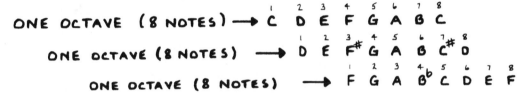

Write notes one octave lower than those in the staff below.

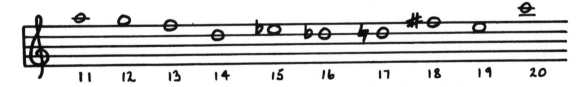

Are the following notes one octave apart? Yes or no.

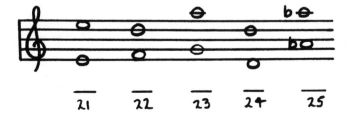

25

CHAPTER REVIEW

Match up each of ten questions from a chapter with a box of ten answers from the same chapter.

CHAPTER 5

1	G F E	A	KEYBOARD	
2	[beamed notes]	B	8 NOTES	
3	SHARPS	C	NOTE C	
4	[beamed notes]	D	NOTES GOING LOUDER	
5	A B C D	E	LOWER NOTES	
6	D♯ AND E♭	F	CANCEL A ♯ or ♭	
7	OCTAVE	G	NOTES GOING HIGHER	
8	NATURALS	H	ENHARMONIC EQUIVALENTS	
9	[beamed notes]	I	RAISE NOTES	
10	FLATS	J	NOTE E	

CHAPTER 2

1	o	A	4	
2	CHANGING NOTE VALUES	B	1	
3	BEATS IN ♪	C	QUARTER NOTE	
4	♩	D	RHYTHM	
5	BEATS IN ♩	E	WHOLE NOTE	
6	UNCHANGING PULSE	F	2	
7	♩	G	HALF NOTE	
8	BEATS IN o	H	EIGHTH NOTE	
9	♪	I	BEAT	
10	BEATS IN ♩	J	½	

CHAPTER 4

1	BEATS IN o. ♩	A	4	
2	A DOT	B	ADDS ½ MORE TO NOTES AND RESTS	
3	BEATS IN ♩ ♩	C	2	
4	BEATS IN o.	D	1½	
5	BEATS IN o ♩	E	6	
6	BEATS IN o. ♪	F	8	
7	BEATS IN ♩.	G	3	
8	BEATS IN ♪	H	7	
9	BEATS IN o. ♩	I	5	
10	BEATS IN ♩ ♩	J	9	

CHAPTER 1

1	TREBLE CLEF	A	SECOND LINE	
2	A	B	THIRD SPACE	
3	[ledger lines]	C	NAMES OF STAFF LINES	
4	G	D	[G clef symbol]	
5	E G B D F	E	LEDGER LINES	
6	TREBLE CLEF'S OTHER NAME	F	NAMES OF STAFF LINES	
7	F A C E	G	FOURTH LINE	
8	D	H	G CLEF	
9	C	I	STAFF	
10	[ledger lines]	J	SECOND SPACE	

CHAPTER 3

1	[rest]	A	½	
2	BEATS IN [rest]	B	QUARTER REST	
3	BEATS IN [rest]	C	WHOLE REST	
4	[rest]	D	2	
5	BEATS IN [rest]	E	1	
6	[rest]	F	HALF REST	
7	BEATS IN [rest]	G	4	
8	BEATS IN [rest]	H	EIGHTH REST	
9	[rest]	I	5	
10	BEATS IN [rest]	J	3	

WHEW!

YOU'RE SMART!

50

NAME _____

BB 5–1

BOREDOM BUSTER

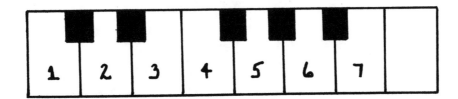

Each white note on the keyboard above has been given a number. On the lines below, write the correct letter name from the keyboard to complete the story.

____ lon ____ tim ____ ____ ____ o, ____ ____ r ____ ____ n ____ 1 ____
  6   5   3 1 5   6   5   3 3   3   4

____ t ____ ____ ____ ____ ____ ____ n ____ ____ 11 ____ sl ____ ____ p
  6   3   6 7 6 2   3 5 5   6   2   4 3   6   3 3

____ or ____ ____ ____ ____ ____ ____ ____ ! ____ urin ____ this tim ____ , th ____
  4   6   2 3 1 6 2 3   2   5   3   3

____ ____ ____ ____ ____ ____ ____ h ____ n ____ ____ ____ th ____ ____ lf into ____
  7 6 2   3 5 5   1   6   5 3 2   3   3   6

r ____ ____ ____ r ____ ____ on. Th ____ monst ____ r wok ____ up, 1 ____ ____ t
   3 2   2   6 5   3   3   3   3 4

his ____ ____ ____ , stu ____ i ____ ____ th ____ s ____ ____ l ____ s on his ____ ____ ____ k,
     7 3 2   2   3 2   3   1 6   3   7 6 1

____ r ____ w lon ____ h ____ ir, ____ n ____ ____ ____ m ____ th ____
  5   3   5   6   6   2   7 3 1 6   3   3

____ or ____ st's ____ irst tr ____ in ____ ____ ro ____ k monst ____ r.
  4   3   4   6   3 2   1   3

BOREDOM BUSTER

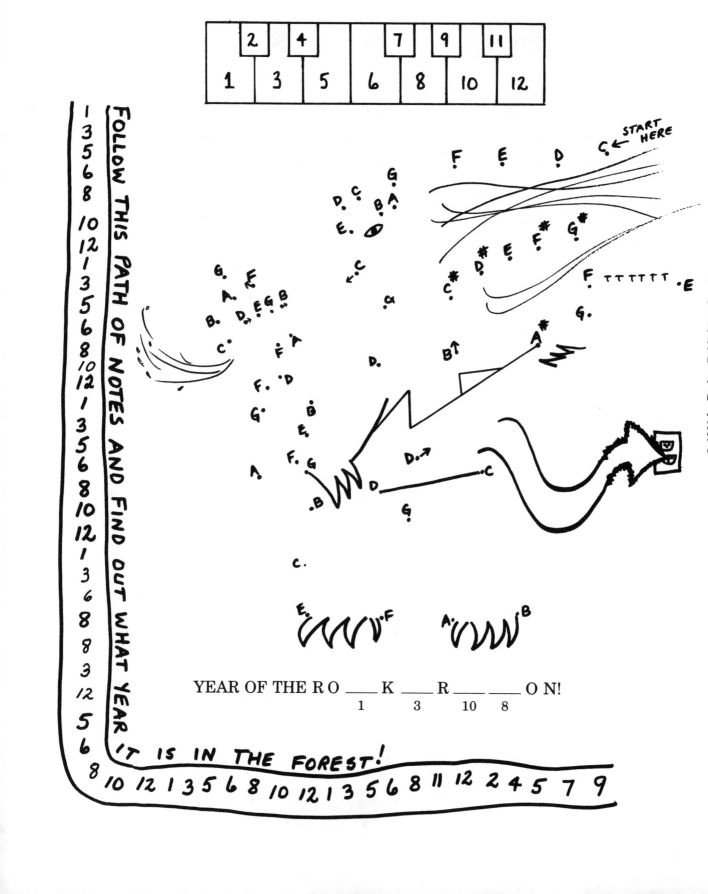

FOLLOW THIS PATH OF NOTES AND FIND OUT WHAT YEAR IT IS IN THE FOREST!

START HERE

YEAR OF THE R O ___ K ___ R ___ ___ O N!
                    1   3   10 8

BOREDOM BUSTER

Some of the words below that cross each other mean the same thing. Circle the letters wherever this happens. Then connect the circled letters.

You have drawn an ____ ____ ____ A G O N! And it's a lady! She has ____ sides.

BOREDOM BUSTER

SEARCH EACH KEYBOARD BELOW FOR A NOTE-NAME ERROR! PLACE THE INCORRECT NOTE OF EACH KEYBOARD IN THE KEYBOARD'S POT.

THEN UNSCRAMBLE THE "POT LETTERS" TO FIND OUT WHAT EACH OF THE KEYBOARDS HAVE THAT'S THE SAME.

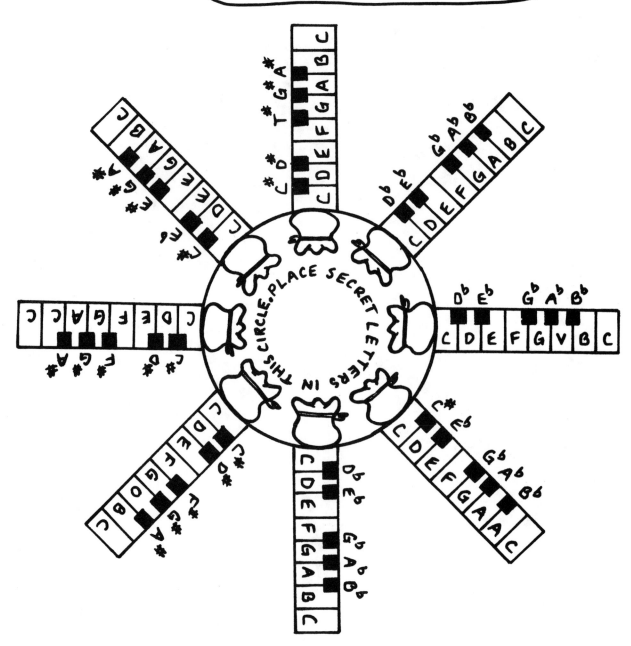

Each keyboard is one _____!
(unscramble letters in the circle)

RULES TO "MUSIC BEE"

This game is similar to the popular "Spelling Bee."

1. Two teams are formed in the class.
2. Each team stands in a line at opposite sides of the room.
3. One at a time, members from opposing teams attempt to guess answers to the Information Cards that are displayed by the teacher.
4. Students who guess cards incorrectly must return to their seats. This continues until one student from one team remains, resulting in a winning team.

Note: When students become increasingly familiar with the material on the cards, ask each student for the answer to two or more cards. This may be necessary to end the game with a single student remaining.

Make laminated cardboard Information Cards (8½″ × 11″).

FRONT	NOTE NAME?	NOTE NAME?	NOTE NAME?	NOTE NAME?	NOTE NAME?	NOTE NAME?	NOTE NAME?	NOTE NAME?
BACK	C	D	E	F	G	A	B	C# OR Db

FRONT	NOTE NAME?	NOTE NAME?	NOTE NAME?	NOTE NAME?	A B C GOING HIGHER OR LOWER?	F E D GOING HIGHER OR LOWER?	B C D GOING HIGHER OR LOWER?	G F E GOING HIGHER OR LOWER?
BACK	D# OR Eb	F# OR Gb	G# OR Ab	A# OR Bb	HIGHER	LOWER	HIGHER	LOWER

FRONT	#	b	♮	WHAT DO #'s DO?	WHAT DO b's DO?	WHAT DO ♮'s DO?	A #, b or ♮ ARE ON WHAT SIDE OF NOTES?	OCTAVE MEANS WHAT?
BACK	A SHARP	A FLAT	A NATURAL	MAKE NOTES GO HIGHER	MAKE NOTES GO LOWER	CANCEL FLATS or SHARPS	LEFT SIDE	8 NOTES

Student Evaluation Sheet

CHAPTER 5
CLASS RECORD SHEET

GRADE   HOMEROOM TEACHER   CLASS PERIOD/DAY   YEAR

Have students complete as many quizzes as necessary. All tests need not be completed. Write in students' names and fill in their marks in the squares below.

STUDENTS' NAMES	SONG				QUIZ 5-1	QUIZ 5-2	QUIZ 5-3	QUIZ 5-4	QUIZ 5-5	QUIZ 5-6	QUIZ 5-7	QUIZ 5-8	QUIZ 5-9	QUIZ 5-10	QUIZ 5-11	BB 5-1	BB 5-2	BB 5-3	BB 5-4	FINAL MARK
	WORDS	MOTIONS	PITCHES	MUSICALITY																

PROGRESS OF CLASSES

A chart is given here to help you keep a record of the tasks your classes complete. After listing the class names in the top squares, indicate with a check mark (✔) or with the date that a task has been accomplished.

CHAPTER 5

LIST OF CLASSES										
HAVE READ THE STORY										
HAVE STARTED THE SONG										
STUDENTS KNOW SONG										
HAVE COMPLETED QUIZ NO.	ACTIVITY	SKILL PRACTICED								
	5–1. Multiple choice	chapter story review								
	5–2. Keyboard study	identifying keyboard notes								
	5–3. Circle arrows	upward and downward movement of notes								
	5–4. Keyboard study	finding keyboard notes								
	5–5. Checking keyboards	looking for wrong notes on keyboards								
	5–6. Writing notes with accidentals	writing staff notes and naming notes without staff								
	5–7. Fill in note names	enharmonic equivalence								
	5–8. Writing notes on the staff	transferring keyboard notes onto the staff								
	5–9. Naming notes having accidentals	accidental rules re: bar lines and naturals								
	5–10. Writing notes on the staff	identifying notes one octave higher and lower								
	5–11. Matching	review of Chapters 1–5								
BOREDOM BUSTER NO.	5–1. Story making	keyboard note identification								
	5–2. Tracing the hidden picture	keyboard note identification								
	5–3. Word puzzle	theory concept equations								
	5–4. Keyboard puzzle	finding errors in keyboard note names								
GAME: MUSIC BEE										

CHAPTER 5 ANSWER KEY

Quiz 5–1

1. b	6. c	11. b	16. b	21. a
2. c	7. a	12. a	17. c	22. a
3. c	8. b	13. b	18. a	23. c
4. b	9. a	14. c	19. c	24. a
5. b	10. a	15. a	20. c	25. a

Quiz 5–2

1. C♯	6. F♯	11. B	16. E♭	21. A♭
2. D	7. G	12. C	17. E	22. A
3. D♯	8. G♯	13. C	18. F	23. B♭
4. E	9. A	14. D♭	19. G♭	24. B
5. F	10. A♯	15. D	20. G	25. C

Quiz 5–3

1. ↑	6. ↑	11. ↑	16. ↑	21. ↑
2. ↑	7. ↓	12. ↓	17. ↓	22. ↑
3. ↑	8. ↑	13. ↓	18. ↓	23. ↓
4. ↓	9. ↑	14. ↓	19. ↓	24. ↓
5. ↓	10. ↓	15. ↓	20. ↓	25. ↓

Quiz 5–4

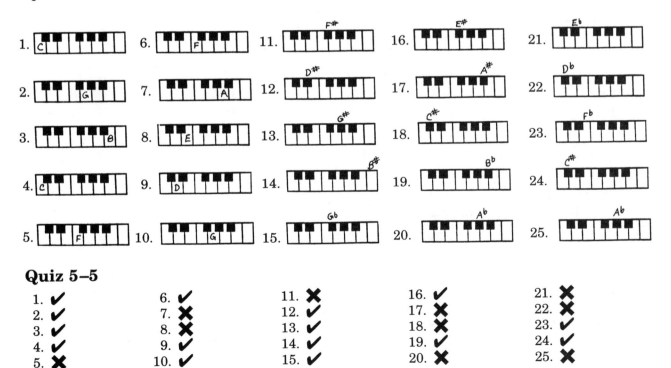

Quiz 5–5

1. ✔	6. ✔	11. ✘	16. ✔	21. ✘
2. ✔	7. ✘	12. ✔	17. ✘	22. ✘
3. ✔	8. ✘	13. ✔	18. ✘	23. ✔
4. ✔	9. ✔	14. ✔	19. ✔	24. ✔
5. ✘	10. ✔	15. ✔	20. ✘	25. ✘

Quiz 5–6

Quiz 5–7

1. D♭	6. C	11. G♯	16. B♯	21. E♭
2. E♭	7. F	12. F♯	17. C♯	22. F
3. G♭	8. D♯	13. E	18. D♭	23. E♯
4. A♭	9. C♯	14. B	19. C♭	24. A♭
5. B♭	10. A♯	15. E♯	20. B♭	25. B♯

Quiz 5–8

Quiz 5–9

1. C	6. B♭	11. F♯	16. A♭	21. B
2. C♯	7. B♭	12. F♯	17. A♭	22. B♭
3. C♯	8. B♭	13. F♯	18. G	23. B
4. C♯	9. A♯	14. F	19. B♭	24. C♯
5. B	10. A	15. A♭	20. B♭	25. C

Quiz 5–10

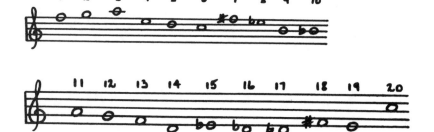

21. Yes	22. No	23. No	24. Yes	25. Yes

Quiz 5–11

Chapter 5	Chapter 4	Chapter 3	Chapter 2	Chapter 1
1. D	1. H	1. C	1. E	1. D
2. C	2. B	2. I	2. D	2. J
3. I	3. C	3. G	3. J	3. E
4. J	4. E	4. F	4. G	4. A
5. G	5. I	5. E	5. F	5. C
6. H	6. H	6. B	6. I	6. H
7. B	7. G	7. D	7. C	7. F
8. F	8. D	8. A	8. A	8. G
9. A	9. F	9. H	9. H	9. B
10. E	10. A	10. J	10. B	10. I

Boredom Buster 5–1

A long time ago, a green elf ate a bad egg and fell asleep for a decade!
During this time, the bad egg changed the elf into a red dragon. The monster
woke up, left his bed, studied the scales on his back, grew long hair, and
became the forest's first trained rock monster.

Boredom Buster 5–2

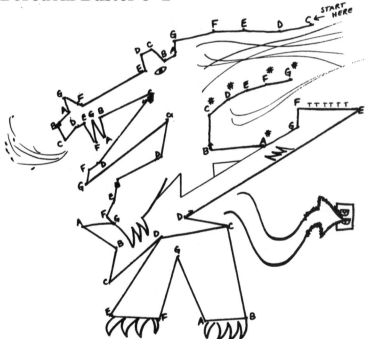

YEAR OF THE ROCK DRAGON!

Boredom Buster 5-3

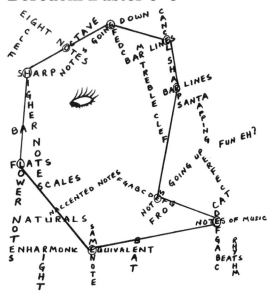

You have drawn an OCTAGON! And it's a lady. She has 8 sides.

Boredom Buster 5-4

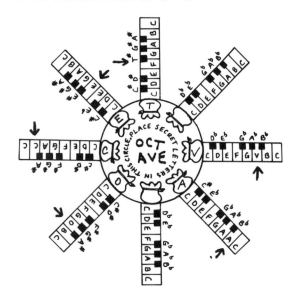

Each keyboard is one octave.

CHAPTER 6

Stuck on a Semitone!

Before reading ask:
1. What happened in the last story?
2. What is ♯? (sharp) ♭? (flat) ♮? (natural)
3. What are black notes? (sharps and flats)
4. What is the musical space between 2 neighboring notes? (semitone)

Mac and Christina had been traveling out of musictown along the magic keyboard, but now found themselves stuck in a dark place where they could hear a very loud sound.

"Where are we?" asked Christina.

"I don't know," replied Mac. "I can't see you! Where are you, Christina?"

"Right in front of you, Mac," answered Christina.

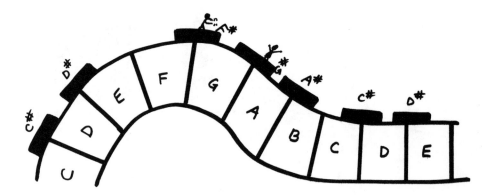

Mac squinted his eyes to see better. Christina was right. Mac could see now that Christina was standing in front of him on the very same black key that he was on.

"Where is that sound coming from?" asked Mac.

"I don't know, but let's try to get out of here," said Christina.

"OK!" said Mac, "Let's jump off this black key, down onto the white keys below."

Christina jumped off the black key down onto the next white key. Immediately, two very loud sounds rang out, clashing with each other.

"Oo," cried Christina.

Play C and C♯ on the piano simultaneously.

"Yeowch!" exclaimed Mac, and then he hopped off his key and landed on Christina's key. Now only one pitch could be heard.

"Mac," said Christina, "I think these keys are making these sounds because we're standing on them!"

"You're right!" boomed a voice whose echo seemed to last forever.

"Who's that?" shouted Mac. He had shivers running down his spine.

"Don't be afraid! I'm the magic keyboard and I want to help you to get home."

"B-b-but how?" asked Christina.

"Well," boomed the magic keyboard, "you are doing very well in getting home, but if you travel upwards one key at a time, it will take you forever. There is a quicker way, you know."

"How?" the children asked. They couldn't see where the voice was coming from.

"By a *semitone!*" answered the invisible voice.

"What do you mean?" questioned Mac.

"You have been traveling up my keyboard one neighboring note after another, or by *semitones*. The distance between any two neighboring notes on the keyboard is a semitone. Traveling by semitones will take you too long to get home."

"Then what should we do?" queried Christina.

"Simply," the magic keyboard stated, "by standing on one note together and jumping onto two notes which are a semitone apart. But you must do this at the same time."

"How come?" Christina asked.

"Two notes which are a semitone apart sound very harsh together. They sound like a shock of musical electricity. If you jump on any two notes a semitone apart, the shock of musical electricity will catapult you all the way home."

"Wow!" exclaimed Mac. "Is it safe?"

"Sure," the magic keyboard reassured Mac, "this is a magic place. . . ."

"Which notes should we jump onto?" asked Christina.

"Pick any two notes a semitone apart," said the magic instrument, "like C and C♯, or B and B♭, or E and F, for example."

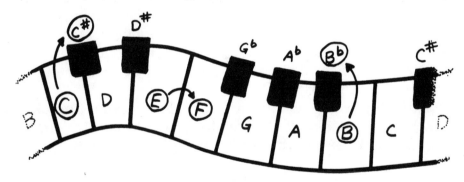

"OK! Let's do it," piped up Christina. "I'm getting pretty hungry."

"OK!" replied Mac.

"What notes shall we jump onto?" asked Christina.

"Well," answered Mac, "we're standing on E right now. Let's climb up onto G♭ so we'll be higher up. Then, let's jump at the same time really hard onto E and F. I'll jump over to E and you jump on F. This will make a really loud clash of semitones and we will be sure to have enough musical electricity to whisk us home."

"OK!" replied Christina.

"OK!" said Mac. "Let's jump *now!*"

Mac and Christina jumped as hard as they could and . . .
Woosh! In a flash of blinding light, they were transported to their Saturday morning class.

"Mac! Christina! I didn't see you come in," said the teacher, seeming quite surprised. "How *did* you come in?"

"By semitones," the children squealed. The class was quiet and so was the teacher. After all, they didn't have the foggiest idea what Mac and Christina were talking about.

Play these notes on the piano while reading them.

Confused, the teacher began to speak. "Well, class," he said, "we were talking about sharps and flats. C to C♯ is a semitone. E down to E♭ is also a semitone. A sharp (♯) raises notes one semitone. A flat (♭) lowers notes one semitone. Any two notes next to each other are a semitone apart!"

The entire class surrounding Mac and Christina let out a big groan and said, "What?"

Just then Mac and Christina giggled because they knew semitones were easy. To them, they were just the order of the keys on the keyboard, one following another.

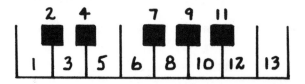

They knew that a semitone was the distance between any two notes that sat together on the keyboard. They started to laugh and began to sing:

Class together.

> The *semitone* is the smallest space
> Between two musical sounds;
> Played together, they surely make
> The strangest sound around.

Music notes which are neighbors,
Living right next door,
Are the distance of a semitone
On the piano keyboard.

Mac and Christina ran up to the piano, played A and A♯, which were a semitone apart. With this strange piercing sound, the entire class sang:

Semitone, half-step,
When together it's a wreck!

The class reads the poems together.

Just then, the teacher began waving his arms frantically, as if pleased that his class understood his lesson about semi-tones.
He sang:

White keys next to white keys,
Black next to white,
Are the distance of a semitone,
Moving left or right.

Mac and Christina jumped on top of the piano and filled the room with song:

Two notes with the same name
And one a flat or sharp—
These two notes will always be
A semitone apart.

Everybody joined in. It sounded like thunder when they sang:

Semitone, half step,
When together it's a wreck!

Just then, amidst the thunderous peal of voices, a giant chain with many links of sharps and flats encircled the singers. Like a serpent, the chain wrapped itself around everyone's feet and hands. Mac and Christina jumped off the piano, but the chain encircled them by their waists. The teacher was stunned. The chain wrapped around him like a hungry python. All were quiet.
Then, a low booming voice slowly spoke, saying:

I am *key signature*.
I am made out of sharps *or* flats.
—and you *must obey* my rules . . .

Ask:
1. What is a semitone? (the musical distance between any 2 neighboring notes on the piano)
2. How can you raise any note a semitone? (add a sharp)
3. How can you lower any note a semitone? (add a flat)
4. How can you erase a ♯ or ♭? (replace a ♯ or ♭ with a ♮)

Everyone screamed. Suddenly, they found themselves in a place of light where they could see nothing, except each other and the chain. . . .

SUGGESTIONS FOR TEACHING THE SONG, *The Semitone*

1. Perform *The Semitone* for your class or play the tape.
2. Go through the lyrics in the song, making sure students understand them. Play samples of semitones from the song so students can hear them. For example, in bar 1 the top notes demonstrate linear semitone motion. Bar 2 in the top line demonstrates simultaneous performance of semitones.
3. Teach each line by rote with a steady, continuous tempo using correct lyric rhythms. Teach body motions at the same time.
4. Remove pitches temporarily for teaching purposes, if this is necessary.
5. The divisi vocal parts are optional (bars 9, 10, 15, 16, 18, 26, 27, 28, 32, 33–35). If necessary have students perform only the upper notes in these measures. Working on both parts will be very beneficial because the students will be able to "experience" the semitone sound. This work will also improve their ability to sing close intervals with notes sung by other students.
6. Have fun!

THE BODY MOTIONS

Verse 1

bar:	
5–6	Hands are brought closer and closer on each beat until hands come together.
7	Hands are held together, pulsing the beat.
9	Play an imaginary piano until you. . . .
10	Place hands over ears.
11–12	Hands over ears and rock head back and forth on the beat.

Verse 2

bar:	
5–6	Hands are brought closer and closer on each beat until hands come together.
7	Hands are held together, pulsing the beat.
9	Hand held up to brow as if looking in the distance.
10	Hands over ears.
13	Play an imaginary piano.
15–16	Hands over ears and rock head back and forth on the beat.
17	Hands over ears for this bar.
18	Hands placed on head as if shocked by a loud dissonant sound.

Verse 1

bar:	
22–23	Two fingers held evenly together.
24–25	One finger held higher (black key) than the other (white key).
27	Hands over ears and . . .
28	Turn left and . . .
29	Turn right.

Verse 2

bar:	
22–23	Hold up 2 fingers.
24	Thumb is pointed downwards.
25	Thumb is pointed upwards.
30–31	Hands over ears and . . .
32–33	Rock head back and forth on the beat.
34	Hands over ears until . . .
35	Hands placed on head as if shocked by a loud dissonant sound.

THE SEMITONE

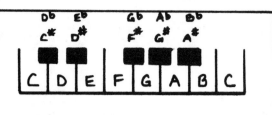

Quiz 6–1

Place a circle on a key showing if it's a semitone higher ↑ or lower ↓ than a given note.

1.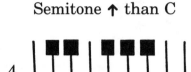
Semitone ↑ than C

2.
Semitone ↑ than D

3.
Semitone ↑ than F

4.
Semitone ↑ than G

5.
Semitone ↑ than E

6.
Semitone ↑ than B

7.
Semitone ↓ than D

8.
Semitone ↓ than E

9.
Semitone ↓ than G

10.
Semitone ↓ than B

11.
Semitone ↓ than A

12.
Semitone ↓ than F

13.
Semitone ↓ than C

14.
Semitone ↑ than C♯

15.
Semitone ↑ than E♭

16.
Semitone ↓ than B♭

17.
Semitone ↑ than A

18.
Semitone ↓ than F♯

19.
Semitone ↑ than F♯

20.
Semitone ↑ than G

21.
Semitone ↓ than A

22.
Semitone ↓ than A♭

23.
Semitone ↓ than C

24.
Semitone ↓ than B

25.
Semitone ↑ than C

25

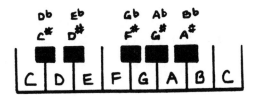

Are the following notes a semitone apart?
Mark ✔ if they are.
Mark ✘ if they are not.

1. C C# ✔	2. D D#	3. F F#	4. G G#	5. A A#
6. D D♭	7. G G♭	8. B B♭	9. D E	10. A B
11. D F	12. G# A	13. B B♭	14. G A	15. F G#
16. F# G#	17. D# E	18. E F	19. B C	20. C# F#
21. E E#	22. D G	23. G G#	24. F E	25. D C

COUNTING SEMITONES

The semitone is the distance between two notes that are right next to each other. Notes further apart must be a few semitones apart. Right?

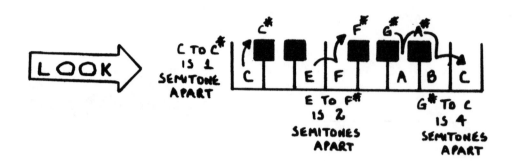

Circle the key that's a number of semitones above or below a given note.

1. 2 semitone ↑ C

2. 3 semitone ↑ C

3. 4 semitone ↑ D

4. 2 semitone ↑ D

5. 3 semitone ↑ D

6. 2 semitone ↑ F

7. 2 semitone ↑ G

8. 1 semitone ↑ B

9. 1 semitone ↑ C♯

10. 1 semitone ↑ D♯

11. 2 semitone ↑ A

12. 3 semitone ↑ C

13. 2 semitone ↑ C

14. 2 semitone ↓ D

15. 2 S.T. ↓ G

16. 2 semitone ↓ A

17. 2 semitone ↓ B

18. 3 semitone ↓ E

19. 3 semitone ↓ F

20. 5 S.T. ↑ C

21. 2 semitone ↑ G

22. 2 semitone ↑ A

23. 2 semitone ↑ F

24. 2 semitone ↑ D

25. 2 S.T. ↑ C

WRITE IN THE TOTAL NUMBER OF SEMITONES BETWEEN THESE NOTES.

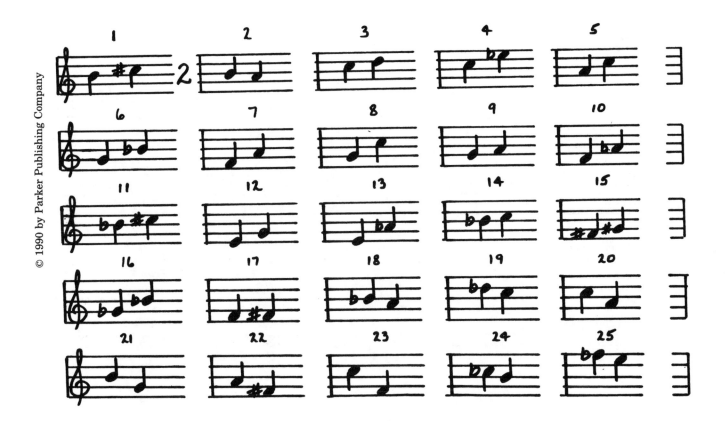

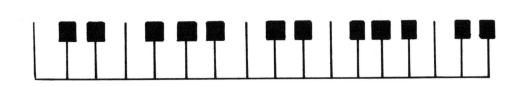

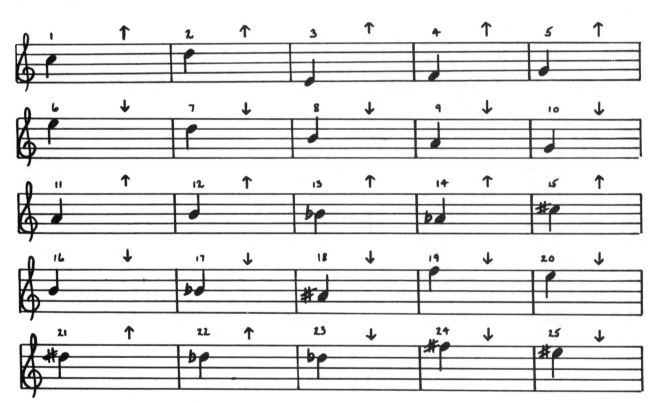

SEMITONES WITH LEDGER LINES

THE TONE

The tone (also called the whole tone) is two semitones added together. The tone is twice as big as the semitone.

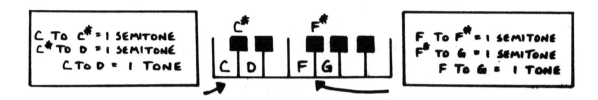

Circle the key that's a tone above or below a given note.

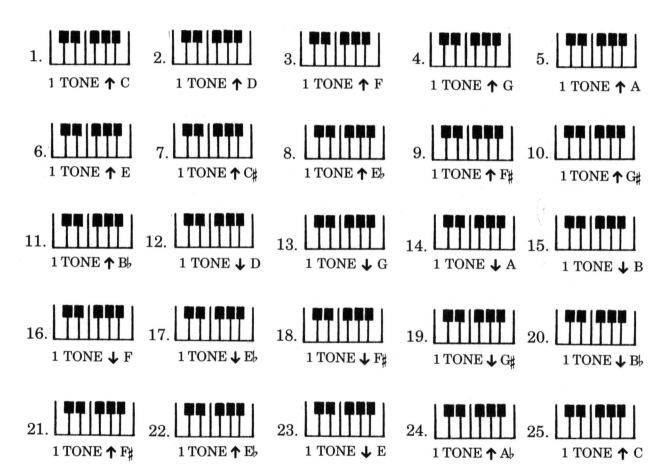

1. 1 TONE ↑ C
2. 1 TONE ↑ D
3. 1 TONE ↑ F
4. 1 TONE ↑ G
5. 1 TONE ↑ A

6. 1 TONE ↑ E
7. 1 TONE ↑ C♯
8. 1 TONE ↑ E♭
9. 1 TONE ↑ F♯
10. 1 TONE ↑ G♯

11. 1 TONE ↑ B♭
12. 1 TONE ↓ D
13. 1 TONE ↓ G
14. 1 TONE ↓ A
15. 1 TONE ↓ B

16. 1 TONE ↓ F
17. 1 TONE ↓ E♭
18. 1 TONE ↓ F♯
19. 1 TONE ↓ G♯
20. 1 TONE ↓ B♭

21. 1 TONE ↑ F♯
22. 1 TONE ↑ E♭
23. 1 TONE ↓ E
24. 1 TONE ↑ A♭
25. 1 TONE ↑ C

25

Place a note name a tone higher or lower than a given note. Higher whole tones go in upper notes. Lower whole tones go in lower notes.

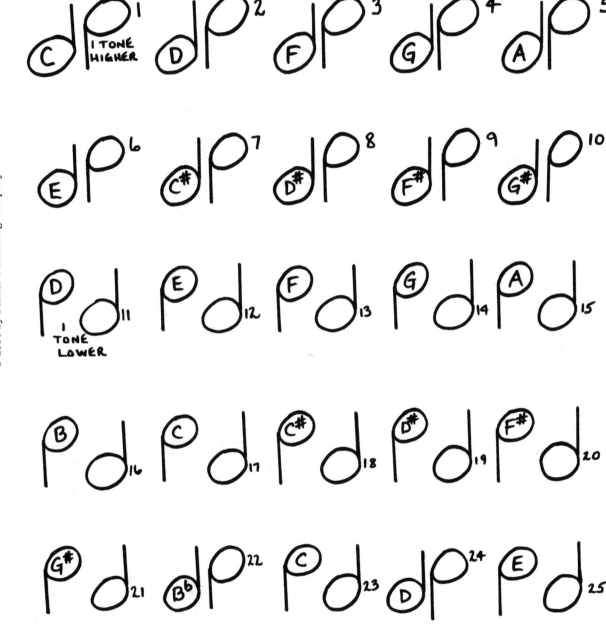

NAME _____

WRITING TONES IN THE STAFF

Draw notes in the staff, *tones* or *semitones* above or below the notes found below.

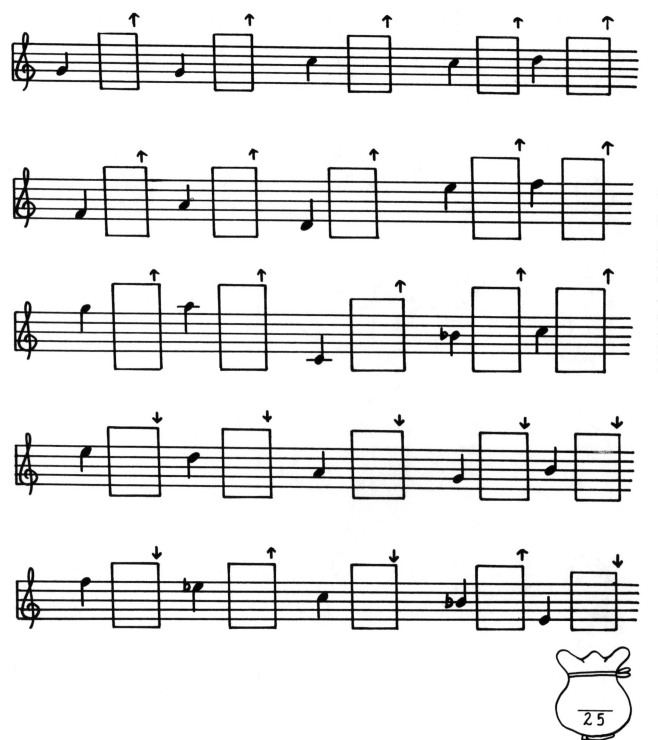

25

1. People play on the piano
    a. seat
    b. keyboard
    c. strings
    ☐

2. The piano is made up of
    a. black keys
    b. white keys
    c. both *a* and *b*
    ☐

3. The smallest distance between 2 notes is a
    a. key
    b. scale
    c. a semitone
    ☐

4. C and C♯ are how far apart?
    a. a tone
    b. a semitone
    c. a keyboard
    ☐

5. C and D are how far apart?
    a. a tone
    b. a semitone
    c. an alphabet
    ☐

6. Sharps change notes
    a. down a semitone
    b. into knives
    c. up a semitone
    ☐

7. Flats change notes
    a. down a semitone
    b. into flat tires
    c. up a semitone
    ☐

8. Naturals cancel
    a. flats
    b. sharps
    c. both *a* and *b*
    ☐

9. Semitones are
    a. two white notes together
    b. a black note next to a white note
    c. both *a* and *b*
    ☐

10. Whole tones are
    a. complete notes
    b. whole tones
    c. 2 semitones
    ☐

11. A sharp added to a note raises the note 1 semitone.
    a. True
    b. False
    ☐

12. A flat added to a note lowers the note 1 semitone.
    a. True
    b. False
    ☐

13. D to E♭ is a semitone.
    a. True
    b. False
    ☐

14. E♭ to D is a semitone.
    a. True
    b. False
    ☐

15. F to F♯ is a semitone.
    a. True
    b. False
    ☐

16. G to G♭ is a semitone.
   a. True
   b. False
☐

17. E to F is a semitone.
   a. True
   b. False
☐

18. D to E is a semitone.
   a. True
   b. False
☐

19. B to C is a semitone.
   a. True
   b. False
☐

20. A natural cancels a flat or sharp on a note.
   a. True
   b. False
☐

21. A semitone is a distance between two notes.
   a. True
   b. False
☐

22. Notes which are neighbors, side by side on the keyboard, are a semitone apart.
   a. True
   b. False
☐

23. White notes having no black note between them are how far apart?
   a. 1 semitone
   b. 2 miles
☐

24. In the staff, sharps, flats, and naturals are written in front of a note.
   a. True
   b. False
☐

25. How are the black notes arranged on the keyboard?
   a. in two's
   b. in three's
   c. in two's and three's
☐

BOREDOM BUSTER

Follow this pattern of tones and semitones: Tone, tone, semitone, tone, tone, tone, semitone. Follow it above C, then D, then F, then C, then D.

Trace your way to the winner's area.

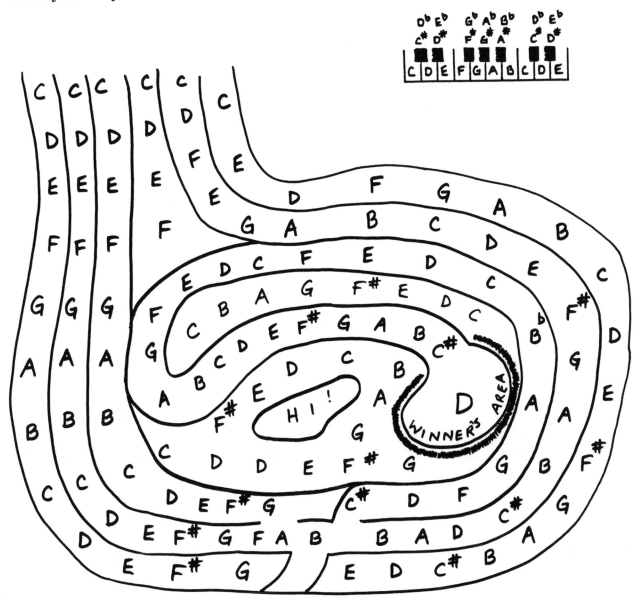

BOREDOM BUSTER

Can you find a line of notes that starts and ends with the same note name and travels upwards by semitones?

C	C#	D#	D	E	F	F#	G	Ab	A	Bb	B	C
C#	Db	D	Db	F	F#	G	G#	A	A#	B	C	C#
D	D#	D#	D#	F#	G	G#	A	Bb	B	C	C#	D
D#	E	E	E	G	G#	A	A#	B	C	C#	D	E
E	F	F	F	G#	A	Bb	B	C	C#	Cb	Eb	F
F#	Gb	F#	F	A	A#	B#	C	C#	D	D#	E	G#
F	G	G	G	A#	B	C	C#	D	Eb	E	F	A
G	G#	G#	G#	A	C	C#	D	D#	E	F	F#	Bb
Ab	A	A	Ab	Ab	C#	D	Eb	E	F	F#	G	B
A	Bb	Bb	A	Db	D	Eb	E	F	F#	G	G#	C
Bb	B	B	Bb	D	D#	E	F#	F#	F#	G#	Ab	C#
B	C	C	B	Eb	E	F	F#	G	G#	A	A#	D
C	C#	C#	C	E	F	F#	G	G	A	Bb	B	Eb

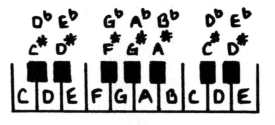

BOREDOM BUSTER

Across

1. The _____ makes notes and rests ½ longer.
3. C D E F G A B are _____ keys.
5. ♯'s make notes _____ up.
6. A tone is the _____ of 2 semitones.
7. Sharps and flats are the _____ keys.
9. The smallest distance between 2 notes is a _____.
11. A _____ sign cancels a sharp or a flat.
12. We _____ our feet to music's beat.
13. A steady even pulse is a _____.
14. Notes on the keyboard a semitone apart are always _____ to each other.
15. A flat makes a note go _____.

Down

2. A beat is the _____ a quarter note takes.
3. Two semitones make a _____ _____.
4. Figuring out notes is easy _____ you have a keyboard.
8. The semitone is the _____ distance between 2 notes.
9. A _____ makes a note go up 1 semitone.
10. A _____ makes a note go down 1 semitone.
13. 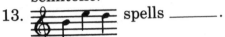 spells _____.

BOREDOM BUSTER

Write in the names of notes on the keyboards below.

On the keyboards below, start on a given note and then follow the pattern: Tone, tone, semitone, tone, tone, tone, semitone.

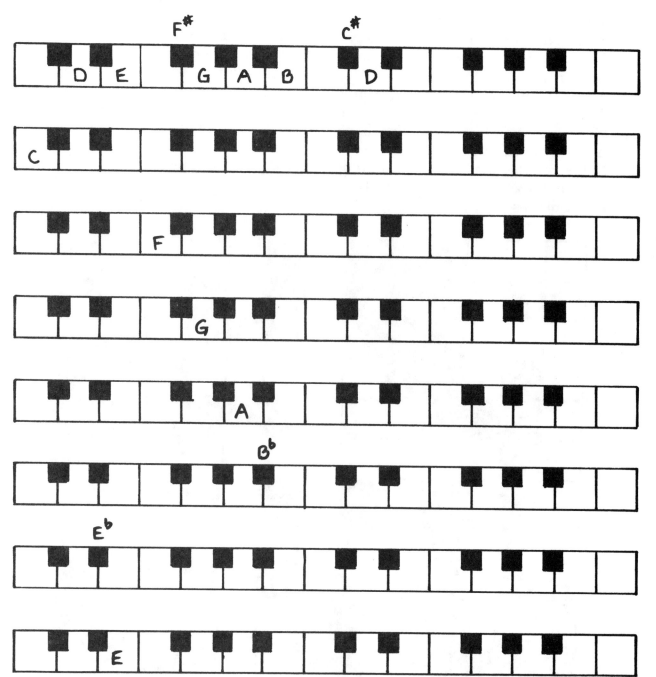

RULES TO "RIP OFF"

1. A partner is chosen for each student. Everyone is grouped in two's and is seated on the floor. (If there is an extra person left over, a group of three is formed.)

2. The teacher lays down an Information Card in front of each group, out of the reach of the students. The cards are question-side-up. Students place their hands behind their backs.

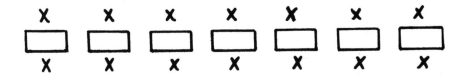

3. The teacher calls out the answer to one of the Card questions. Students who think the card in their group has the question, try to pick up the card before their partner does. Students who pick up a wrong card are disqualified, as are students who attempt to grab a correct card, but are slower than their eager partner.

4. As students are disqualified, new groups are formed from remaining students.

5. The game continues until only one student remains.

Make 8½″ × 11″ laminated cardboard Information Cards.

FRONT	A SEMITONE ABOVE C IS	A SEMITONE ABOVE D IS	A SEMITONE ABOVE E IS	A SEMITONE ABOVE F IS	A SEMITONE ABOVE G IS	A SEMITONE ABOVE A IS	A SEMITONE ABOVE B IS
BACK	C# or Db	D# or Eb	F or E#	F# or Gb	G# or Ab	A# or Bb	C or B#

FRONT	A SEMITONE BELOW C IS	A SEMITONE BELOW D IS	A SEMITONE BELOW E IS	A SEMITONE BELOW F IS	A SEMITONE BELOW G IS	A SEMITONE BELOW A IS	A SEMITONE BELOW B IS
BACK	B or Cb	Db or C#	Eb or D#	E or Fb	Gb or F#	Ab or G#	Bb or A#

FRONT	A TONE ABOVE C IS	A TONE ABOVE D IS	A TONE ABOVE E IS	A TONE ABOVE F IS	A TONE ABOVE G IS	A TONE ABOVE A IS	A TONE ABOVE B IS
BACK	D	E	F# or Gb	G	A	B	C# or Db

FRONT	A TONE BELOW C IS	A TONE BELOW D IS	A TONE BELOW E IS	A TONE BELOW F IS	A TONE BELOW G IS	A TONE BELOW A IS	A TONE BELOW B IS
BACK	Bb	C	D	Eb or D#	F	G	A

NAME _____

Student Evaluation Sheet

EXCELLENT!

PERFECT!

VERY GOOD!

HOW HIGH DO YOU STAND?
NOW COLOR   YOUR MAN!
(or balloons!)

GOOD!

FAIR!

OH, OH!

%

CHAPTER 6
CLASS RECORD SHEET

GRADE   HOMEROOM TEACHER   CLASS PERIOD/DAY   YEAR

Have students complete as many quizzes as necessary. All tests need not be completed. Write in students' names and fill in their marks in the squares below.

STUDENTS' NAMES	SONG				QUIZ 6-1	QUIZ 6-2	QUIZ 6-3	QUIZ 6-4	QUIZ 6-5	QUIZ 6-6	QUIZ 6-7	QUIZ 6-8	QUIZ 6-9	QUIZ 6-10	BB 6-1	BB 6-2	BB 6-3	BB 6-4	FINAL MARK
	WORDS	MOTIONS	PITCHES	MUSICALITY															

PROGRESS OF CLASSES

A chart is given here to help you keep a record of the tasks your classes complete. After listing the class names in the top squares, indicate with a check mark (✔) or with the date that a task has been accomplished.

CHAPTER 6

LIST OF CLASSES											
HAVE READ THE STORY											
HAVE STARTED THE SONG											
STUDENTS KNOW SONG											

HAVE COMPLETED QUIZ NO.	ACTIVITY	SKILL PRACTICED								
	6–1. Keyboard study	finding notes up and down a semitone								
	6–2. Correct semitones	the semitone								
	6–3. Keyboard study	counting semitones								
	6–4. Staff note study	counting semitones								
	6–5. Staff note writing	writing semitones								
	6–6. Ledger line note writing	writing semitones								
	6–7. Keyboard study	finding upward and downward whole tones								
	6–8. Keyboard study	finding upward and downward whole tones								
	6–9. Staff note writing	writing whole tones								
	6–10. Multiple choice	review of Chapter 6								
BOREDOM BUSTER NO.	6–1. Trace the maze	writing major scales								
	6–2. Note name puzzle	finding a chromatic scale								
	6–3. Crossword puzzle	review of Chapter 6								
	6–4. Keyboard fun	finding major scales								
GAME: RIP OFF											

CHAPTER 6 ANSWER KEY

Quiz 6–1

1. 6. 11. 16. 21.
2. 7. 12. 17. 22.
3. 8. 13. 18. 23.
4. 9. 14. 19. 24.
5. 10. 15. 20. 25.

Quiz 6–2

1. ✔	6. ✔	11. ✖	16. ✖	21. ✔
2. ✔	7. ✔	12. ✔	17. ✔	22. ✖
3. ✔	8. ✔	13. ✔	18. ✔	23. ✔
4. ✔	9. ✖	14. ✖	19. ✔	24. ✔
5. ✔	10. ✖	15. ✖	20. ✖	25. ✖

Quiz 6–3

1. 6. 11. 16. 21.
2. 7. 12. 17. 22.
3. 8. 13. 18. 23.
4. 9. 14. 19. 24.
5. 10. 15. 20. 25.

Quiz 6–4

1. 2	6. 3	11. 3	16. 4	21. 4
2. 2	7. 4	12. 3	17. 1	22. 3
3. 2	8. 5	13. 4	18. 1	23. 7
4. 3	9. 2	14. 2	19. 1	24. 0
5. 3	10. 3	15. 2	20. 3	25. 0

Quiz 6–8

1. D	6. F♯ (G♭)	11. C	16. A	21. F♯ (G♭)
2. E	7. D♯ (E♭)	12. D	17. B♭ (A♯)	22. C
3. G	8. E♯ (F)	13. E♭ (D♯)	18. B	23. B♭
4. A	9. G♯ (A♭)	14. F	19. C♯ (D♭)	24. E
5. B	10. A♯ (B♭)	15. G	20. E	25. D

Quiz 6–9

Quiz 6–10

1. b	6. c	11. a	16. a	21. a
2. c	7. a	12. a	17. a	22. a
3. c	8. c	13. a	18. b	23. b
4. b	9. c	14. a	19. a	24. a
5. a	10. c	15. a	20. a	25. c

Boredom Buster 6–1

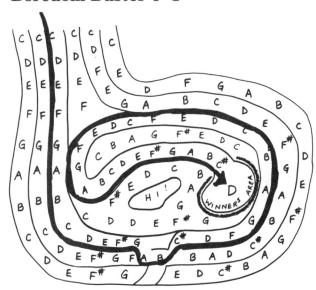

Boredom Buster 6–2

C	C♯	D♭	D	E	F	F♯	G	A♭	A	B♭	B	C
C♯	D♭	D	D♭	F	F♯	G	G♯	A	A♯	B	C	C♯
D	D♭	D♯	D♯	F♯	G	G♯	A	B♭	B	C	C♯	D
D♯	E	E	E	G	G♯	A	A♯	B	C	C♯	D	E
E	F	F	F	G♯	A	B♭	B	C	C♯	C♭	E♭	F
F♯	G♭	F♯	F	A	A♯	B♭	C	C♯	D	D♯	E	G♯
F	G	G	G♯	B	C	C♯	D	E♭	E	F	A
G	G♯	G♯	G♯	A	C	C♯	D	D♯	E	F	F♯	B♭
A♭	A	A	A♭	A♭	C♯	D	E♭	E	F	F♯	G	B
A	B♭	B♭	A	D♭	D	E♭	E	F	F♯	G	G♯	C
B♭	B	B	B♭	D	D♯	E	F♯	F♯	F♯	G♯	A♭	C♯
B	C	C	B	E♭	E	F	F♯	G	G♯	A	A♯	D
C	C♯	C♯	C	E	F	F♯	G	G	A	B♭	B	E♭

Boredom Buster 6–3

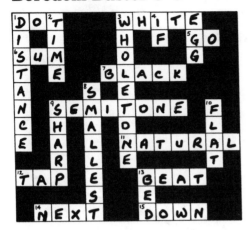

Boredom Buster 6–4

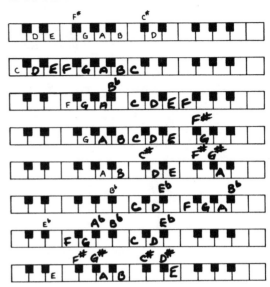

CHAPTER 7
The Great
Ruler of Notes

204

The giant chain of sharps and flats was tangled around everyone. The children and the teacher were starting to tremble. Again, a great voice boomed out:

I am *Key Signature.*
KEY SIGNATURE!
I am made out of sharps *or* flats,
And you *must follow* my rules.

Before reading ask:
1. What happened in the last story?
2. What is a ♯ (sharp), ♭ (flat), ♮ (natural)?
3. What is a semitone? (musical distance between two neighboring notes)
4. How can you raise notes a semitone? (add a ♯)
5. How can you lower any note a semitone? (add a ♭)
6. How can you erase a ♯ or ♭? (replace a ♯ or ♭ with a natural)

"Good grief," cried Mac. "I can't think. . . . What's a *key signature?*"

"Key signatures are made out of sharps or flats, kids," said the teacher. "You find them at the beginning of the staff." The teacher pointed to the blackboard where key signatures were written down.

A KEY SIGNATURE

ANOTHER KEY SIGNATURE

All of a sudden the chain started to shake all over and a low booming voice thundered, "Correct!" and to everyone's surprise, started to sing:

At the start of every song in the staff,
A group of sharps or flats
Tells us the notes to change as you play,
Throughout the song, in fact!

Class together.

205

Sharps or flats you find in a group,
Are called a *key signature*.
Up to seven sharps or flats you can find—
Or *none* at all, for sure!

Natural signs still do their task
And cancel any sharp or flat.
Even a sharp or flat from key signatures—
A natural changes *that*!

"Chain, Chain, Chain!" screamed Mac.

"I am not Chain. I am Key Signature!"

"Sorry," apologized Mac. "But if you don't mind me asking, why are you, the Key Signature, so important?"

"Because," the Key Signature boomed, "I tell you the correct notes to play all the way through a musical piece. I tell you what notes to play sharp or flat."

"Oh, you are important, Key Signature," said Christina. "We'd better remember to look at you before playing any piece of music."

"Cor-rect!" boomed the Key Signature chain.

And then it jingled:

A note on a line
Or space in a song
Will get a flat or sharp
The whole music long.

Just look at the start
Flats and the sharps
Won't let you go wrong . . .

Rumble. Jingle. Clatter. The Key Signature trembled while it sang its key signature song.

And with that, everybody began to sing the key signature song. The chain rattled right along with everyone. As the teacher and the children sang more and more, they began to know the words by heart. As soon as the last person knew the words, the giant chain stopped rattling.

All grew quiet. Again, a great thunderous voice boomed:

You know my rules.
You've sung my song.
You're free to read music,
You'll never go wrong!

And then the chain disappeared. Everyone now knew that

key signatures were very important. Without looking at the key signature, people wouldn't be able to play correct notes.

As soon as Christina finished saying, "I guess Key Signature left because we understand how important he is for us to read music notes correctly," all of the students and the teacher disappeared from sight. Suddenly they found themselves lost in a place of light.

Looking around, they began to see strange signs in the distance.

"How are we going to get out of here?" asked Christina.

"I don't know!" shuddered Mac. "Let's look at those signs up ahead. . . ."

Ask:
1. What do key signatures do? (tell what notes have flats or sharps throughout the music)
2. How many sharps or flats can you have in key signatures? (0–7)
3. What is a *key*? (the alphabet name of a certain key signature)

SUGGESTIONS FOR TEACHING THE SONG,
KEY SIGNATURES

1. Play the song, *Key Signatures*, for your students yourself or play the tape.
2. Go through the words with your students making sure the lyrics are clearly understood.
3. Teach the song by rote. Maintain a steady, continuous beat while maintaining the correct rhythms of the lyrics.
4. Extract pitches whenever necessary while teaching the song. Replace pitches when students are ready.
5. The "key" is, *have a ball!*

THE BODY MOTIONS

Verse 1

bar: 5   On "staff," hold out 5 fingers.

6   On "sharps," hold a thumb up. On "flats" hold thumb down.

9–11   Hold out one hand of five fingers (the staff). The other hand continually points further and further to the right (the changing notes).

Verse 2

bar: 5   Thumb up on "sharp." Thumb down on "flat."

9–10   Hold out 1 to 7 fingers successively, each on a beat.

11   Make a "zero."

Verse 3

bar: 5   Make each part of a natural sign, each on a beat.

9   Hold up a thumb on "sharp." Hold a thumb down on "flat."

10   Hold out 5 fingers (the staff) with one hand and point to where the key signature would be with the other.

11   Make each part of the natural sign, each on a beat.

KEY SIGNATURES

start of ev - 'ry song in the staff,   a group   of sharps   or flats
2. Sharps or flats you find in   a group   are called a key sig - na - ture:
3. Nat - 'ral signs   will do their task   and can - cel a sharp   or flat

tells us all the notes to change___ as you play,   through -
One to sev - en sharps or flats ___ you will find...   or
E - ven notes changed by key___ sig - na - tures:

1. Key signatures are made up of

    a. sharps or flats
    b. no sharps or flats
    c. both *a* and *b* ☐

2. Key signatures are found

    a. at the beginning
       of the staff
    b. at the end
       of the staff
    c. in the middle
       of bars ☐

3. Key signatures can have up to how many sharps or flats?

    a. 5
    b. 7
    c. 6 ☐

4. Key signatures tell you what notes are

    a. sharped or flatted
    b. sharped or flatted
       throughout
       a piece
    c. missing ☐

5. A natural sign in front of a note

    a. won't cancel sharps
       or flats from a key
       signature
    b. makes it bigger
    c. cancels any sharp
       or flat ☐

6. In   the note is

    a. F
    b. F♯
    c. F♮ ☐

7. In   the note is

    a. C♮
    b. C♯
    c. C♭ ☐

8. In   the note is

    a. G♯
    b. G♮
    c. G♭ ☐

9. In   the note is

    a. D♭
    b. D♯
    c. D♮ ☐

10. In   the note is

    a. A♮
    b. A♯
    c. A♭ ☐

11. In   the note is

    a. E♯
    b. E♭
    c. E♮ ☐

12. In the note is

    a. B♮
    b. B♭
    c. B♯

13. In 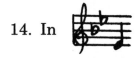 the note is

    a. B♭
    b. B♮
    c. B♯

14. In 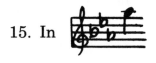 the note is

    a. E♯
    b. E♮
    c. E♭

15. In  the note is

    a. B♭
    b. A
    c. A♭

16. In  the note is

    a. D
    b. D♭
    c. E

17. In 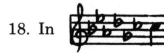 the note is

    a. G♯
    b. G
    c. G♭

18. In  the note is

    a. B♭
    b. C♭
    c. C

19. In the note is

    a. F
    b. E♭
    c. F♭

20. In  the second note is

    a. C♯
    b. C
    c. C♭

21. In  the second note is

    a. A♯
    b. A
    c. A♭

22. In  the third note is

    a. E
    b. F
    c. F♯

23. In  the fourth note is

    a. C♯
    b. C♮
    c. C♭

24. In the second note is

    a. G
    b. G♯
    c. A

25

KEY SIGNATURES CHANGE NOTES IN ANY OCTAVE

Do you remember that an octave is a distance of 8 notes? Two notes an octave apart have the same note name.

Since the piano has 88 keys, there are over 7 octaves. There are many C's, many D's, and so on. . . .

> So your new rule is:
>
> *A note in any octave is changed by A♯ or A♭ in a key signature.*

Name the following:

Draw five nice sharps.

And now, five flats!

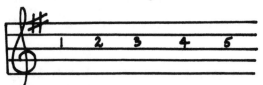 

Draw sharps right over the dots in the staff.

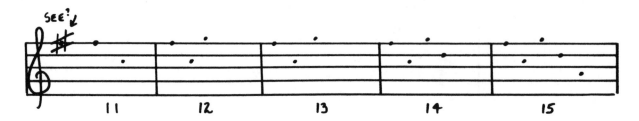

Now, flats!

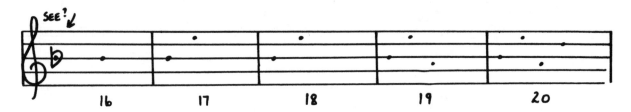

Studying the order of dots, decide if you should write sharps or flats.

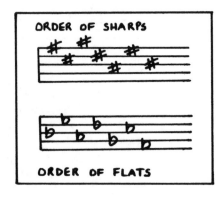

WRITE THE FOLLOWING MUSIC, BY FOLLOWING THE GIVEN INSTRUCTIONS.

DON'T FORGET WHAT KEY SIGNATURES DO!

1 2 3 4 5 6 7 8 9 10 11 12 13 14 15 16

1. DRAW A TREBLE CLEF . . . .
2. DRAW A SHARP ON LINE F .
3. DRAW A SHARP ON SPACE C .
4. DRAW A QUARTER NOTE D ON A LINE . . . . .
5. DRAW A C# QUARTER NOTE ON A SPACE . . . . .
6. DRAW A QUARTER D ON A LINE . . . .
7. DRAW A QUARTER F# ON A SPACE . . . .
8. DRAW A G FOR 1 BEAT . .
9. DRAW AN A FOR 1 BEAT . .
10. DRAW AN E ON A SPACE FOR 2 BEATS . . .
11. DRAW AN F# FOR 1 BEAT ON A LINE . . .
12. DRAW A G JUST ABOVE THE STAFF FOR 1 BEAT . .
13. DRAW A QUARTER NOTE C# .
14. DRAW A QUARTER NOTE D . . .
15. DRAW A Bb FOR 3 BEATS .
16. DRAW A REST HAVING 1 BEAT . . . . .

17 18 19 20 21 22 23 24 25

17. DRAW A TREBLE CLEF . . . . .
18. DRAW A SHARP ON LINE F . .
19. DRAW A SHARP ON SPACE C . .
20. DRAW AN Eb QUARTER NOTE ON A SPACE . . .
21. DRAW A Bb QUARTER NOTE . .
22. DRAW AN Eb QUARTER NOTE ON A SPACE . .
23. DRAW A C# QUARTER NOTE . . . .
24. DRAW A 4-BEAT D IN THE STAFF . . . .
25. PLACE A BAR LINE AFTER EVERY 4 BEATS .

25

Name all of the notes in the staff and . . .

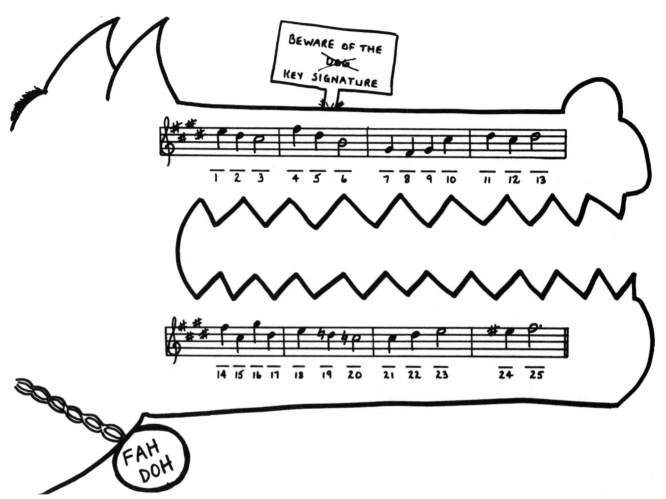

NAME THE NOTES WITH STARS ON TOP! ⭐ ⭐

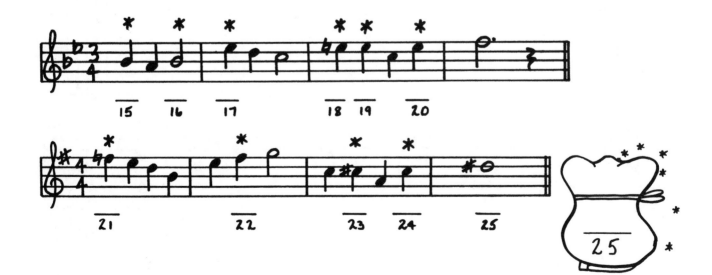

Match up questions and answers in each box.

1	(music staff) IS NOTE	C	A	E♭	16	(dotted half note) IS		A	6 BEATS
2	(music staff) IS NOTE		B	B♭	17	(dotted half + eighth) IS		B	5 BEATS
3	(music staff) IS NOTE		C	F♯	18	(two half notes) IS		C	3 BEATS
4	(music staff) IS NOTE		D	G♯	19	(half + eighth) IS		D	7 BEATS
5	(music staff) IS NOTE		E	C♯	20	(dotted half) IS		E	2 BEATS

PLACE ANSWERS   PLACE ANSWERS

6	C TO C♯ IS A	A	TONE	21	(rest) IS		A	2 BEATS
7	A SEMITONE SOUNDS	B	TWO SEMITONES	22	(rest) IS A		B	3 BEATS
8	A TONE IS	C	RAISES A NOTE A SEMITONE	23	(rest) IS		C	STAFF
9	A SHARP	D	SEMITONE	24	(rest) IS		D	6 BEATS
10	C TO D IS A	E	HARSH	25	(rests) IS		E	4 BEATS

PLACE ANSWERS

11	A NATURAL SIGN	A	CHANGES THAT NOTE FOR THE WHOLE BAR
12	A FLAT	B	C♯
13	A SHARP ADDED TO A NOTE IN A BAR	C	C
14	(music staff) IS	D	CANCELS ANY SHARPS OR FLATS ON A NOTE
15	(music staff) IS	E	LOWERS A NOTE ONE SEMITONE

25

BOREDOM BUSTER

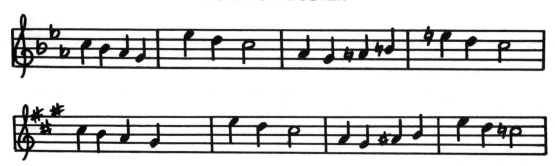

Follow the notes above and trace your way to the star in the maze below.

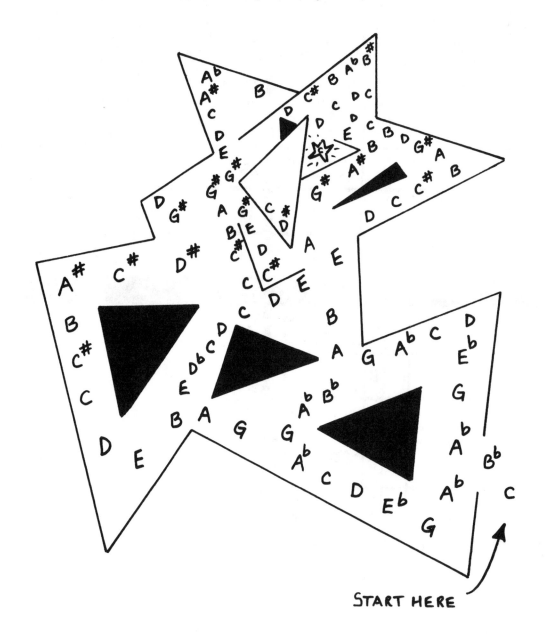

START HERE

NAME _____

BOREDOM BUSTER

Completely color the sections having correct information.

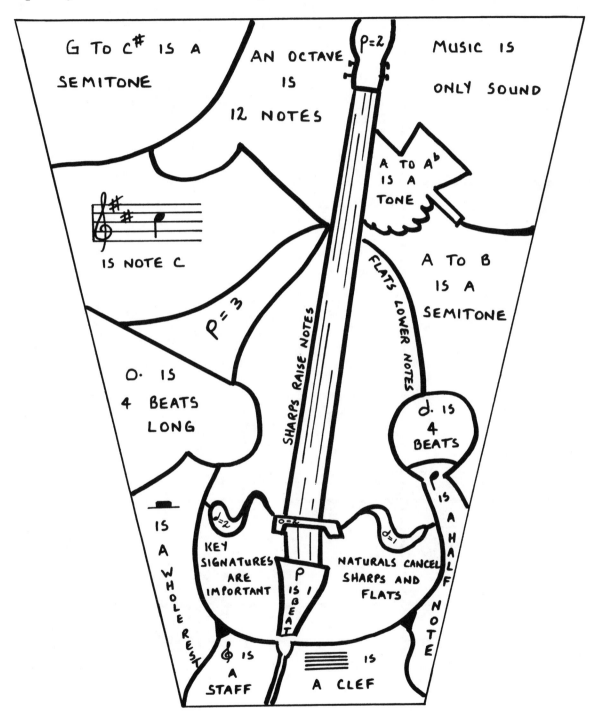

You have drawn a _____ _____!

© 1990 by Parker Publishing Company

BOREDOM BUSTER

Choose a partner and play this music tic-tac-toe game. One person ✘'s out the wrong information blocks. One person ✔'s the correct information blocks. Taking turns, the first person to find 3 blocks across, down, up, or diagonally, wins!

IS F♯	IS A TREBLE CLEF	IS A BAR OF MUSIC	IS NOTE F♯	IS NOTE B♭	A TONE IS TWO SEMITONES
○· IS 6 BEATS	♩· IS 3 BEATS	BLACK NOTES ARE NATURAL NOTES	TIES MAKE NOTES SHORTER	D♭ IS LOWER THAN C	A FLAT LOWERS A NOTE 1 SEMITONE
▬ IS 2 BEATS	♪♪ IS 3 BEATS	BAR LINES ARE BARS	BAR LINES ARE MEASURES	♩ IS A QUARTER NOTE	ON THE KEYBOARD, C IS LEFT OF ANY 2 BLACK NOTES
IS F	E TO F IS A WHOLE TONE	BLACK NOTES ARE SHARPS AND FLATS	IS NOTE E♭	○·♪ GETS 7 BEATS	IS NOTE C
▬ IS 2 BEATS	IS A STAFF	BLACK NOTES ARE GROUPED IN 2's ON THE KEYBOARD	NATURALS CANCEL SHARPS AND FLATS	MUSIC IS SILENCE	IS NOTE C
C TO D IS A SEMITONE	A♯ RAISES A NOTE A SEMITONE	A♯ LOWERS NOTES	IS NOTE B	IS NOTE E	A FLAT RAISES NOTES

When you want to play the game again, just ask your teacher for another game chart.

BOREDOM BUSTER: *CIRCLE WORD PUZZLE*

Clockwise

1. F to G is a _____ tone.
2. F to F♯ is a semi_____.
3. Key signatures can have up to 7 sharps or flats or _____ sharps or flats.
5. A _____ raises a note a semitone.
7. _____ lower notes 1 semitone.
9. _____ _____ change notes throughout a piece.
12. E to F is a _____ _____.
14. _____ is _____ A.

Towards the Center

2. _____ is a _____ clef.
4. _____ The first note is F♯. All of the _____ are F♯.
6. _____ an instrument is fun!
8. _____ This key signature is full of _____.
10. Natural _____ cancel sharps or flats.
11. Notes moving to the _____ on the keyboard go higher.
13. Key signatures are very _____!
15. ♮ is a _____ sign.

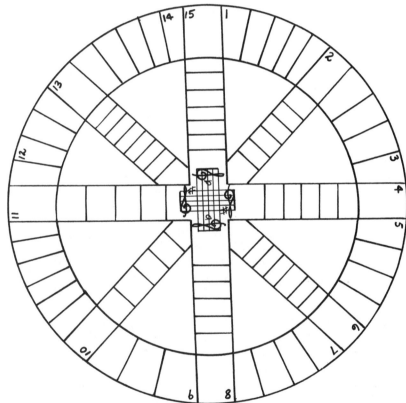

Now that you've completed this puzzle, start at square 1 and count through the following pattern of squares to find out why key signatures are so important.

Counting square 1 as 1, count 15, 11, 1, 18, 4, 4 (clockwise), then 1, 2, 2 (towards the center).

Key signatures tell us the _____ _____!

RULES TO "CIRCLE MARCH CARD"

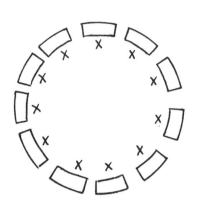

1. A large number of Information Cards are placed in a large circle on the floor (about 30 cards) question side up.
2. Students form a circle inside the circle of cards, facing the cards. Each student is given a number 1 or 2 and then told they are in team number 1 or team number 2.
3. Students hold hands. When the teacher begins to clap an even beat, students step sideways to the beat. The teacher then calls out an answer to a card on the floor. As soon as a student sees the corresponding question card, he breaks from his circle and grabs the correct card or cards. If he is correct, he yells the answer and a point is given to his team. If not, a mark is subtracted from his team's score. The team with the highest mark wins.
4. The game ends at the conclusion of a time period predetermined by the teacher.

Make cardboard laminated Information Cards 8½″×11″ (2 of each).

IS A	IS NOTE	IS NOTE	IS NOTE	IS NOTE	IS NOTE	IS NOTE	IS NOTE
KEY SIGNATURE	F♯	F♯	C♯	C♯	B♭	B♭	E

IS NOTE E♭	IS NOTE E♭	IS NOTE D♯	IS NOTE G♯	IS NOTE G♯	IS NOTE A♭	THERE CAN BE UP TO ____ SHARPS OR FLATS IN A KEY SIGNATURE	THE SMALLEST NO. OF SHARPS OR FLATS IN A KEY SIGNATURE IS:
						7	0

CHAPTER 7
CLASS RECORD SHEET

GRADE	HOMEROOM TEACHER	CLASS PERIOD/DAY	YEAR

Have students complete as many quizzes as necessary. All tests need not be completed. Write in students' names and fill in their marks in the squares below.

STUDENTS' NAMES	SONG				QUIZ 7-1	QUIZ 7-2	QUIZ 7-3	QUIZ 7-4	QUIZ 7-5	QUIZ 7-6	QUIZ 7-7	QUIZ 7-8	QUIZ 7-9	QUIZ 7-10	BB 7-1	BB 7-2	BB 7-3	BB 7-4	FINAL MARK
	WORDS	MOTIONS	PITCHES	MUSICALITY															

PROGRESS OF CLASSES

A chart is given here to help you keep a record of the tasks your classes complete. After listing the class names in the top squares, indicate with a check mark (✔) or with the date that a task has been accomplished.

CHAPTER 7

LIST OF CLASSES										
HAVE READ THE STORY										
HAVE STARTED THE SONG										
STUDENTS KNOW SONG										

HAVE COMPLETED QUIZ NO.	ACTIVITY	SKILL PRACTICED							
	7–1. Multiple choice	chapter story review							
	7–2. Naming notes	naming notes in any octave altered by key signature							
	7–3. Drawing sharps and flats	placing ♯'s and ♭'s in proper places on staff							
	7–4. Writing music	writing notes using key signatures							
	7–5. Naming notes	key signature and accidental note changes							
	7–6. Naming notes	key signature and accidental note changes							
	7–7. Circling errors	key signature and accidental note changes							
	7–8. Naming notes	key signature and accidental note changes in any octave							
	7–9. Reason search	key signature and accidental note changes							
	7–10. Matching	review of Chapters 1–7							
BOREDOM BUSTER NO.	7–1. Note name puzzle	key signature and accidental note changes							
	7–2. Information jigsaw	review of Chapters 2–7							
	7–3. Tic-Tac-Toe	review of Chapters 1–7							
	7–4. Circle-word puzzle	review of Chapters 6 and 7							
GAME: CIRCLE MARCH CARD										

CHAPTER 7 ANSWER KEY

Quiz 7–1

1. c	6. b	11. a	16. b	21. b
2. a	7. b	12. c	17. c	22. c
3. b	8. a	13. a	18. b	23. b
4. b	9. b	14. c	19. c	24. b
5. c	10. b	15. c	20. b	

Quiz 7–2

1. F♯	6. C♯	11. E♭	16. G♯	21. B♭
2. F♯	7. B♭	12. E♭	17. G♯	22. F♯
3. F♯	8. B♭	13. A♭	18. G♯	23. C♯
4. C♯	9. B♭	14. A♭	19. G♯	24. E♭
5. C♯	10. E♭	15. A♭	20. E♭	25. F♯

Quiz 7–3

Quiz 7–4

Quiz 7–5

1. E	6. B	11. D♯	16. G♯	21. C♯
2. D♯	7. G♯	12. C♯	17. D♯	22. D♯
3. C♯	8. F♯	13. D♯	18. C	23. E
4. F♯	9. G♯	14. F♯	19. D	24. E♯
5. D♯	10. C♯	15. C♯	20. C	25. F♯

Quiz 7–6

1. F♯	6. C	11. B♭	16. B♭	21. F
2. C♯	7. C♯	12. B♭	17. E♭	22. F♯
3. A♯	8. F♯	13. B	18. E	23. C♯
4. F♯	9. F	14. B	19. E	24. C♯
5. F♯	10. C♯	15. B♭	20. E	25. D♯

Quiz 7–7

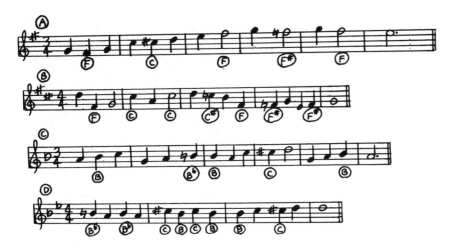

Quiz 7–8

1. B	6. B♭	11. F	16. B	21. D♭
2. F♯	7. E♭	12. C	17. E	22. B♭
3. C♯	8. A♭	13. C♯	18. B♭	23. D♯
4. G♯	9. D♭	14. C♯	19. F	24. C
5. D♯	10. G	15. C	20. C	25. C♯

Quiz 7–9

Quiz 7–10

1. C	6. D	11. D	16. A	21. D
2. E	7. E	12. E	17. D	22. C
3. D	8. B	13. A	18. E	23. E
4. B	9. C	14. B	19. B	24. A
5. A	10. A	15. C	20. C	25. B

Boredom Buster 7–1

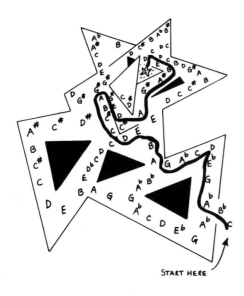

START HERE

Boredom Buster 7–2

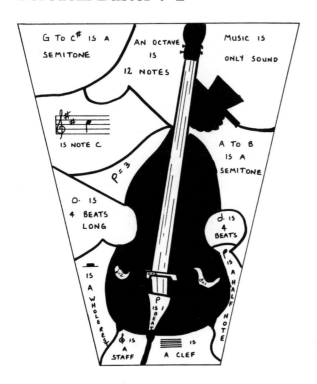

You have drawn a string bass.

Boredom Buster 7–3

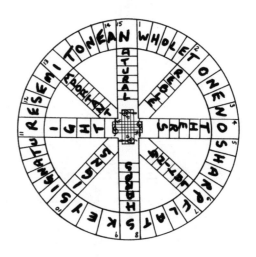

Boredom Buster 7–4

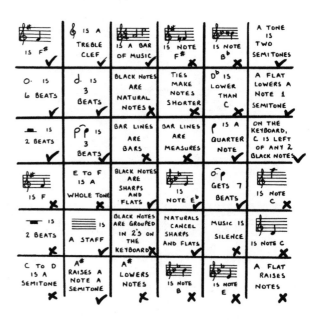

CHAPTER 8
Dancing Signs
Guide Space Travel

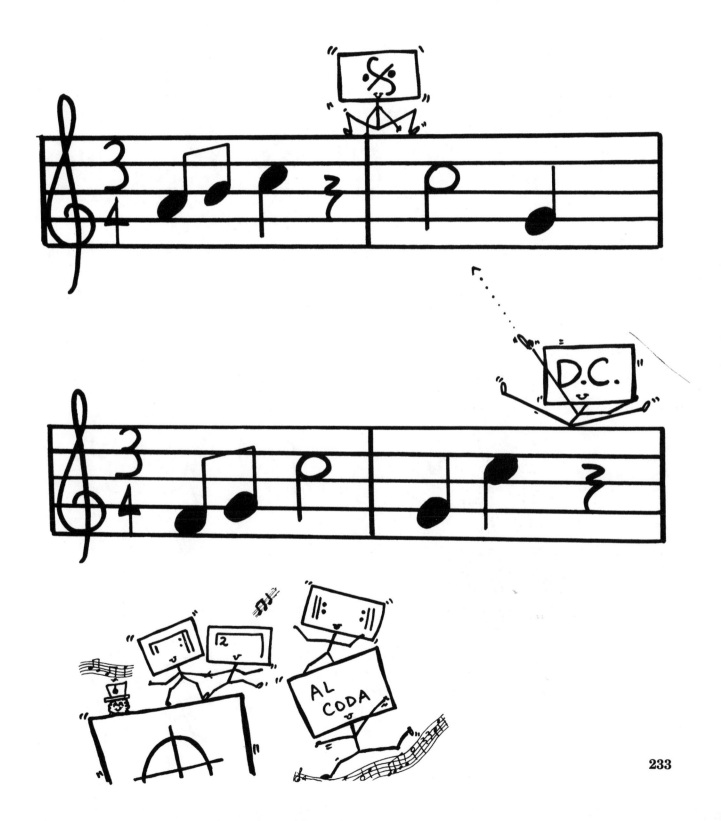

Before reading ask:
1. What happened in the last story?
2. What do key signatures do? (tell what notes have ♯'s or ♭'s throughout a piece)
3. What's a *key*? (the name of a key signature)

Mac, Christina, the other children, and the teacher were puzzled and worried. How would they be able to escape this place of light? The children were starting to see signs of some sort, but they couldn't figure out what they were. They really felt stuck.

"Hey, there are more signs up ahead!" cried Christina. "But they don't seem to tell us how to get out of here."

"Maybe they will," said the teacher. "These are all signs that we see in music. Each one tells you to travel to a certain place in the music."

"What do you mean?" asked Mac.
"Well, for example, these two signs are called *repeat signs*."

234

"They say to repeat any music that's found between them. If you find G-A-G between them, you play G-A-G, G-A-G."

Clarify if necessary.

"Often, you find these signs *with* repeats."

"These are called *first* and *second endings*. You use these when you want to repeat some music but change some of it too!"

Clarify if necessary.

"Let's say you write:

> You are nice.
> You are OK.
> You are nice.
> Have a nice day.

"If you used repeat signs (‖: :‖) with first and second endings, you could write this poem like this:

Clarify if necessary.

YOU ARE NICE. |¹YOU ARE O.K.:‖ |²HAVE A NICE DAY.|

The whole class was listening. It seemed pretty clear to them what repeats and first and second endings were. Repeats mean to repeat. To do it again. Endings changed the endings of repeated music. Everybody understood this, but how would repeat signs and first and second endings help them out of here?

"What about these other signs? Can they get us out of here?" asked Christina.

"I don't know," answered the teacher. "Let's see . . . *al coda* means 'go to the coda (⊕) sign.'"

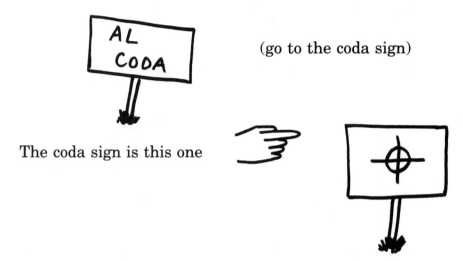

(go to the coda sign)

The coda sign is this one

"So you jump from the music at *al coda* to the music that has the coda (⊕) sign."

Clarify if necessary.

"Right!" said the teacher. "You start at *al coda*, disappear and immediately come out at the coda (⊕). The coda sign looks like a spaceship, doesn't it?"

"What about these two signs?" asked Christina.

"*D.C.* means *Da Capo*, which means 'Go back to the top (or the beginning of the piece),'" answered the teacher.

"How can I remember that?" asked Mac.

"Well," said the teacher, "You wear a cap on your head, right? And your head is on top of your body! So, *Da Capo* means 'Go to the top of the music.'"

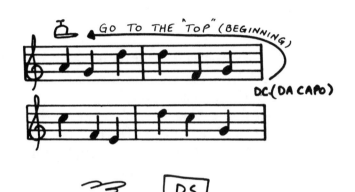

Clarify if necessary.

"This sign  means *Dal Segno*, which means 'Go back to the sign!'"

"What sign?" Christina and Mac asked together.

"This one," answered the teacher.

Then the teacher continued, "So *D.S.* means 'Jump from the music with the *D.S.* sign to the music with the 𝄋 sign.'"

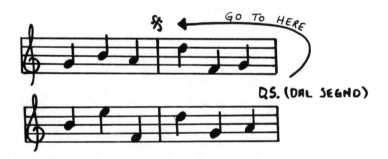

Clarify if necessary.

"*D.C.* and *D.S.* are almost the same thing. *D.C.* means 'Go to the top' and *D.S.* means 'Go to the sign.' And with that explanation kids, I'm *Fine!*" (pronounced *feeneh*)

Everybody looked up. Everybody asked, "What do you mean, *Fine*? Do you mean *finished*?"

"Sort of," explained the teacher. "In music, *Fine* means 'The End.'"

Clarify if necessary.

"Wow!" said Christina. "That seems like a lot to remember. No wonder we're lost! How can we find our way around music if we can't remember the directions?"

As soon as Christina asked this question, all of the signs started to move a little. More and more they became agitated, until they appeared to be dancing. The signs all started to shout:

> Learn about us.
> We signs are no fuss—
> And we can send you home!

And then the signs sang:

Class together.

> Repeats are two dots and lines.
> Notes between, play *two* times.
> First time first ending play;
> Repeat! Go second ending way.
>
> *D.C.* means "Go to top."
> *Al coda*, to the sign (⊕) we hop.
> Jump to the next one that you find,
> Play the notes which are behind.
>
> *D.S.* means "Go back to sign."
> "S" with two dots and line.
> *D.S.* with *al Fine*:
> "To sign, then to End play!"

The sign song was so catchy that the children and the teacher forgot where they were and started to sing along. Over and over they sang the song. The signs danced and danced and began to change their positions with each other. The land of light began to dim. The music began to slow down. Then, for the last time, the class and the teacher heard the signs slowly chant:

> Where oh where do my notes go?
> Follow signs and you will know.

And the signs lined themselves up so that it seemed to everyone that they pointed a way out of the land of light. Everyone began to follow what the signs said. Can you figure how they found their way out?

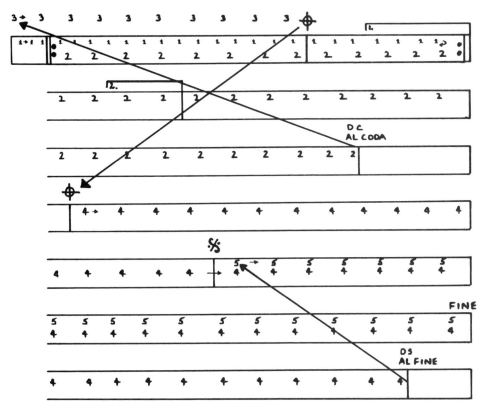

Place on overhead and explain how they found their way out, using the music signs.

Ask:
What is:
1. ‖:? (repeat sign)
2. ‖:   :‖? (first and second endings)
3. *D.C.*? (*Da Capo*—go to beginning)
4. *D.S.*? (*Dal Segno*—go to sign 𝄋)
5. *al coda*: (play to coda and jump to next ⊕)
6. *Fine*? (The End)

SUGGESTIONS FOR TEACHING THE SONG, *Following Signs*

1. Review the musical material by discussing the story events.
2. Play the tape of *Following Signs* or perform it for your students. Then explain the words, making sure they understand what the words mean.
3. Let them hear the song again. (Students in Grades 2–6 can follow the words.)
4. Teach each line by rote, repeating each one several times successively. Maintain an unbroken, steady beat, retaining the lyric rhythms (with or without pitches as necessary).
5. Teach the hand motions while teaching the words. You can follow the pictures on the music.

6. Have all students *completely* memorize the song, through repetition over time.
7. Have students perform as soloists, in duets, and in other interesting combinations. Have the girls compete with the boys, or rows against each other for marks you announce. Kids love competitions.
8. Have a lot of fun!

THE BODY MOTIONS

Verse 1
bar:

8	Hold up 2 fingers on the fourth beat.
9	Hold up 2 fingers on the second beat.
10	Two hands each point two fingers towards the other.
13	Point 2 fingers on the first beat.

Verse 2
bar:

9	On "top," point to the top of your head.
11	Point a finger on the first beat. Move your hand (indicating hopping) arriving at another position on the third beat.
12	On "play," two hands play an imaginary piano.

Verse 3
bar:

8	Point a thumb behind you on "back to sign."
10	Draw on "S" on beat 1 from the top down.
11	Draw a diagonal line downwards from left to right on "line."

Chorus
Line 1
bar:

14	Place hand up to face as if searching, on "where."
16	Arms outstretched, palms up as if puzzled.

Line 2
bar:

14	Point two hands downwards with two fingers on each hand. On "follow" have your fingers "walk," starting on beat 1.
19	Point to your temple with an index finger.

FOLLOWING SIGNS

1. ‖: :‖ are
   a. notes
   b. repeat signs
   c. lines and dots

2. Any music between ‖: :‖ is
   a. lost
   b. repeated
   c. damaged

3. ⌐1 :‖ ⌐2 ⌐ are
   a. one and two squares
   b. boxes
   c. first and second endings

4. x ⌐1 y :‖ ⌐2 z ⌐ means
   a. XYZ
   b. XYXZ
   c. XZY

5. ab ⌐1 c :‖ ⌐2 de ⌐ means
   a. abcde
   b. abdec
   c. abcabde

6. I like ⌐1 Tom and :‖ ⌐2 you ⌐ means
   a. I like Tom and you.
   b. I like Tom and I like you.
   c. I like Tom I like.

7. First and second endings help
   a. change parts of repeated music
   b. music sound louder
   c. end music quickly

8. *Al coda* means
   a. go to the coda (⊕) sign.
   b. you have a bad cold.
   c. *al coda* is a mean man.

9. ⊕ is a
   a. telescope viewer
   b. space ship
   c. coda sign

10. *D.C.* means
    a. go back to Corny Street
    b. go back to the beginning of the music
    c. go away

11. *D.C. al coda* would mean
    a. repeat
    b. play loudly
    c. go to the beginning and play to the coda (⊕) sign.

12. *D.S.* means
    a. go back to the sign (𝄋)
    b. go back to the beginning
    c. repeat

13. *D.S. al coda* would mean
    a. go back to the sign (𝄋) and play to the coda (⊕)
    b. repeat
    c. go back to the beginning

14. *Fine* in music means
    a. the end of the music
    b. the music is fine
    c. everything is OK

15. *D.C. al Fine* would mean
    a. go to the beginning and play to the end
    b. repeat
    c. go back to the sign □

16. *D.S. al Fine* would mean
    a. go back to the sign and play to the end
    b. repeat
    c. go back to the beginning □

17.
A B C D D.C.
E F G H
  means
    a. A B C D E F G H
    b. A B C D E F G H, A B C D E F G H
    c. E F G H, A B C D □

18.
A B C D D.S.
E F G H
  means
    a. A B C D E F G H, C D E F G H
    b. A B C D E F G H
    c. C D E F G H □

19.
A B C
D E F D.C. al
G H I Coda
  means
    a. A B C D E F G H I, A B, G H I
    b. A B C D E F G H I
    c. G H I, D E F, A B C □

20.
A B C
D E F D.S. al
G H I Coda
  means
    a. A B C D E F G H I, C D E, G H I
    b. A B C D E F G H I
    c. A B C, G H I, D E F □

21.
A B C Fine
D E F D.C. al
G H I Fine
  means
    a. A B C D E F G H I
    b. A B C E F G H I, A B C D E F
    c. G H I, A B C, D E F □

22.
║:A B :║: C D:║
E F G H
I J K L D.S.
  means
    a. AB, AB, CD, CD, EFGHIJKL, IJKL
    b. IJKL, EFGH, ABCD
    c. ABCD, ABCD, EFGHIJKKL □

23.
A B C
D E F D.C. al
G H I Coda
  means
    a. A B C D E F G H I, A B C D E, G H I
    b. A B C D E F G H I
    c. A B C, E F, G H I □

24.
A B C
D E F D.S. al
G H I Fine
Fine
  means
    a. A B C D E F G H I, F G H
    b. A B C D E F G H I
    c. A B C D E H I

25. Music signs make *writing* music
    a. faster to complete
    b. shorter to write
    c. both *a* and *b* □

25

The following music poem is written in a code using repeats and first and second endings. Figure out the code and write the poem out in full to discover its secret.

MUSIC IS ⟦1.EASY,:‖ ⟦2.FUN.

MUSIC MAKES ME ⟦1.EXCITED,:‖ ⟦2.RUN.

MUSIC ⟦1.MAKES ME SLEEPY.:‖ ⟦2.CAN MAKE ME SAD.:‖

⟦3.USUALLY ACCOMPANIED THE BEST TIMES
    I'VE EVER HAD.

MUSIC CAN BE ⟦1.FIERY,:‖ ⟦2.QUIET.

MUSIC, ⟦1.CAN BE RENTED.:‖ ⟦2.YOU CAN BUY IT.

IT CAN ⟦1.SOOTHE YOUR SPIRIT.:‖ ⟦2.MAKE YOU GLAD.:‖

⟦3.CHANGE A NICE MOVIE INTO ONE THAT'LL
    MAKE YOU MAD.

‖:MUSIC:‖:MUSIC:‖

I COULD SAY IT ⟦1.ALL DAY.:‖ ⟦2.ALL NIGHT TOO
                          IF I HAD MY WAY.

MUSIC FROM ⟦1.TV'S,:‖ ⟦2.RADIOS,:‖ ⟦3.GHETTO

BLASTERS,:‖ ⟦4.STEREOS,:‖ ⟦5.WALKMANS,:‖ ⟦6.MOVIES,:‖

⟦7.CHOIRS,:‖ ⟦8.BANDS,:‖ ⟦9.BIRDS,:‖ ⟦10.ME.‖

I WOULD SING MUSIC ALL DAY LONG.
IF EVERYONE WOULD AGREE!

1	Music is
1	
1	
1	
1	
1	
1	
1	
1	
1	
1	
1	
1	
1	
1	
4	
1	
1	

5 marks
for each
2 lines

_____
_____

25

NAME _____

Quiz 8–3

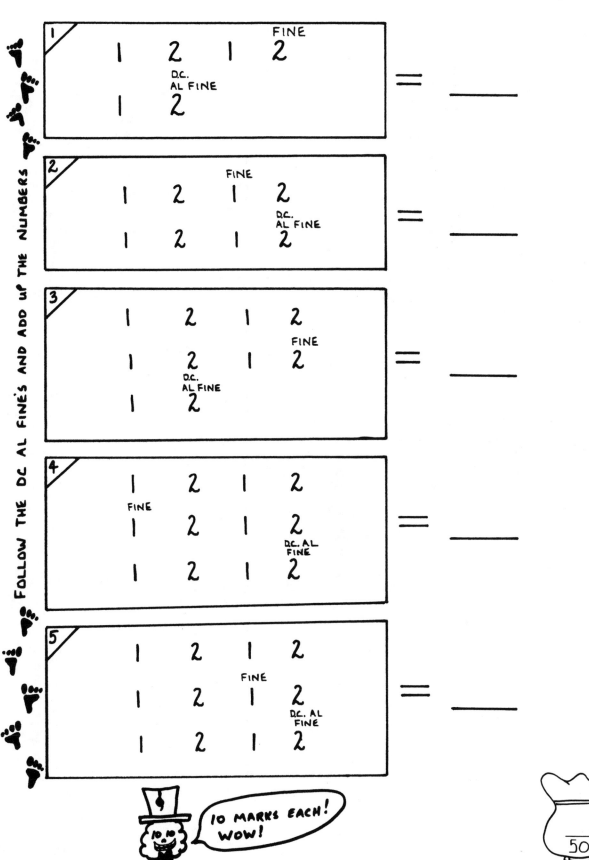

FOLLOW THE DC AL FINE'S AND ADD UP THE NUMBERS

© 1990 by Parker Publishing Company

10 MARKS EACH! WOW!

50

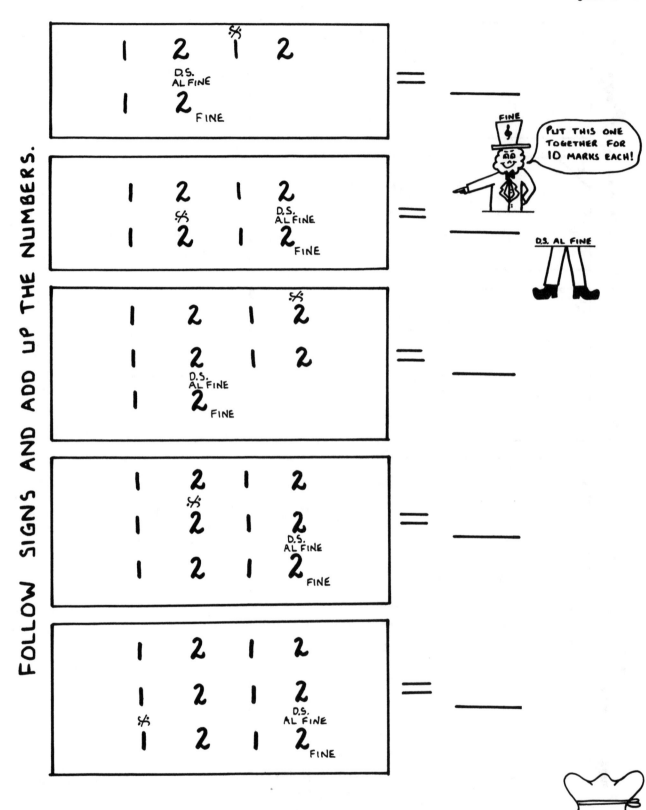

FOLLOW SIGNS AND ADD UP THE NUMBERS.

PUT THIS ONE TOGETHER FOR 10 MARKS EACH!

Start at the first letter M and jump from coda to coda, writing the letter below each coda at the bottom of the page.

1	2	3	4	5	6
	⊕	⊕	⊕	⊕	⊕

MAY UMBRELLAS OPEN IN AN ICY FISH!

7	8	9	10	11
⊕	⊕	⊕	⊕	⊕

HE'S THROWN EVERY ELM OUT! VIKKY EGG...

12	13	14	15	16
⊕	⊕	⊕	⊕	⊕

ARE YOU A LOBSTER LONGER WITH TAH?

17	18	19	20	21
⊕	⊕	⊕	⊕	⊕

HAPPY YEARS ARE AS NICE IN FALL

22	23	24
⊕	⊕	⊕

WE WILL IN THE STADIUM.

M __ __ __ __   __ __   __ __ __ __ __
1 2 3 4 5   6 7   8 9 10 11 12

__ __ __ __ __ __   __ __ __ __ __ __ __
13 14 15 16 17 18   19 20 21 22 23 24 25

A free mark if your secret makes "crazy" sense!

25

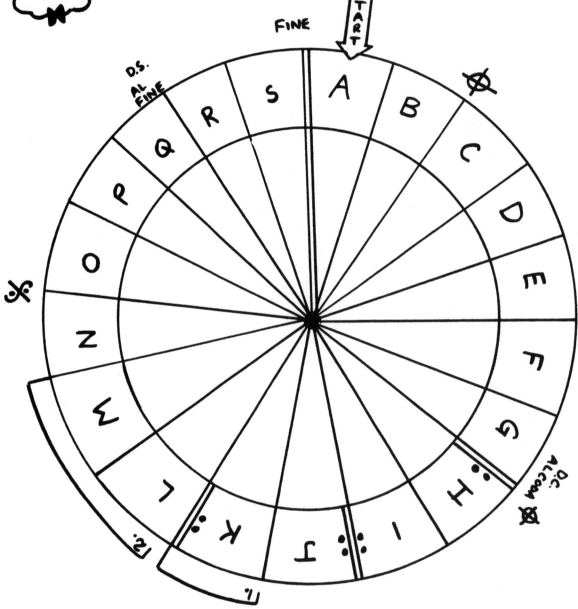

A B ___ ___ ___ ___ ___ ___ ___ ___ ___ ___
     1   2   3   4   5   6   7   8   9   10

___ ___ ___ ___ ___ ___ ___ ___ ___ ___
11 12 13 14 15 16 17 18 19 20

___ ___ ___ ___ ___
21 22 23 24 25

Follow the signs in the music above and write out this music in full below.

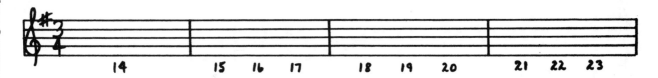

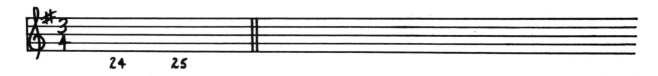

Signs are used in the music above. Write out the music in full *below* without using the signs.

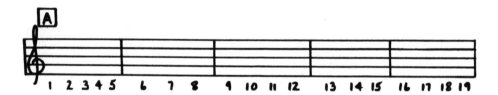

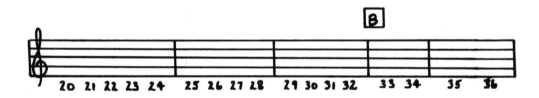

NAME _____

Quiz 8–9

Write the above song below, but without using signs.

"ONE MARK PER ITEM (JUST LIKE BEFORE.) OPEN YOUR BRAIN TO GET A GREAT SCORE!"

50

Match up questions and answers in each of boxes A, B, C, D, and E.

Box A

	Letters		Questions
A	GO BACK TO THE BEGINNING	1.	‖:‖ (G)
B	KEY SIGNATURE	2.	𝄞 (C)
C	TREBLE CLEF	3.	o.
D	8 BEATS	4.	[notes on staff]
E	NOTE D	5.	D.S.
F	STAFF	6.	[staff notation]
G	REPEAT SIGN	7.	⌢o
H	6 BEATS	8.	D.C.
I	NATURAL SIGN	9.	♮
J	GO BACK TO SIGN (𝄋)	10.	

Box B

	Letters		Questions
A	SHARP	1.	♭
B	½ BEAT	2.	[staff notation]
C	FLAT	3.	[notation]
D	KEY SIGNATURE	4.	♯
E	1 BEAT	5.	[rest]
F	6 BEATS	6.	CHANGING VALUES
G	RHYTHM	7.	[dotted note]
H	2 BEATS	8.	[notation]
I	BAR OF MUSIC	9.	[rest]
J	¾ BEAT	10.	[rest]

Box C

	Letters		Questions
A	MEANS PLAY F#'s AND C#'s	1.	[first ending / repeat]
B	THIRD LINE ON THE 𝄞 STAFF	2.	[staff notation]
C	BAR LINE	3.	[notation]
D	LINES IN THE 𝄞 STAFF	4.	[notation]
E	FIRST ENDING	5.	B
F	NOTE HEAD	6.	FACE
G	NOTE TAIL	7.	F
H	SPACES IN THE 𝄞 STAFF	8.	[notation]
I	FIRST SPACE IN THE STAFF	9.	EGBDF
J	NOTE STEM	10.	[note]

Box D

	Letters		Questions
A	3 BEATS	1.	LINES
B	1 BEAT	2.	AL CODA
C	JUMP TO THE CODA (⊕)	3.	[note]
D	EGBDF	4.	[staff notation]
E	KEY SIGNATURE	5.	[notation]
F	4 BEATS	6.	FINE
G	2 BEATS	7.	[rest]
H	THE END OF A PIECE	8.	[note]
I	1½ BEATS	9.	SPACES
J	FACE	10.	o

Box E

	Letters		Questions
A	KEY SIGNATURE WITH FLATS	1.	EVEN PULSE
B	EIGHTH NOTES	2.	[note]
C	BEAT	3.	[staff notation]
D	3 BEATS	4.	♪♪♪♪
E	WHOLE REST	5.	[rest]
F	EIGHTH REST	6.	[note]
G	2 BEATS	7.	[staff notation]
H	KEY SIGNATURE WITH A SHARP	8.	[note]
I	DOTTED QUARTER NOTE	9.	[staff notation]
J	FLAT SIGN	10.	[dotted note]

BOREDOM BUSTER

Follow the musical signs and trace your way to *"Fine."*

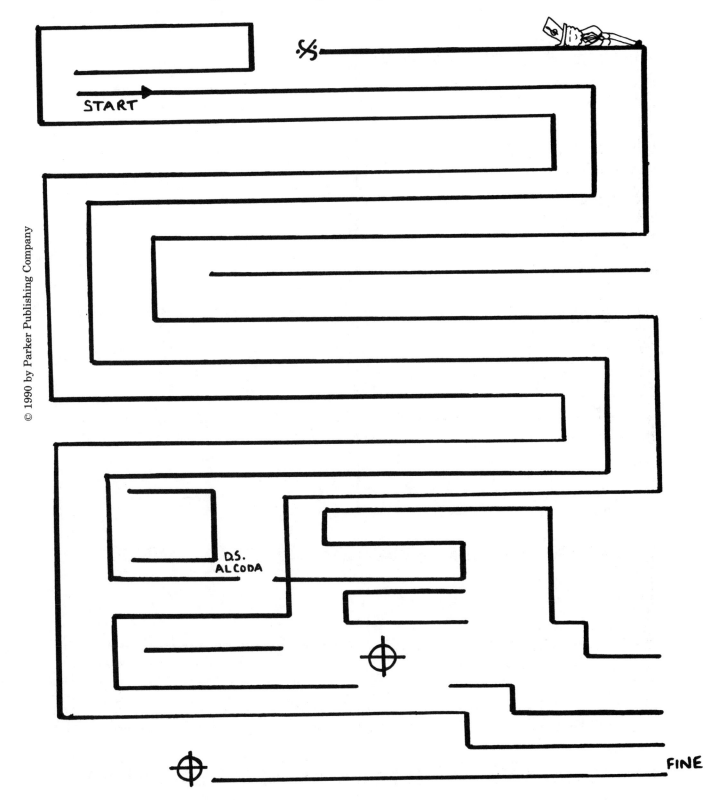

START

D.S.
AL CODA

FINE

NAME _____

BB 8–2

BOREDOM BUSTER

Musical Jewelry

Follow the words, with music directions, found below and rewrite the poem IN FULL HERE.

Our world is ⌜1·a wonderful place.:‖
 ⌜2·floating in space!⌝
A diamond ⊕ ⌜1·resting in the sky,:‖
 ⌜2·twinkling in God's eye.⌝
And‖: on our ⌜1·jewel,:‖ ⌜2·ground,⌝
So much of beauty can be found . . .
Things to ⌜1·smell,:‖ ⌜2·study,:‖ ⌜3·share,
 with a very best buddy.:‖
⌜4·see,:‖ ⌜5·touch,‖ ⌜6·love so very much.‖

A more precious place
Could ne'r be discovered . . .
_____ ⊕ where there's music!
D.S. al coda
Don't you just love it?

© 1990 by Parker Publishing Company

BOREDOM BUSTER

This game can be played with 2 or more players. Each player begins at the START square. Each player takes a turn rolling a die and moving the number of squares shown on the die. As players move through the squares, they must follow the musical directions on the game. The first player to get to the END square wins.

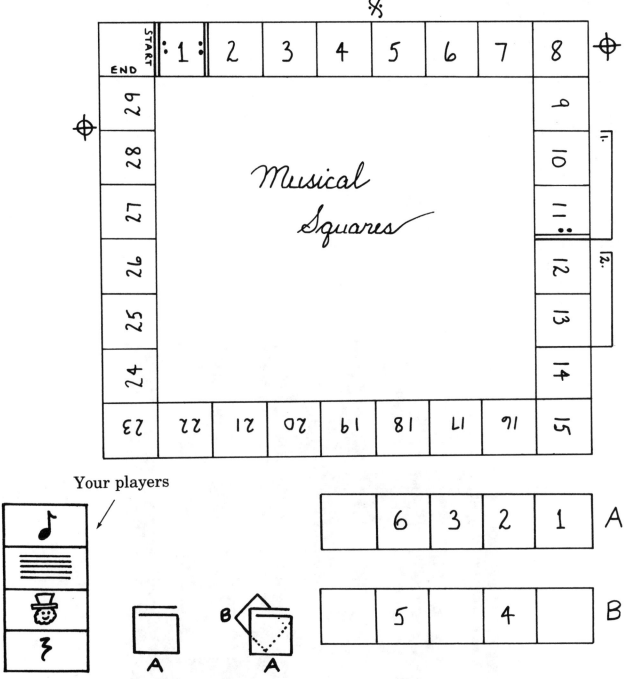

Your players

MAKE A DIE FROM PAPER! Tape A1 over B block crosswise. Fold B strip around A strip and tape two strips together. (Fold last B blank inside A strip.)

BOREDOM BUSTER

Across

1. *D.C.* means "Go _____ _____ _____ _____."
7. ‖:C:‖ *D.C.* is played _____ _____ _____ _____.
9. ‖:JET:‖ means JET _____.
10. A musical sign _____ musicians time writing music.
11. For "back to the sign" write _____.
13. ‖:S:‖T is a short form for _____ _____.
14. ⌐‾‾:‖ is a _____ ending.
16. ⌐2‾‾⌐ is a second _____.
17. Does *D.S.* mean go back to the start of the piece?
18. Does *D.C.* mean go back to the sign?
19. *D.C.* means "_____ back to the start."
20. Does "*Fine*" mean repeat?
24. How do you write "Go back to the start and play to the end?"
25. Is ⊕ a coda sign?

Down

1. ‖:HI:‖ means HI HI _____ there are repeat signs.
2. ⊕ is a _____ sign.
3. *D.C.* means go back _____ the start.
4. Musical signs save _____ writing music.
5. ⌐‾‾⌐ is a _____ ending.
6. ‖: :‖ are _____ _____.
8. Does "*Fine*" mean "the end"?
12. "*Fine*" means _____ _____.
14. How do we write "the end" in music?
15. ℅ is called the _____.
21. _____ means "Go back to the start."
22. ‖:OF:‖ means OF _____.
23. ⌐‾‾⌐ is _____ ending. (Note that there's no 1 or 2 inside it.)

RULES TO "SECOND GUESS"

1. Two teams are formed and are seated in single file on the floor. A number of cards are placed in two piles of equal numbers on the opposite side of the room. A student monitor sits with each pile of cards.

2. This is a timed relay. The teacher says "go" and the first student in each team runs to his pile of cards and has 15 seconds to guess as many cards correctly as he can. After each guess, the student turns the answer side of the card towards the card monitor for confirmation that he is correct. At the end of 15 seconds, the student runs back, touching the team leader, at which time the next person repeats the process.

3. Card monitors keep track of correct guesses. The highest scoring team wins.

Note: Shortening the time period in the game will add more excitement.

Make laminated cardboard Information Cards (8½″ × 11″).

‖: :‖ MEANS	1. :‖ IS A	2. IS A	⊕ IS A	AL CODA MEANS	𝄋 IS CALLED	D.S. MEANS
REPEAT	FIRST ENDING	SECOND ENDING	CODA SIGN	JUMP TO THE CODA (⊕) SIGN	THE SIGN	GO BACK TO THE SIGN 𝄋

D.C. MEANS	D.S. AL CODA MEANS	D.C. AL CODA MEANS	D.S. IS SHORT FOR	D.C. IS SHORT FOR	FINE MEANS
GO BACK TO THE BEGINNING	BACK TO SIGN + JUMP TO CODA (⊕)	BACK TO START AND JUMP TO CODA (⊕)	DEL SEGNO	DA CAPO	THE END OF A PIECE

NAME ______________________________

Student Evaluation Sheet

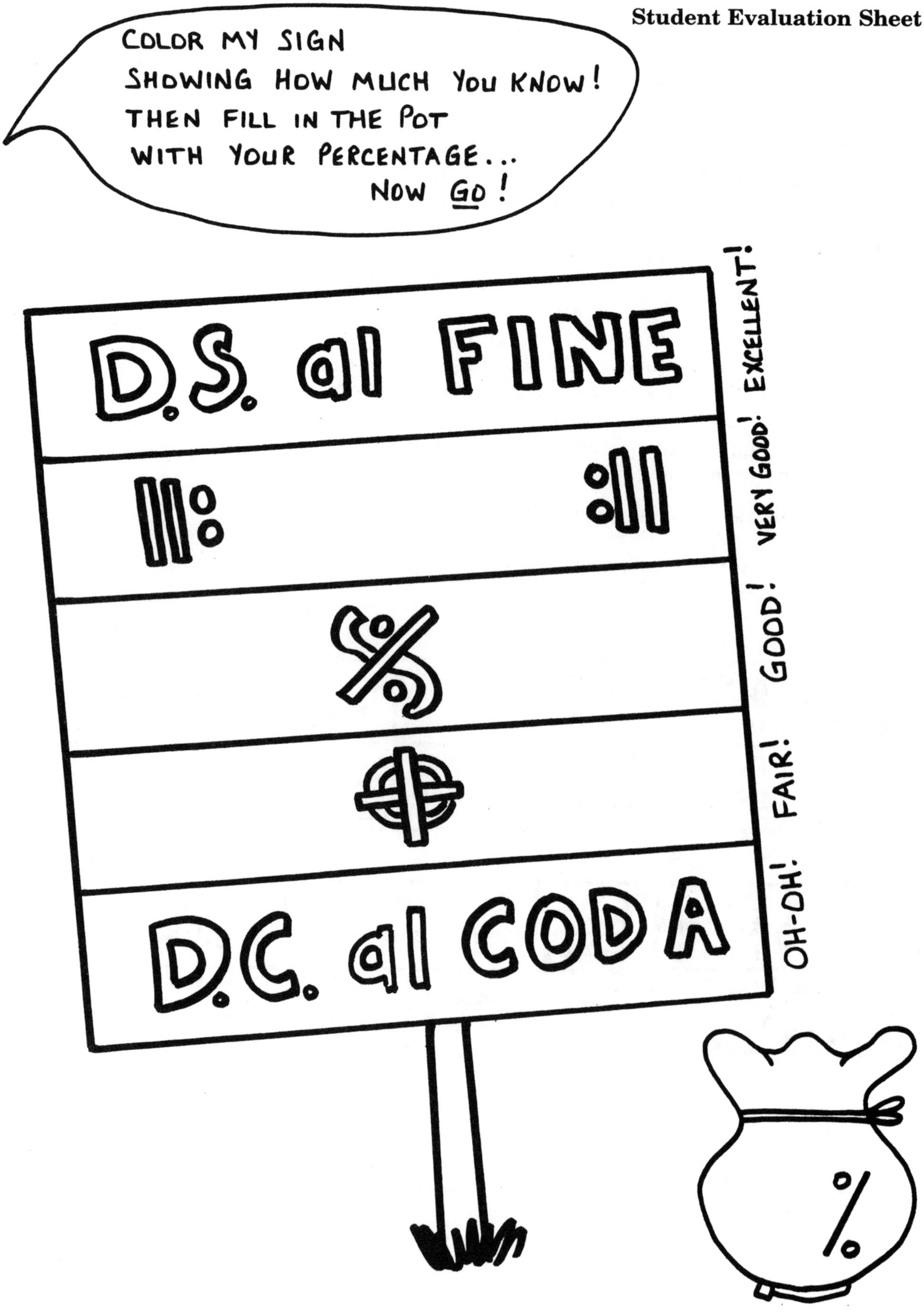

CHAPTER 8
CLASS RECORD SHEET

GRADE	HOMEROOM TEACHER	CLASS PERIOD/DAY	YEAR

Have students complete as many quizzes as necessary. All tests need not be completed. Write in students' names and fill in their marks in the squares below.

SONG

STUDENTS' NAMES	WORDS	MOTIONS	PITCHES	MUSICALITY	QUIZ 8–1	QUIZ 8–2	QUIZ 8–3	QUIZ 8–4	QUIZ 8–5	QUIZ 8–6	QUIZ 8–7	QUIZ 8–8	QUIZ 8–9	QUIZ 8–10	BB 8–1	BB 8–2	BB 8–3	BB 8–4	FINAL MARK

PROGRESS OF CLASSES

A chart is given here to help you keep a record of the tasks your classes complete. After listing the class names in the top squares, indicate with a check mark (✔) or with the date that a task has been accomplished.

CHAPTER 8

LIST OF CLASSES										
HAVE READ THE STORY										
HAVE STARTED THE SONG										
STUDENTS KNOW SONG										
HAVE COMPLETED QUIZ NO.	ACTIVITY	SKILL PRACTICED								
	8–1. Multiple choice	chapter story review								
	8–2. Writing a poem	repeats, 1st and 2nd endings								
	8–3. Adding numbers	*D.C.*, al *Fine*								
	8–4. Adding numbers	*D.S.*, al *Fine*								
	8–5. Discovering a secret message	the coda sign								
	8–6. A wheel puzzle	*D.C.*, *D.S.*, al *Fine*, 1st and 2nd endings, *al coda*								
	8–7. Writing music	repeats, 1st and 2nd endings, *D.C.*, *al coda*								
	8–8. Writing music	repeats, 1st and 2nd endings, ℅, ⊕								
	8–9. Writing music	repeats, 1st and 2nd endings, ℅, ⊕								
	8–10. Matching	review of Chapter 8								
BOREDOM BUSTER NO.	8–1. Tracing the maze	*D.S.*, al coda, Fine								
	8–2. Writing a poem	1st, 2nd . . . 6th endings, *D.S. al coda*								
	8–3. Game for friends	1st and 2nd endings, *D.S. al coda*, *D.C.*								
	8–4. Crossword puzzle	review of Chapter 8								
GAME: SECOND GUESS										

CHAPTER 8 ANSWER KEY

Quiz 8–1

1. b	6. b	11. c	16. a	21. a
2. b	7. a	12. a	17. a	22. a
3. a	8. a	13. a	18. a	23. a
4. b	9. c	14. a	19. a	24. a
5. c	10. b	15. a	20. b	25. c

Quiz 8–2

1. Music is easy,
   Music is fun.
   Music makes me excited,
   Music makes me run.
   Music makes me sleepy,
   Music can make me sad.
   Music usually accompanied
   The best times I've ever had.

2. Music can be fiery,
   Music can be quiet.
   Music, can be rented,
   Music, you can buy it.
   It can soothe your spirit;
   It can make you glad.
   It can change a nice movie
   Into one that'll make you mad.

3. Music music music music,
   I could say it all day,
   I could say it all night too,
   If I had my way.

4. Music from TVs
   Music from radios
   Music from "ghetto blasters"
   Music from stereos
   Music from Walkmans
   Music from movies
   Music from choirs
   Music from bands
   Music from birds
   Music from me.
   I would sing music all day long
   If everyone would agree!

Quiz 8–3

1. 15	2. 16	3. 27	4. 25	5. 28

Quiz 8–4

1. 15	2. 17	3. 26	4. 29	5. 24

Quiz 8–5

Music is never always silent.

Quiz 8–6

1. C	6. A	11. I	16. M	21. O
2. D	7. B	12. J	17. N	22. P
3. E	8. H	13. K	18. O	23. Q
4. F	9. I	14. J	19. P	24. R
5. G	10. H	15. L	20. Q	25. S

Quiz 8–7

Quiz 8–8

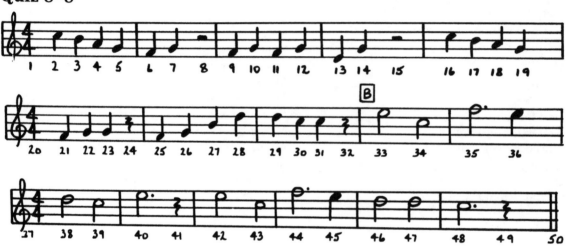

Quiz 8–9

Quiz 8–10

Box A	Box B	Box C	Box D	Box E
1. G	1. C	1. E	1. D	1. C
2. C	2. D	2. A	2. C	2. E
3. H	3. B	3. C	3. B	3. A
4. B	4. A	4. F	4. E	4. B
5. J	5. E	5. B	5. A	5. F
6. E	6. G	6. H	6. H	6. D
7. F	7. F	7. I	7. I	7. H
8. D	8. I	8. G	8. G	8. J
9. A	9. H	9. D	9. J	9. G
10. I	10. J	10. J	10. F	10. I

Boredom Buster 8–1

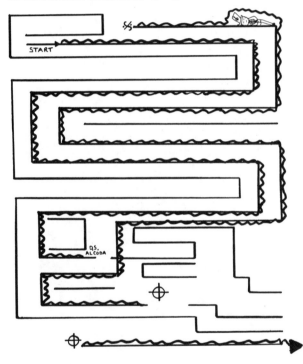

Boredom Buster 8–2

Musical Jewelry

Our world is a wonderful place
Our world is floating in space!
A diamond resting in the sky,
A diamond twinkling in God's eye.

And on our jewel,
And on our ground,
So much of beauty can be found. . . .

Things to smell,
Things to study,
Things to share with your very best buddy.

Things to see,
Things to touch,
Things to love so very much.

A more precious place
Could n'er be discovered . . .
A diamond where there's music!
Don't you just love it?

Boredom Buster 8–3

Have fun!

Boredom Buster 8–4

Lost in Time!

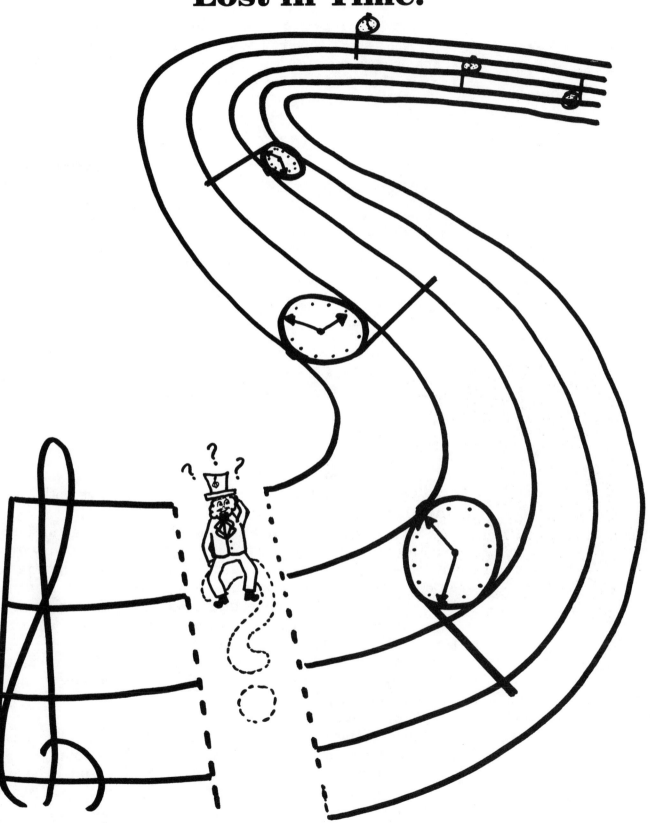

Before reading ask:
1. What happened in the last story?
2. What is
a. ‖: (repeat sign)
b. (first and second endings) ⌐1 :‖ ⌐2.
c. D.C.? (Da Capo—go back to the beginning)
d. D.S.? (Dal Segno—go back to sign 𝄋)
e. al coda? (play to coda and jump to next one ⊕, ⊕)
f. Fine? (The End)

The last of the members of the music class made it to the end of the path leading out of the land of light. They were finally at the *Fine* but they still could not see home.

"I see a sign that says 'home' over there," shouted Christina. "Let's go over there and see," and they all agreed. When they arrived, they found a long tunnel behind the sign. The tunnel seemed to go on forever.

"Is this our way home?" questioned Mac.

"Guess so," answered the teacher.

"Well, let's go then! It's the only choice we've got!" cried Christina.

They all slowly entered the tunnel. Soon they found themselves slipping down the tunnel, and then they slipped upwards! Faster and faster they traveled. They now were moving so quickly that the tunnel began to disappear from sight. In no time they found themselves all traveling at the same speed but with no tunnel to be seen at all! It seemed to them that they were just hanging freely in the air.

In a blink of an eye, they began to see strange sights. *Now* they could see an old man wearing a top hat riding a horse-drawn buggy.

"This is right out of a history book!" said Mac.

Right alongside, a spaceship quietly sped by. The past, present, and future were appearing at the same time.

"This is strange," remarked Christina. "We seem to be lost in time! How can we find our way out without time? After all, it takes time to go from one place to another."

266

"I've got an idea," said Mac. "Since we keep winding up in different parts of Musictown, maybe we have to use *musical time* to get out."

"How do we do that?" asked Christina.

"I've got it!" exclaimed the teacher. "Normal time is measured by a clock in seconds, minutes, and hours. Music time is measured in *beats*."

"Beats are even claps or taps!" said Mac. "They're always even, but they can be fast or slow."

"Right!" said the teacher. "And it takes *time* to tap or clap them."

"If we make beats," said Christina, "maybe we can make music time and move forward out of here!"

"OK! Let's try it," said Mac. "Let's all clap a steady beat and make some musical time."

And so they all clapped to a steady beat, but they still didn't move!

"I don't understand!" exclaimed Mac. "We're still not moving!"

"I know why," said the teacher. "Beats are always notes of value. We need to use a certain note type for a beat, like a quarter note, for example. This way, our beats will have a certain length of time. Let's use a quarter note beat."

So everybody clapped quarter note beats. They sang "Tah" each time, on the beat, because quarter notes are sung "Tah." They felt like they were moving forward, but they couldn't be sure.

"We've got nothing beside us to tell us if we're traveling. It's like being in a plane; you go fast but you can't tell, because you can't see the ground going by," said Christina.

"We need *bar lines*," said the teacher.

"What are bar lines?" asked Mac.

"Bar lines are drawn from the top to the bottom of the staff."

Start clapping a steady, even beat.

Have students clap a steady, even beat *very quietly*.

Have students clap a steady, even beat *very quietly*.

"What are they for?" asked Mac.

"They help you to measure time and let you see the music better. You write bar lines after every two, three, or maybe four beats of music. They help you to keep track of where you are."

Demonstrate this →

"The top number at the beginning of the staff tells you how many beats there are in each bar. The bottom number tells you what kind of note the beat is. Look!"

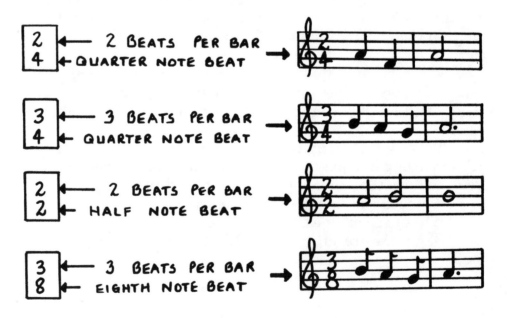

"Is there a name for the two numbers that tell us all this?" asked Christina.

"It's called a *time signature*," answered the teacher.

"Well, how will all of this help us to get moving?" asked Christina. She was getting a bit dizzy from floating in the air.

"Let's make a big $\frac{4}{4}$ time signature and some bar lines, with the chain," suggested the teacher. "We'll clap and march quarter note beats. As we sound four quarter note beats in each bar, we'll see the bar lines go by, and we'll know we're going forward."

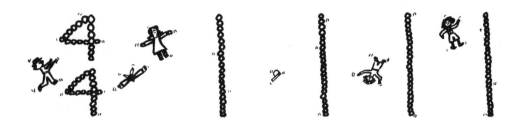

And so they did. They soon found that by *accenting* (or making a bit louder) the first beat in every bar, it sounded pleasant and it helped them keep a steady beat too. Bar after bar floated by, one after another. The time signature helped them remember what to do and the bar lines helped them to keep track of the number of beats they made. Steadily, the group floated forward.

Soon they were approaching a blue valley far below them. They could see . . . blue cows grazing in long green grass! There were many little blue boys playing too, and in the middle of all of this was a gigantic man, who was very, very fat. And, "Goodness," said Christina, "that man looks like an ear!"

Crash! They all landed in the blue valley below. This place seemed very peaceful, but it sure wasn't home.

But what was that very low sound that they could hear now? It seemed so low. . . .

Ask:
1. What are the two numbers at the beginning of the staff? (time signature)
2. What does the top number do? (tells how many beats there are in a bar)
3. What's a bar line? (vertical line drawn in the staff)
4. What's a bar? (all the music between 2 bar lines)
5. What does the bottom number in the time signature do? (tells what kind of note is the beat)

SUGGESTIONS FOR TEACHING THE SONG,
Time Signatures

1. Review the musical material by discussing the story events.
2. Play the tape of *Time Signatures* or perform it for your students. Then explain the words, making sure they understand what the words mean.
3. Let them hear the song again. (Students in Grades 2–6 can follow the words.)
4. Teach each line by rote, repeating each one several times successively. Maintain an unbroken, steady beat, retaining the lyric rhythms (with or without pitches as necessary).

5. Teach the hand motions while teaching the words. You can follow the pictures on the music.

6. Have all students *completely* memorize the song, through repetition over time.

7. Have students perform as soloists, in duets, and in other interesting combinations. Have the girls compete with the boys, or rows against each other for marks you announce. Kids love competitions.

8. Have a lot of fun!

THE BODY MOTIONS

Verse 1
bar: 6 Hold hands apart as if making bar lines.
7 Raise your "bar lines" on the word "top."
8 Lower your "bar lines" on the word "staves."
10 Point two fingers together.

Verse 2
bar: 5 On each of beats 1 to 4, hold up 1, 2, 3, and 4 fingers consecutively.
7 On "bars," make 2 "bar lines" with hands.
8 Move hands as if playing the piano.
10 On each of beats 1 to 4, hold up 1, 2, 3, and 4 fingers consecutively.
11 Hold up 2 fingers on one hand on "time." Add 4 fingers with the other hand and place below the first hand. Do this on the second beat.

Verse 3
bar: 5 Point upwards on beat 1.
6 Count 1, 2, 3, 4 on fingers, on each beat.
7 Place hand over eyes as if looking for something.
8 Make "bar lines" with your hands.
9 Point downwards.
10 Place index finger up to temple as if thinking.
11 Make a quarter note on beat 1, half note on beat 2, and whole note on beat 4.

Verse 4
bar: 5 Place 2 fingers over 2 fingers.
6 Make a "half note."
7 Place 2 fingers over 4 fingers.
8 Make a "quarter note."
9 Make a "2" with one hand on beat 1 about eye level. Make an "8" on beat 2, at chest level.
10 Draw an eighth note on beat 1.
11 Place index finger at temple on "know."

Chorus
bar: 13 On the first beat, hold a "2" over a "4."
14 On the first beat, hold a "2" over a "4."
15 On the first beat, hold a "2" over a "4."
16 Hold hands as if reading a page of music.
17 Hold a "2" over a "4."
19 Hold hands apart, making the "bar lines."

TIME SIGNATURES

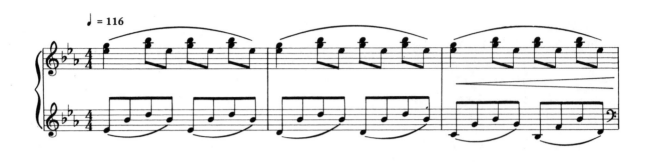

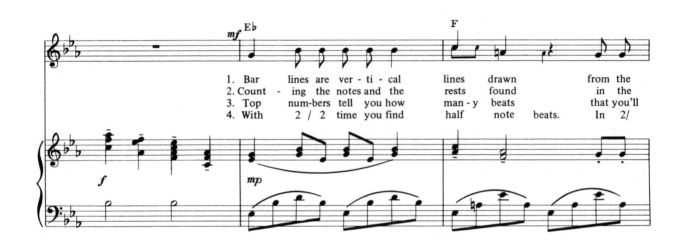

1. Bar lines are ver-ti-cal lines drawn from the
2. Count - ing the notes and the rests found in the
3. Top num-bers tell you how man-y beats that you'll
4. With 2 / 2 time you find half note beats. In 2/

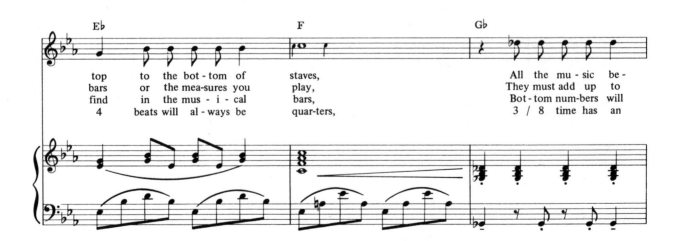

top to the bot-tom of staves,
bars or the mea-sures you play,
find in the mus - i - cal bars,
4 beats will al - ways be quar-ters,

All the mu - sic be -
They must add up to
Bot - tom num-bers will
3 / 8 time has an

NAME _____

Quiz 9–1

1. Real time is measured by the clock
   but music time is measured in
   a. seconds
   b. rhythms
   c. beats
   □

2. Music, like words, is read from
   a. upside down
   b. left to right
   c. right to left
   □

3. What is found at the beginning of the
   staff, that tells about music time?
   a. a key signature
   b. a time signature
   c. a clock
   □

4. A time signature has how many
   numbers?
   a. 4
   b. 3
   c. 2
   □

5. The top number in a time signature
   tells you
   a. the number of beats per bar
   b. what time it is
   c. where the bottom number is
   □

6. The bottom number in a time
   signature tells you
   a. what kind of note the beat is
   b. the number of beats per bar
   c. where the bottom is
   □

7. Time signatures can be $\frac{2}{4}, \frac{3}{4}, \frac{4}{4}$
   a. True
   b. False
   □

8. $\frac{2}{4}$ time has
   a. four beats per bar
   b. three beats per bar
   c. two beats per bar
   □

9. $\frac{3}{4}$ time has
   a. two beats per bar
   b. three beats per bar
   c. four beats per bar
   □

10. $\frac{4}{4}$ time has
    a. two beats per bar
    b. three beats per bar
    c. four beats per bar
    □

11. $\frac{3}{4}$ time has
    a. a quarter note beat
    b. a half note beat
    c. a whole note beat
    □

12. $\frac{3}{2}$ time has
    a. a quarter note beat
    b. a half note beat
    c. a whole note beat
    □

13. $\frac{3}{8}$ time has
    a. a quarter note beat
    b. an eighth note beat
    c. a half note beat
    □

© 1990 by Parker Publishing Company

NAME _____

14. The order of things here is
a. key signature, treble clef, time signature
b. treble clef, key signature, time signature
c. time signature, key signature, treble clef □

15. Each bar in a musical piece will usually have the same number of beats in it. a. True b. False □

16. This bar is a. correct b. incorrect □

17. This bar is a. correct b. incorrect □

18. This bar is a. correct b. incorrect □

19. This bar is a. correct b. incorrect □

20. This bar is a. correct b. incorrect □

21. This bar is a. correct b. incorrect □

22. This bar is a. correct b. incorrect □

23. This bar is a. correct b. incorrect □

24. This bar is a. correct b. incorrect □

25. This bar is a. correct b. incorrect □

NAME _____

© 1990 by Parker Publishing Company

Quiz 9–3

Mark ✔ if the following bars (measures) have the correct number of beats. If not, mark ✘.

WELL, GEE! WELL, HECK! NOW COUNT UP ALL YOUR WELL-EARNED CHECKS!

25

Write the correct time signature in each bar below.

Look at the time signatures in the bars (measures) below. Fill in each bar with the notes or rests that are asked for.

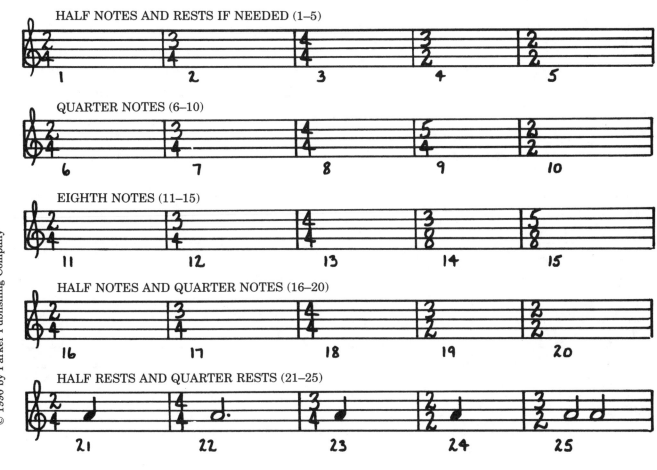

HALF NOTES AND RESTS IF NEEDED (1–5)

QUARTER NOTES (6–10)

EIGHTH NOTES (11–15)

HALF NOTES AND QUARTER NOTES (16–20)

HALF RESTS AND QUARTER RESTS (21–25)

YOUR MARK IS ...

Mark in the beats in each bar, with a *stroke* (|). Remember:

1. The top number in the time signature tells the number of beats in each bar.
2. *The bottom number tells what kind of note the beat is.*

Complete the following measures with notes. Always complete each beat by writing smallest note values to largest note values. Use as few notes as possible.

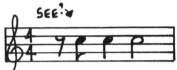

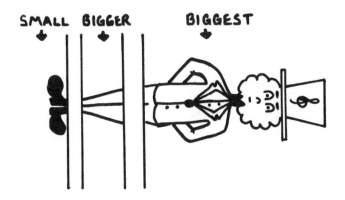

A WHOLE REST WILL COMPLETELY FILL A BAR IN ANY TIME SIGNATURE.

SMALL BIGGER   BIGGEST

Complete the following measures (bars) with rests. Remember: Always complete each beat by writing smallest rest values to largest rest values.

Look at the following time signatures in each staff of music. Now write in bar lines in the right places for each staff.

Make a beautiful piece of music by following the directions and writing music on the staff at the bottom of the page.

Draw:

1. A vertical line at the beginning of the staff
2. A treble clef
3. A key signature with flats on B, E (space), and A in the staff
4. A $\frac{4}{4}$ time signature
5. A quarter note G (on a line)
6. 4 eighth notes of B♭ on a line
7. A quarter note B♭ on the line
8. A quarter note C in the staff
9. A quarter note A♭ in the staff
10. A quarter rest
11. 2 eighth notes of G in the staff
12. A bar line between your notes
13. Repeat signs to repeat bars 1 and 2
14. A first ending around bar 2

15. A half note C in the staff
16. A half rest
17. A vertical line and a treble clef at the start of the next staff
18. A key signature of 3 flats as in No. 3
19. Quarter rest and 4 eighth notes of D♭ on a line
20. Quarter note D♭ on a line
21. Quarter note D♭ on a line
22. Quarter note A♭ on a space
23. Half rest
24. Double bar line to show the music is finished
25. A missing bar line and write a second ending over this bar

Write your music here:

50

BOREDOM BUSTER

Trace your way into the winner's triangle. Follow the pattern of time signatures below. In the maze, you will find bars of notes and rests that follow the pattern of the time signatures. Good luck!

$\frac{4}{4}$ $\quad$ $\frac{3}{4}$ $\quad$ $\frac{2}{4}$ $\quad$ $\frac{4}{4}$ $\quad$ $\frac{3}{4}$ $\quad$ $\frac{4}{4}$ $\quad$ $\frac{5}{4}$ $\quad$ $\frac{7}{4}$ $\quad$ $\frac{2}{4}$ $\quad$ $\frac{6}{8}$ $\quad$ $\frac{4}{4}$ $\quad$ $\frac{3}{4}$

NAME _____

BOREDOM BUSTER

Across

3. $\frac{2}{4}$ means there are _____ beats in each bar.

4. Bar lines make music _____ to read.

6. A bar of $\frac{2}{4}$ time can have one _____ note in it.

7. In $\frac{4}{4}$ time, you could have one whole _____ in a bar.

9. In a bar of $\frac{6}{8}$ time, you could have _____ eighth notes.

10. $\frac{3}{4}$ time means there are _____ beats in a bar.

13. $\frac{4}{4}$ ♩ ♩ ♩ | is right or wrong?

14. In a bar of $\frac{4}{4}$ time you could write o _____ 𝄼 .

15. The _____ _____ tells you how many beats are in each bar and what kind of note gets the beat.

Down

1. Another name for bar is _____.

2. With $\frac{4}{4}$ time there is a _____ note beat.

3. In $\frac{3}{4}$ time there are _____ beats in each measure.

5. In $\frac{6}{8}$ time there can be _____ eighth notes in a bar.

8. In $\frac{5}{4}$ time there can be _____ eighth notes in a bar.

11. In $\frac{5}{4}$ time there are _____ beats in a bar.

12. In $\frac{4}{2}$ time there are _____ beats in a bar.

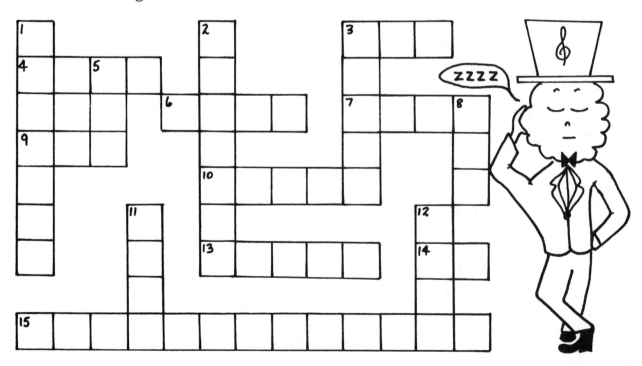

BOREDOM BUSTER: *SONGWRITING*

Songs usually have words. The rhythm found in a song melody is created from the natural rhythm of the song *lyrics* (words).

See if you can write music rhythms for the following *lyrics*. Don't use rests. Use only quarter and eighth notes. Use any pitches you want.

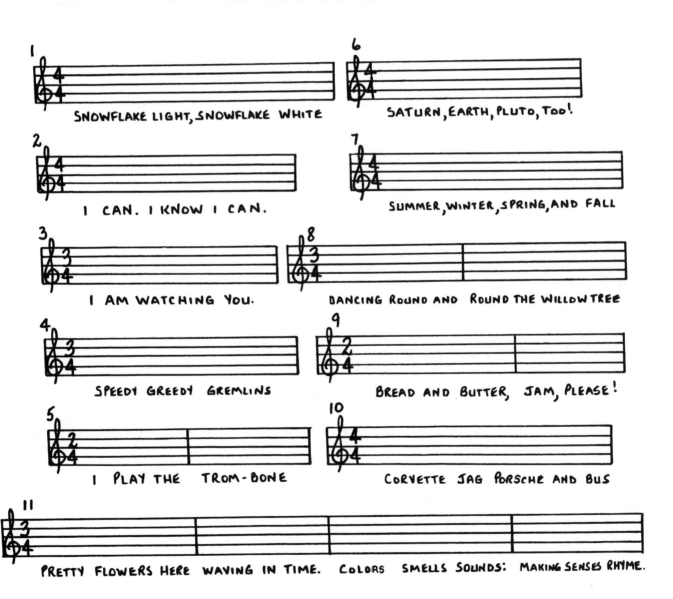

BOREDOM BUSTER: *ACCENTS*

Usually the first beat in a bar is *accented* more than the other beats. (Accent means to play *louder*.)

In the following lines, place strokes over words to show where the beats fall. Then circle the strokes that you think would be the loudest beats.

Example: Ⓘ   I   I
Forest in the sky,

Ⓘ   I   I
How I wonder why.

1. Hugs can make your day great.

2. Spacemen can be green, only when they're seen.

3. Spider hanging from my wall, I'm afraid that you might fall.

4. Mary Joan Edna Chris all have names that start with "Miss."

5. Accents make the notes sound strong.

   Even when the notes are wrong!

6. Guitar drums and bass, really do sound "ace."

7. TV, Walkman, Cars, and Food,

   Many times can change my mood.

Time signatures tell you how many beats are in each bar. Now you know that the first beat in each bar is accented.

Go back and write the time signature of each line above by grouping beats into patterns.

Example: $\frac{3}{4}$ Ⓘ   I   I
Forest in the sky,
1   2   3

Ⓘ   I   I
How I wonder why.
1   2   3

MUSICAL "X'S AND O'S"

1. Divide the class into two equal parts.
2. Draw a large tic-tac-toe that has 6 lines on the board.

1	2	3	4
5	6	7	8
9	10	11	12
13	14	15	16

3. Have a student from each team alternately guess the answers to Information Cards that the teacher or a student shows the class.
4. A team is either an "X" team or an "O" team. If the "X" team member guesses an Information Card correctly, he is allowed to place an X anywhere on the grid. If an "O" team member guesses an Information Card incorrectly, she is not allowed to place an "O" on the grid, giving team "X" the advantage.
5. To win, 4 squares are completed up, down, diagonally, or in a "box"; i.e., a "box" would be squares 1, 2, 5, 6, or 10, 11, 14, 15.

Make laminated cardboard cards (8½" × 11"). Make 2 of each.

FRONT	HOW MANY BEATS IN A BAR OF $\frac{4}{4}$?	HOW MANY BEATS IN A BAR OF $\frac{3}{4}$?	HOW MANY BEATS IN A BAR OF $\frac{2}{4}$?	HOW MANY BEATS IN A BAR OF $\frac{4}{2}$?	HOW MANY BEATS IN A BAR OF $\frac{3}{2}$?	HOW MANY BEATS IN A BAR OF $\frac{2}{2}$?	HOW MANY BEATS IN A BAR OF $\frac{5}{4}$?	HOW MANY BEATS IN A BAR OF $\frac{7}{4}$?
BACK	4	3	2	4	3	2	5	7

FRONT	WHAT KIND OF NOTE GETS THE BEAT IN $\frac{3}{8}$?	WHAT KIND OF NOTE GETS THE BEAT IN $\frac{3}{4}$?	WHAT KIND OF NOTE GETS THE BEAT IN $\frac{2}{4}$?	WHAT KIND OF NOTE GETS THE BEAT IN $\frac{3}{2}$?	THE TOP NUMBER IN A TIME SIGNATURE TELLS YOU	THE BOTTOM NUMBER IN A TIME SIGNATURE TELLS YOU	WHAT BEAT IN ANY BAR IS ACCENTED?
BACK	EIGHTH NOTE	QUARTER NOTE	QUARTER NOTE	HALF NOTE	HOW MANY BEATS ARE IN A BAR	WHAT KIND OF NOTE GETS THE BEAT	THE FIRST BEAT

Student Evaluation Sheet

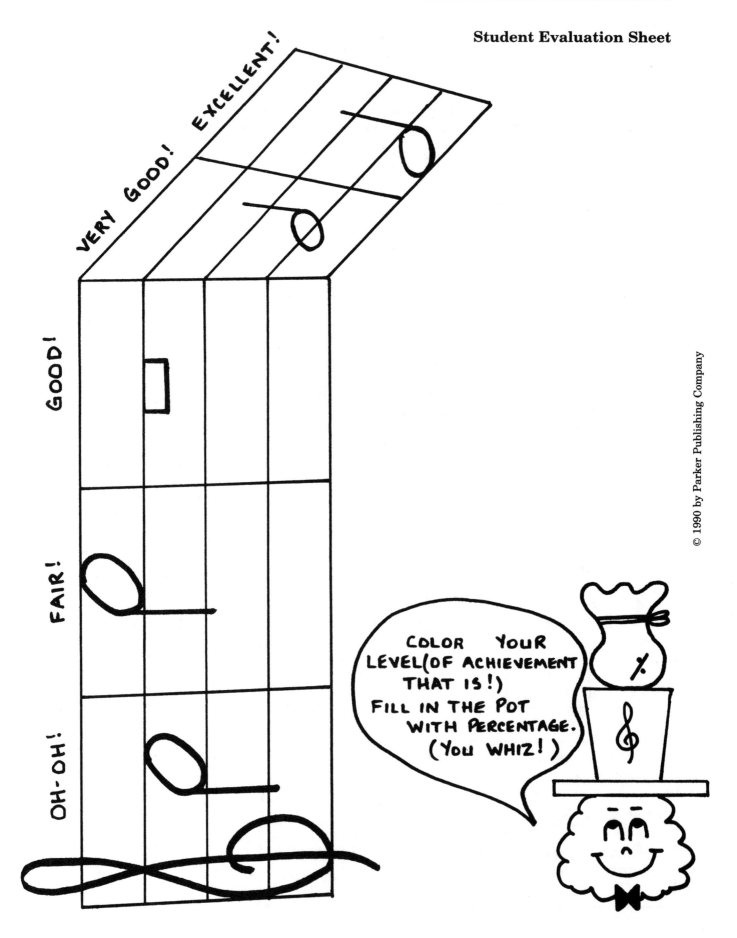

CHAPTER 9
CLASS RECORD SHEET

GRADE

HOMEROOM TEACHER

CLASS PERIOD/DAY

YEAR

Have students complete as many quizzes as necessary. All tests need not be completed. Write in students' names and fill in their marks in the squares below.

STUDENTS' NAMES	SONG				QUIZ 9–1	QUIZ 9–2	QUIZ 9–3	QUIZ 9–4	QUIZ 9–5	QUIZ 9–6	QUIZ 9–7	QUIZ 9–8	QUIZ 9–9	QUIZ 9–10	BB 9–1	BB 9–2	BB 9–3	BB 9–4	FINAL MARK
	WORDS	MOTIONS	PITCHES	MUSICALITY															

PROGRESS OF CLASSES

A chart is given here to help you keep a record of the tasks your classes complete. After listing the class names in the top squares, indicate with a check mark (✔) or with the date that a task has been accomplished.

CHAPTER 9

LIST OF CLASSES											
═══════════════════════════											
HAVE READ THE STORY											
HAVE STARTED THE SONG											
STUDENTS KNOW SONG											
HAVE COMPLETED QUIZ NO.	**ACTIVITY**	**SKILL PRACTICED**									
	9–1. Multiple choice	chapter story review									
	9–2. Marking beats	beat recognition in bars									
	9–3. Marking ✔ or ✖	recognizing correct number of beats in bars									
	9–4. Writing time signatures	identifying time signatures given bars									
	9–5. Writing music	bar completion given time signature, notes, rests									
	9–6. Marking beats	beat recognition given 3/4, 3/8, 2/2, 3/2									
	9–7. Writing music	bar completion with notes									
	9–8. Writing music	bar completion with rests									
	9–9. Writing music	placing bar lines									
	9–10. Writing music	review of Chapters 1–8									
BOREDOM BUSTER NO.	9–1. Fun maze	correct numbers of beats in bars given time signatures									
	9–2. Crossword puzzle	time signature information									
	9–3. Songwriting	writing rhythms given words									
	9–4. Word study	beats and accents									
GAME: MUSICAL X'S AND O'S											

CHAPTER 9 ANSWER KEY

Quiz 9–1

1. c	6. a	11. a	16. b	21. b
2. b	7. a	12. b	17. b	22. b
3. b	8. c	13. b	18. a	23. b
4. c	9. b	14. b	19. b	24. a
5. a	10. c	15. a	20. b	25. b

Quiz 9–2

Quiz 9–3

1. ✔	6. ✔	11. ✔	16. ✘	21. ✔
2. ✔	7. ✔	12. ✘	17. ✔	22. ✔
3. ✔	8. ✘	13. ✘	18. ✔	23. ✘
4. ✔	9. ✔	14. ✘	19. ✔	24. ✘
5. ✔	10. ✘	15. ✘	20. ✘	25. ✘

Quiz 9–4

1. $\frac{3}{4}$	6. $\frac{2}{4}$	11. $\frac{3}{4}$	16. $\frac{2}{4}$	21. $\frac{3}{4}$
2. $\frac{4}{4}\left(\frac{2}{2}\right)$	7. $\frac{4}{4}\left(\frac{2}{2}\right)$	12. $\frac{4}{4}\left(\frac{2}{2}\right)$	17. $\frac{2}{4}$	22. $\frac{3}{4}$
3. $\frac{2}{4}$	8. $\frac{4}{4}\left(\frac{2}{2}\right)$	13. $\frac{4}{4}\left(\frac{2}{2}\right)$	18. $\frac{2}{4}$	23. $\frac{2}{4}$
4. $\frac{3}{4}$	9. $\frac{4}{4}\left(\frac{2}{2}\right)$	14. $\frac{4}{4}\left(\frac{2}{2}\right)$	19. $\frac{4}{4}\left(\frac{2}{2}\right)$	24. $\frac{3}{4}$
5. $\frac{4}{4}\left(\frac{2}{2}\right)$	10. $\frac{3}{4}$	15. $\frac{4}{4}\left(\frac{2}{2}\right)$	20. $\frac{4}{4}\left(\frac{2}{2}\right)$	25. $\frac{3}{8}$

Quiz 9–5

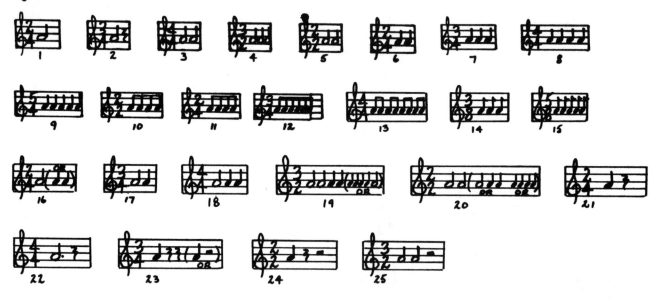

Quiz 9–6

Quiz 9–7

Quiz 9–8

Quiz 9–9

Quiz 9–10

Boredom Buster 9–1

Boredom Buster 9–3

Boredom Buster 9–2

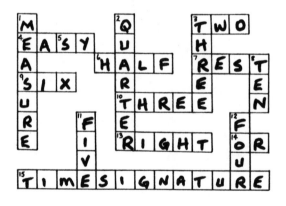

Boredom Buster 9–4

1. $\frac{4}{4}$ Hugs can make your day great.

2. $\frac{3}{4}$ Spacemen can be green, only when they're seen.

3. $\frac{4}{4}$ Spider hanging from my wall, I'm afraid that you might fall.

4. $\frac{4}{4}$ Mary Joan Edna Chris all have names that start with "Miss."

5. $\frac{4}{4}$ Accents make the notes sound strong.

   Even when the notes are wrong!

6. $\frac{3}{4}$ Guitar drums and bass, really do sound "ace."

7. $\frac{4}{4}$ TV, Walkmen, Cars, and Food,

   Many times can change my mood.

Meet Mr. Treble Clef's Partner

Before reading ask:
1. What happened in the last story?
2. What are the 2 numbers at the beginning of the staff? (time signature)
3. What does the top number do? (tells the no. of beats per bar)
4. What's a bar line? (vertical line in the staff)
5. Bar? (all the music between 2 bar lines)
6. What does the bottom number in the time signature do? (tells what kind of note is the beat)

Mac and Christina, the children, and their teacher looked around this very unusual place where they had just landed.

"Where are we now?" asked Christina.

"Everything's blue, except for that big fat man over there. He's black and *looks like an ear*!" exclaimed Mac.

"Let's ask that strange-looking man where we are," said the teacher.

"Excuse me, Mr. Ear," said Christina, "but where are we?"

"A special place in Musictown," answered the ear-man. "Allow me to introduce myself. I am Mr. Bass Clef!"

"How do you do! I am Christina. This is Mac, our teacher, and our music class. Do you know Mr. Treble Clef?"

"But of course," said Mr. Bass Clef. "We work together all the time. When Mr. Treble Clef sits on a staff, people play higher notes, but when Mr. Bass Clef sits on the staff, people play low notes."

"Do bass clef lines and spaces and treble clef lines and spaces have the same names?" asked Mac.

"Nope!" Mr. Bass Clef answered. "When I sit on the staff, the lines are G B D F A. The spaces are A C E G !"

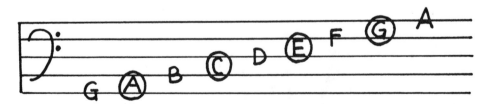

"Why are bass clef lines and spaces named differently from those in the treble clef?" asked Christina.

"Because, four billion years ago, the treble clef staff and

the bass clef staff were joined together by a single line in the middle, called *middle C*. The top lines and spaces were for *high notes* and the bottom lines and spaces were for *low notes*.

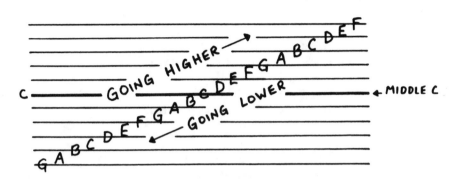

"People had a hard time reading notes because there were so many lines and spaces. So, an ancient king who was called *common sense*, ordered the middle C to disappear. The king then hired Mr. Treble Clef to sit on the top five lines and Mr. Bass Clef to sit on the bottom five lines. Notes with the treble clef were high and notes with the bass clef were low."

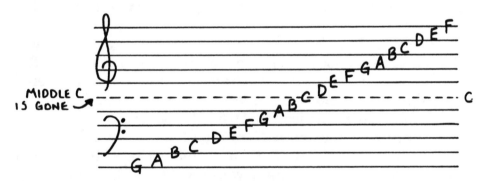

"So that's why my bass clef lines and spaces are named differently from those in the treble clef staff."

"But how can we possibly remember the new names of the bass clef lines and spaces?" asked Christina.

"Simple!" boomed Mr. Bass Clef. "Just like Mr. Treble Clef, I have two names. You could call me Mr. F Clef if you wanted to. This is because my two dots sit around the fourth line, which is F."

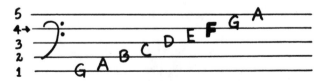

Show how the lines and spaces are named in relation to fourth line F.

"From this F, you can go to the right in the alphabet when notes go higher! Go backwards in the alphabet from F, as notes go lower. *And* you can sing my own magic song to help you to remember the names of my lines and spaces."

Mr. Bass Clef opened his mouth wide, took a deep breath, and boomed:

Class together.

> Bass clef, the F clef
> Looks like an ear with two dots
>   around the F line.
> Bass clef, the F clef,
> It has low notes in the staff
>   all the time.
>
> Bass clef notes are low,
> Bass clef notes are low,
> Bass clef has the low notes,
>   is the ear with two dots,
> F clef is the . . .

Mr. Bass Clef sang his magic song over and over again.

"But how can we remember the names of the lines and spaces?" complained Christina. "And why are those little boys playing over there and why are there so many cows eating grass?"

"The little boys having fun and the cows eating grass will help you to remember the names of the lines and spaces. The bass clef lines are G B D F A. These letters can be remembered by thinking 'Good Boys Deserve Fun Always.' The first letter in each of these words is G B D F A!"

"What about the spaces?" quizzed Mac.

"The spaces are A C E G. Remember that 'All Cows Eat Grass.' The first letters of these words are A C E G, the names of the spaces," answered Mr. Bass Clef.

Just then, the little blue boys in the field and the blue cows all began to sing:

Good Boys Deserve Fun Always
Tells you the bass clef *lines'* names
Words All Cows Eat Grass
Tells you the *spaces* in the staff.

G-B-D-F-A, A-C-E-G,
Good Boys Deserve Fun Always.
All Cows . . . Eat Grass!

Class together.

After the playing boys and grass-eating cows sang their verses for a while, the teacher and the music class began to sing different verses at the same time, singing:

G-B-D-F-A are the *lines*
A-C-E-G are the *spaces*
G-B-D-F-A are the *lines*
A-C-E-G are the *spaces* . . .
G-B-D-F-A, A-C-E-G
G-B-D-F-A, A-C-E-G

Class together.

Afterwards, Mr. Bass Clef joined in, crooning:

Bass clef, the F clef
It looks like an ear with two
      dots around the F line.
Bass clef, the F clef,
It has low notes in the staff
      all the time.

Class together.

G-B-D-F-A, A-C-E-G,
Good Boys Deserve Fun Always.
All Cows Eat Grass!

Everybody was singing different verses at the same time, and the music sounded exciting. The beat stayed the same, even though everyone sang so many different rhythms. Round and round the song went, it seemed like forever. Everybody accented the first of every four beats. (The music must have been in $\frac{4}{4}$ time!) It was easy to imagine bar lines floating by. Mr. Bass Clef snapped his fingers and right away, the teacher and his class found their eyes closed. In their minds, they could *really* see bar lines whisking by. They soon began to move forward and out of the blue valley, soon leaving the boys, cows, and Mr. Bass Clef far behind. Beat by beat they traveled, until they finally began to see home again! Closer and closer home came into sight. They first passed over Christina's house. There was Mac's bike. There was the music school. And in a flash, everybody landed right back in their classroom, with the teacher standing up in front. To everyone's surprise, each of the students' chairs now had a very fancy sign written on it. Each sign said *Musician*. This was a special day for the kids. Mac and Christina and all of their classmates now knew a lot about music and how music works. They now truly could call themselves, with great pride, now and forever, *musicians*.

Ask:
1. What are the two clefs you know? (treble and bass)
2. Which clef has the lower notes? (bass)
3. What's another name for the bass clef? (F clef)
4. Why? (the two dots surround F)

SUGGESTIONS FOR TEACHING THE SONG,
Bass Clef Blues

1. Review the musical material by discussing the story events.
2. Play the tape of *Bass Clef Blues* or perform it for your students. Then explain the words, making sure they understand what the words mean.
3. Let them hear the song again. (Students in Grades 2–6 can follow the words.)
4. Teach each line by rote, repeating each one several times successively. Maintain an unbroken, steady beat, retaining the lyric rhythms (with or without pitches as necessary).
5. Teach the hand motions while teaching the words. You can follow the pictures on the music.
6. Have all students *completely* memorize the song, through repetition over time.

7. Have students perform as soloists, in duets, or in any other interesting combinations. Have the girls compete with the boys, or rows against each other for marks you announce. Kids love competitions.
8. Have a lot of fun!

THE BODY MOTIONS

Verse 1

bar:	7	Pull your ear lobe on "ear."
	8	Point fingers on "dots." On "F line" open one hand and point to the index finger on the other hand.
	12	Draw 𝄢 on "staff" and point out two dots, one over the other on each of the third and fourth beats.
13 & 14		Point a finger down on beat 1. Move hand downwards, stopping on the third beat.
15 & 16		Rock head to the left and right making one motion per beat.

Verse 2

bar:	5	Raise hands increasingly higher on each of "G B D F A."
	6	Open a hand showing 5 "lines."
	7	Raise hands increasingly higher on each of "A C E G."
	8	Open one hand, revealing four spaces. Point the index finger of the other hand at the first, second, third, and fourth "spaces" on each beat.
	9	Raise hands increasingly higher on each "G B D F A."
	10	Open one hand, revealing five lines.
	11	Raise hands increasingly higher on each of "A C E G."
	12	Pulse an open hand (with spaces) on each beat.
13, 15		Close a hand.
14, 16		Open a hand.

Verse 3

bar:	5	Make a "halo" over your head.
	7	Point a finger on each beat.
	8	Open a hand.
9, 10		Rock head from left to right on beats 1 and 3.
	11	Point on beat 1. Open a hand on beat 3.
	13	Close a hand (revealing lines).
	14	Open a hand (revealing spaces).
	15	Place hands over head making a "halo" on beat 1.

BASS CLEF BLUES

Perform lines 1, 2 and 3 consecutively, then as a round.

1. A

Bass   clef, ___   the   F   clef, ___   it

2.

G   B   D   F   A   are   the   lines,

3.

Good   boys   de-serve   fun   al   -   ways

Play 3 times

1. The bass clef looks like
   - a. an ear with two dots
   - b. a cow
   - c. a treble clef

2. The two dots on the bass clef sit around
   - a. line G
   - b. eating grass
   - c. line F

3. The lines in the bass clef staff are
   - a. F A C E
   - b. G B D F A
   - c. A C E G

4. The spaces are
   - a. A C E G
   - b. B L U E
   - c. F A C E

5. Bass clef notes are
   - a. low
   - b. high
   - c. loud

6. "All Cows Eat Grass" helps you to remember
   - a. that cows produce milk
   - b. the bass clef spaces
   - c. the bass clef lines

7. "Good Boys Deserve Fun Always" helps you to remember
   - a. the bass clef spaces
   - b. that they really deserve fun!
   - c. the bass clef lines

8. The treble clef staff and bass clef staff were once joined.
   - a. True
   - b. False

9. The line between these two staves was
   - a. high C
   - b. the Twiline Zone
   - c. middle C

10. Middle C was taken out
    - a. to make better sounding music
    - b. to make notes easier to read
    - c. because it misbehaved

11. The top five lines of the 11-line staff always have
    - a. wings
    - b. a treble clef
    - c. a bass clef

12. The bottom five lines of the 11-line staff always have
    - a. a treble clef
    - b. sore muscles
    - c. a bass clef

NAME _____

13. Space two in the bass clef staff is
    a. C
    b. A
    c. F
□

14. Space four is
    a. F
    b. E
    c. G
□

15. Line one is
    a. B
    b. D
    c. G
□

16. Line three is
    a. B
    b. D
    c. G
□

17. Line five is
    a. B
    b. G
    c. A
□

18. [music notation] is
    a. A
    b. C
    c. F
□

19. [music notation] is
    a. F
    b. A
    c. C
□

20. [music notation] is
    a. B
    b. G
    c. E
□

21. [music notation] is
    a. F
    b. D
    c. B
□

22. [music notation] is
    a. F
    b. D
    c. B
□

23. A) [music notation] B) [music notation]
Which note is higher?
    a. A
    b. B
□

24. A) [music notation] B) [music notation]
Which note is higher?
    a. A
    b. B
    c. they're the same
□

25. is
    a. right
    b. wrong
□

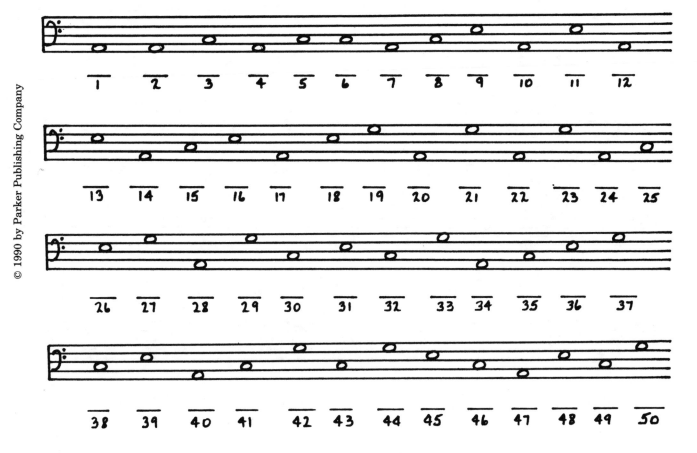

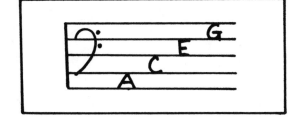

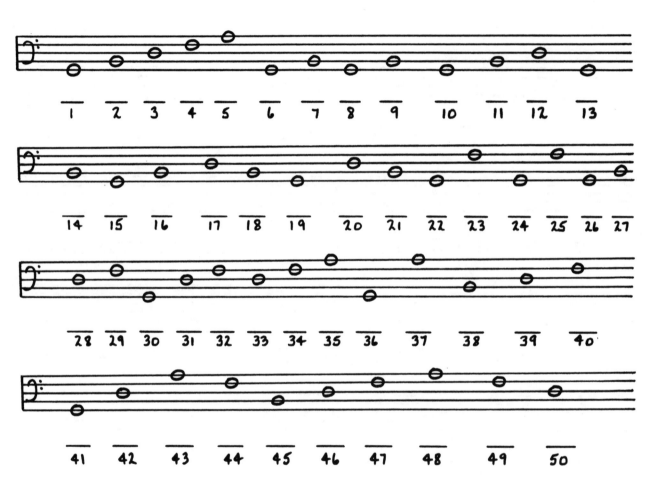

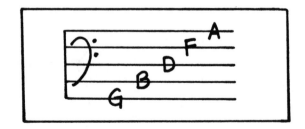

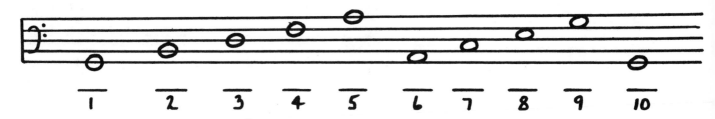

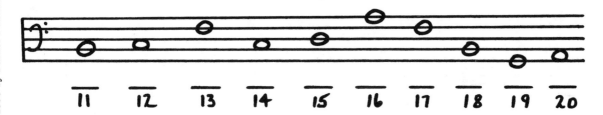

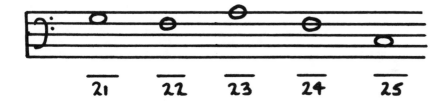

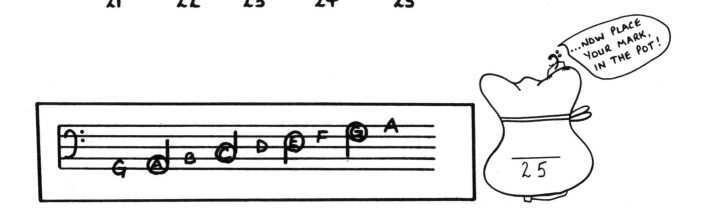

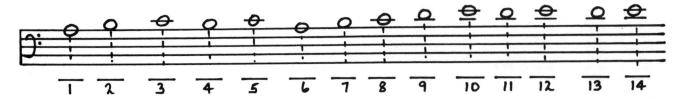

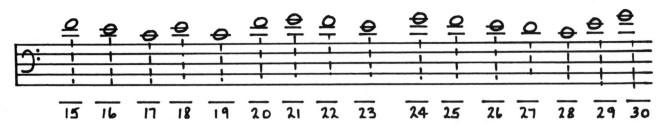

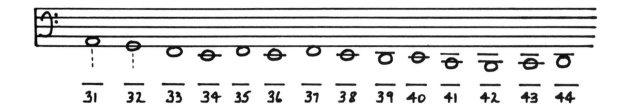

For every note you find in one staff, write a note that has *the same name* in another staff. *Watch your clefs!*

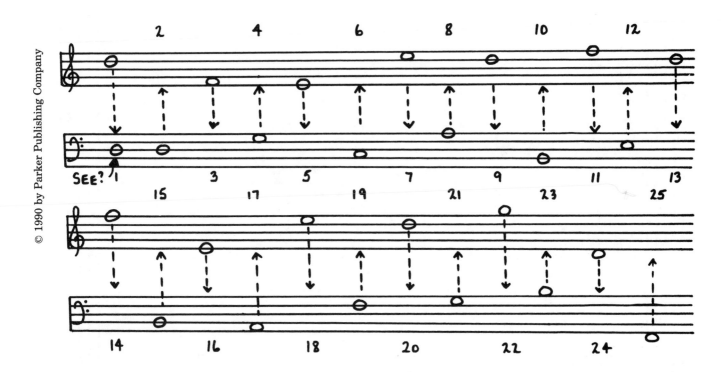

In each bar, you will find one note. After it, write a note which is one semitone higher. Complete 1–25 this way.

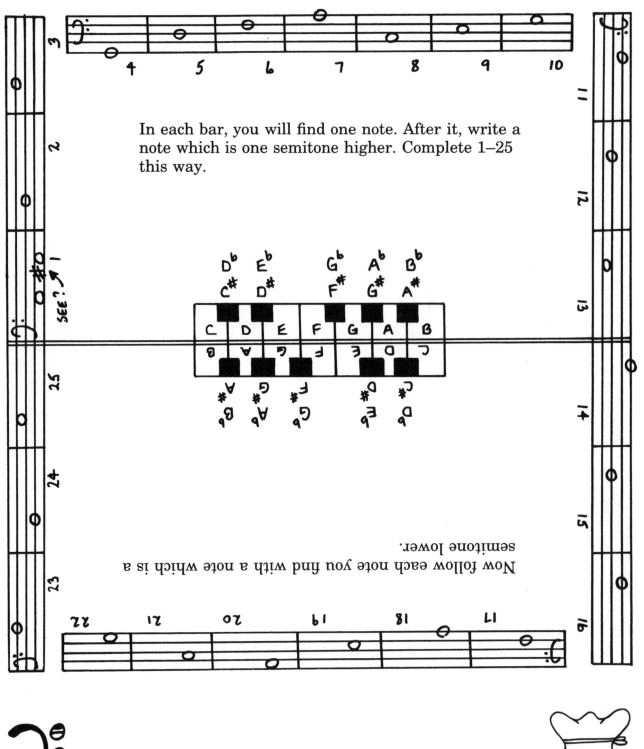

Now follow each note you find with a note which is a semitone lower.

50

HERE ARE LINES AND SPACES
AND LEDGER LINES
ALL MIXED UP!

HAVE A GOOD TIME
AND NAME ALL OF THESE
NOTES!

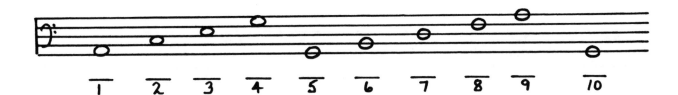

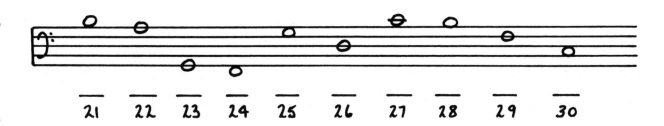

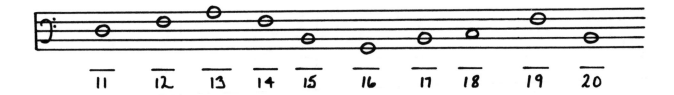

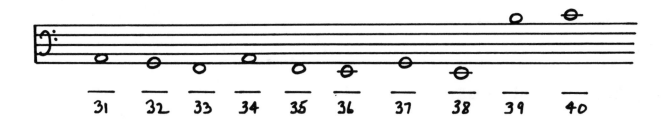

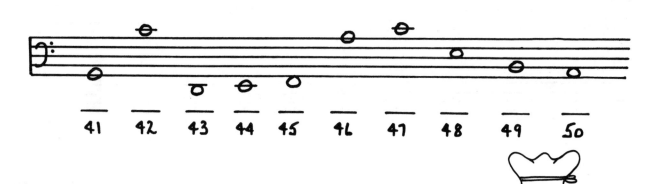

Follow these instructions and write beautiful music below. Write a:

1	BAR LINE AT THE START OF THE STAFF	**13**	B♭ ON A LINE FOR ONE BEAT	**25**	G ON A LINE FOR 1 BEAT	**38**	C BELOW THE STAFF FOR ½ BEAT
2	BASS CLEF	**14**	G ON A LINE FOR ONE BEAT	**26**	F BELOW THE STAFF FOR 1 BEAT	**39**	C BELOW THE STAFF FOR ½ BEAT
3	4/4 TIME SIGNATURE	**15**	E BELOW THE STAFF FOR ONE BEAT	**27**	E BELOW THE STAFF FOR 1 BEAT	**40**	C BELOW THE STAFF FOR ½ BEAT
4	C BELOW THE STAFF FOR 1 BEAT	**16**	1 BEAT OF SILENCE	**28**	D BELOW THE STAFF FOR ½ BEAT	**41**	C BELOW THE STAFF FOR ½ BEAT
5	½ BEAT OF SILENCE	**17**	F BELOW THE STAFF FOR 1 BEAT	**29**	G ON A LINE FOR ½ BEAT	**42**	C BELOW THE STAFF FOR ½ BEAT
6	1½ BEATS OF E BELOW THE STAFF	**18**	½ BEAT OF SILENCE	**30**	F BELOW THE STAFF FOR 1 BEAT	**43**	C BELOW THE STAFF FOR ½ BEAT
7	G ON A LINE – ONE BEAT	**19**	1½ BEATS OF A ON A SPACE	**31**	E BELOW THE STAFF FOR 1 BEAT	**44**	REPEAT SIGNS AROUND THE LAST 4 BEATS
8	REPEATS AROUND THESE NOTES	**20**	C ON A SPACE FOR 1 BEAT	**32**	D BELOW THE STAFF FOR 1 BEAT	**45**	FILL IN THE MISSING BAR LINE ON STAFF 1
9	C BELOW THE STAFF FOR ONE BEAT	**21**	REPEATS ON THE LAST 4 BEATS OF MUSIC	**33**	C BELOW THE STAFF FOR ½ BEAT	**46**	WRITE "DS AL CODA" ABOVE AND AT THE END OF BAR 4
10	E BELOW THE STAFF FOR ONE BEAT	**22**	BAR LINE AT THE START OF NEXT STAFF	**34**	F BELOW THE STAFF FOR ½ BEAT	**47**	WRITE "THE SIGN" ABOVE AND AT THE BEGINNING OF BAR 2
11	G ON A LINE FOR ONE BEAT	**23**	BASS CLEF ON THIS STAFF	**35**	BAR LINE BETWEEN NOTES IN STAFF 2	**48**	WRITE A CODA SIGN ABOVE AND AT THE END OF BAR 3
12	A ON A SPACE FOR ONE BEAT	**24**	4/4 TIME SIGNATURE	**36**	C BELOW THE STAFF FOR ½ BEAT	**49**	WRITE A CODA SIGN ABOVE AND AT THE END OF BAR 6
				37	C BELOW THE STAFF FOR ½ BEAT	**50**	HAVE A FREE MARK!

WRITE YOUR MUSIC HERE

MATCH UP THE SQUARES IN EACH BOX

BOX A

#			
1	FLATS	A	SEMITONE
2	C TO C♯ IS A	B	RAISE NOTES A SEMITONE
3	KEYBOARD BLACK NOTES ARE THE	C	LOWER NOTES A SEMITONE
4	[notes] IS	D	SHARPS AND FLATS
5	C TO D IS A	E	WHOLE TONE
6	[music notation] IS A	F	A SLEEPY MR. T.C.
7	SHARPS	G	TIME SIGNATURE
8	⁴₄ IS A	H	3
9	IN ³₄ THERE ARE ___ BEATS PER BAR	I	2
10	IN ²₄ THERE ARE ___ BEATS PER BAR	J	KEY SIGNATURE

BOX B

#			
11	‖: :‖ ARE	A	GO BACK TO THE SIGN 𝄋
12	DS MEANS	B	CODA SIGN
13	DC MEANS	C	REPEAT SIGNS
14	⊕ IS A	D	FIRST ENDING
15	"FINE" MEANS	E	GO BACK TO THE BEGINNING
16	[1. :‖] IS A	F	SECOND ENDING
17	AL CODA MEANS	G	THE END
18	[2.] IS A	H	GO TO THE CODA SIGN (⊕)
19	[rabbit] IS A	I	RABBIT
20	♩· IS	J	ONE BEAT

BOX C

#			
21	♩ IS	A	4 BEATS
22	o IS	B	3 BEATS
23	𝅗𝅥 IS	C	2 BEATS
24	𝅗𝅥· IS	D	½ BEAT
25	♩ IS	E	6 BEATS
26	♩♩ IS	F	5 BEATS
27	♫ IS A	G	MR. BASS CLEF
28	DOTS ADD	H	TIE
29	𝄢 IS	I	½ MORE TO NOTES AND RESTS
30	[rest] IS	J	2 BEATS

BOX D

#			
31	𝄾 IS	A	4 BEATS
32	[rest] IS	B	½ BEAT
33	𝄾 IS	C	6 BEATS
34	[rest]· IS	D	1 BEAT
35	[rest]· IS	E	1½ BEATS
36	o [rest] GETS	F	3 BEATS
37	𝄾· IS	G	8 BEATS
38	[bow tie] IS A	H	NOTE B♭
39	[music notation] IS	I	BOW TIE
40	[music notation] IS	J	NOTE A♭

BOX E

#			
41	[music notation] IS	A	NOTE A
42	[music notation] IS	B	NOTE B
43	[music notation] IS	C	NOTE C
44	[music notation] IS	D	NOTE C♯
45	[music notation] IS	E	NOTE B♭
46	[music notation] IS	F	NOTE G
47	[music notation] IS	G	NOTE E
48	[music notation] IS	H	NOTE F♯
49	𝄢 IS A	I	TREBLE CLEF
50	𝄞 IS A	J	BASS CLEF

25

BOREDOM BUSTER

BOREDOM BUSTER

Across

1. $\frac{4}{4}$ is a _____ signature.
3. __ __ __ __ __ __ are the treble clef staff lines.
5. ♩ gets _____ beats.
9. ▤ is a _____ _____ .
12. ▤← is the _____ line.
14. ▬ gets _____ beats.
15. ▤ is B flat _____ if a flat sign changes it.
16. We sing _____ to a quarter note.
17. A dot adds half _____ to notes and rests.
20. ▤ spells __ __ __ .

Down

1. Two eighth notes are sung _____ _____ .
2. ▤ spells __ __ __ .
4. The treble clef staff spaces are __ __ __ __ .
6. ▤ spells _____ .
7. A steady, unchanging pulse is a _____ .
8. In the base clef staff, A is the _____ line.
11. _____ is the changing value of notes you hear in songs.
12. A _____ lowers a note 1 semi-tone.
13. ♩ is a _____ note.
18. There are white and black keys _____ the keyboard.
19. ▤ spells __ __ __ .

BOREDOM BUSTER

Follow the notes on the staff below. Trace their letter names around the circle, to get to the E in the middle.

START HERE

BOREDOM BUSTER

Fill in the note letter names found in the staves below into the correct spaces in the words of the secret story.

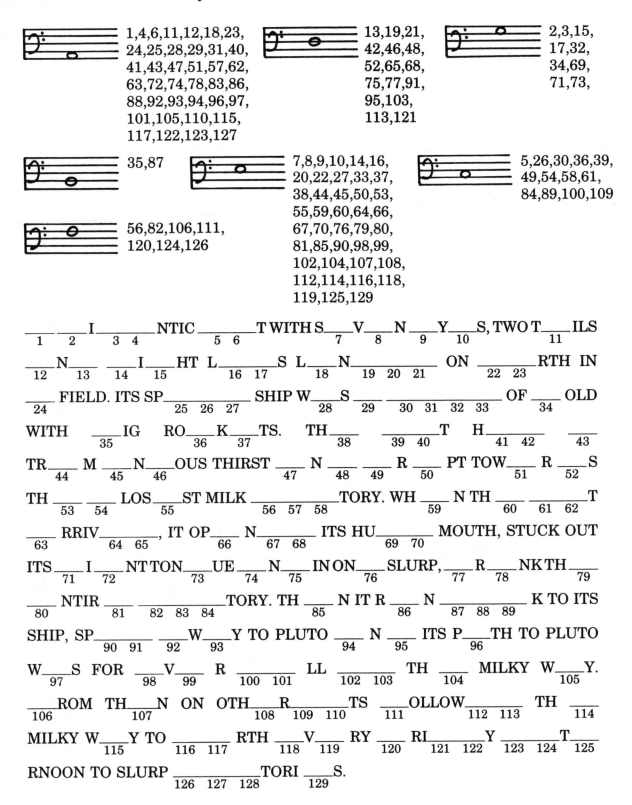

1,4,6,11,12,18,23,
24,25,28,29,31,40,
41,43,47,51,57,62,
63,72,74,78,83,86,
88,92,93,94,96,97,
101,105,110,115,
117,122,123,127

13,19,21,
42,46,48,
52,65,68,
75,77,91,
95,103,
113,121

2,3,15,
17,32,
34,69,
71,73,

35,87

7,8,9,10,14,16,
20,22,27,33,37,
38,44,45,50,53,
55,59,60,64,66,
67,70,76,79,80,
81,85,90,98,99,
102,104,107,108,
112,114,116,118,
119,125,129

5,26,30,36,39,
49,54,58,61,
84,89,100,109

56,82,106,111,
120,124,126

___ ___ I ___ ___ NTIC ___ ___ T WITH S ___ V ___ N ___ Y ___ S, TWO T ___ ILS
1   2   3 4   5 6   7   8   9   10   11

___ N ___ ___ I ___ HT L ___ ___ S L ___ N ___ ___ ___ ON ___ ___ RTH IN
12   13   14 15   16 17   18   19 20 21   22 23

___ FIELD. ITS SP ___ ___ ___ SHIP W ___ S ___ ___ ___ ___ ___ OF ___ OLD
24   25 26 27   28   29 30 31 32 33   34

WITH ___ IG RO ___ K ___ TS. TH ___ ___ ___ T H ___ ___ ___ ___
     35   36   37   38   39 40   41 42   43

TR ___ M ___ N ___ OUS THIRST ___ N ___ ___ R ___ PT TOW ___ R ___ S
   44   45   46   47   48 49   50   51   52

TH ___ ___ LOS ___ ST MILK ___ ___ ___ TORY. WH ___ N TH ___ ___ ___ T
   53 54   55   56 57 58   59   60 61 62

___ RRIV ___ ___ ___, IT OP ___ N ___ ___ ITS HU ___ ___ MOUTH, STUCK OUT
63   64 65   66   67 68   69 70

ITS ___ I ___ NT TON ___ UE ___ N ___ IN ON ___ SLURP, ___ R ___ NK TH ___
    71   72   73   74   75   76   77   78   79

___ NTIR ___ ___ ___ ___ TORY. TH ___ N IT R ___ N ___ ___ ___ K TO ITS
80   81 82 83 84   85   86   87 88 89

SHIP, SP ___ ___ ___ W ___ Y TO PLUTO ___ N ___ ITS P ___ TH TO PLUTO
         90 91 92   93   94   95   96

W ___ S FOR ___ V ___ R ___ ___ LL ___ ___ TH ___ MILKY W ___ Y.
  97   98   99   100 101   102 103   104   105

___ ROM TH ___ N ON OTH ___ R ___ ___ TS ___ OLLOW ___ ___ TH ___
106   107   108   109 110   111   112 113   114

MILKY W ___ Y TO ___ ___ RTH ___ V ___ RY ___ RI ___ ___ Y ___ ___ T ___
        115   116 117   118   119   120   121 122   123 124   125

RNOON TO SLURP ___ ___ ___ TORI ___ S.
               126 127 128   129

RULES TO "SPIN THE MUSIC"

1. This is a variation on the game "Spin the Bottle."
2. Students sit in a circle and hold Information Cards with the question sides of them facing away from the students.
3. One student sits in the middle of the circle and spins a bottle. (How about a maraca?)
4. When the "bottle" points to a student in the circle, the spinner must guess the answer to the Information Card. If he is correct, the person holding the guessed card becomes "it" in the middle.
5. The spinner is allowed 3 incorrect guesses. After the third incorrect guess, he must sing the entire song that corresponds to the Information Cards. This will help him to learn the material. A new spinner is chosen by the teacher or by a student monitor.

Make 8½ × 11 laminated cardboard Information Cards (2 of each).

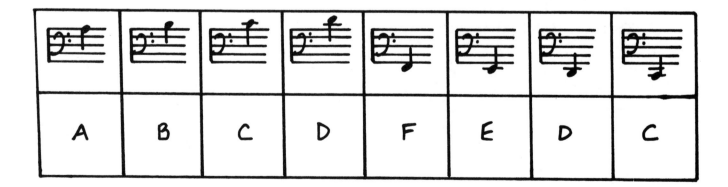

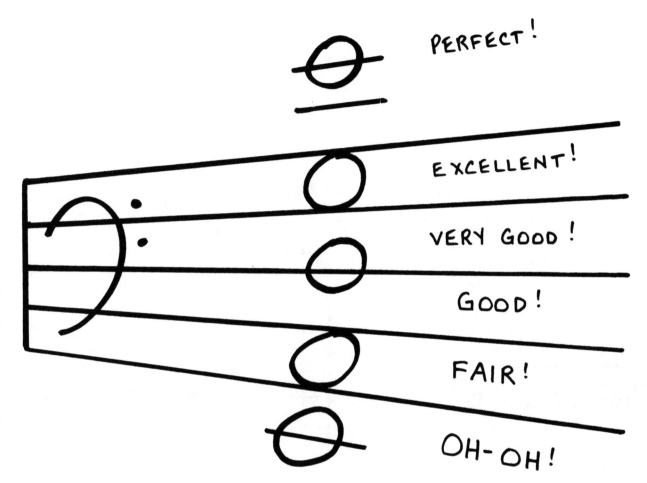

CHAPTER 10
CLASS RECORD SHEET

GRADE [   ] HOMEROOM TEACHER [   ] CLASS PERIOD/DAY [   ] YEAR [   ]

Have students complete as many quizzes as necessary. All tests need not be completed. Write in students' names and fill in their marks in the squares below.

STUDENTS' NAMES	SONG				QUIZ 10-1	QUIZ 10-2	QUIZ 10-3	QUIZ 10-4	QUIZ 10-5	QUIZ 10-6	QUIZ 10-7	QUIZ 10-8	QUIZ 10-9	QUIZ 10-10	BB 10-1	BB 10-2	BB 10-3	BB 10-4	FINAL MARK
	WORDS	MOTIONS	PITCHES	MUSICALITY															

PROGRESS OF CLASSES

A chart is given here to help you keep a record of the tasks your classes complete. After listing the class names in the top squares, indicate with a check mark (✔) or with the date that a task has been accomplished.

CHAPTER 10

LIST OF CLASSES										
= =										
HAVE READ THE STORY										
HAVE STARTED THE SONG										
STUDENTS KNOW SONG										
HAVE COMPLETED QUIZ NO.	ACTIVITY	SKILL PRACTICED								
	10–1. Multiple choice	chapter story review								
	10–2. Naming notes	bass clef staff spaces								
	10–3. Naming notes	bass clef staff lines								
	10–4. Naming notes	bass clef lines and spaces								
	10–5. Naming notes	bass clef ledger lines								
	10–6. Note recognition	transferring notes from bass to/from treble clef								
	10–7. Writing semitones	bass clef staff notes								
	10–8. Naming notes	bass clef staff lines, spaces, ledger lines								
	10–9. Writing music	review of Chapters 1–10								
	10–10. Matching	review of Chapters 1–10								
BOREDOM BUSTER NO.	10–1. Finding the hidden picture	bass clef staff notes								
	10–2. Crossword puzzle	review of Chapters 1–10								
	10–3. Circle puzzle	bass clef staff notes								
	10–4. Secret story	bass clef staff notes								
GAME: SPIN THE MUSIC										

CHAPTER 10 ANSWER KEY

Quiz 10–1

1. a	6. b	11. b	16. b	21. b
2. c	7. c	12. c	17. c	22. c
3. b	8. a	13. a	18. b	23. a
4. a	9. c	14. c	19. b	24. c
5. a	10. b	15. c	20. b	25. b

Quiz 10–2

1. A	11. E	21. G	31. E	41. C
2. A	12. A	22. A	32. C	42. G
3. C	13. E	23. G	33. G	43. C
4. A	14. A	24. A	34. A	44. G
5. C	15. C	25. C	35. C	45. E
6. C	16. E	26. E	36. E	46. C
7. A	17. A	27. G	37. G	47. A
8. C	18. E	28. A	38. C	48. E
9. E	19. G	29. G	39. E	49. C
10. A	20. A	30. C	40. A	50. G

Quiz 10–3

1. G	11. B	21. B	31. D	41. G
2. B	12. D	22. G	32. F	42. D
3. D	13. G	23. F	33. D	43. A
4. F	14. B	24. G	34. F	44. F
5. A	15. G	25. F	35. A	45. B
6. G	16. B	26. G	36. G	46. D
7. B	17. D	27. B	37. A	47. F
8. G	18. B	28. D	38. B	48. A
9. B	19. G	29. F	39. D	49. F
10. G	20. D	30. G	40. F	50. D

Quiz 10–4

1. G	6. A	11. B	16. A	21. G
2. B	7. C	12. C	17. F	22. F
3. D	8. E	13. F	18. B	23. A
4. F	9. G	14. C	19. G	24. F
5. A	10. G	15. D	20. A	25. C

Quiz 10–5

1. A	11. D	21. G	31. A	41. C
2. B	12. E	22. F	32. G	42. B
3. C	13. D	23. E	33. F	43. C
4. B	14. E	24. G	34. E	44. D
5. C	15. F	25. F	35. F	45. C
6. A	16. E	26. E	36. E	46. B
7. B	17. C	27. D	37. F	47. A
8. C	18. E	28. C	38. E	48. B
9. D	19. C	29. E	39. D	49. G
10. E	20. F	30. G	40. E	50. C

Quiz 10–6

Quiz 10–7

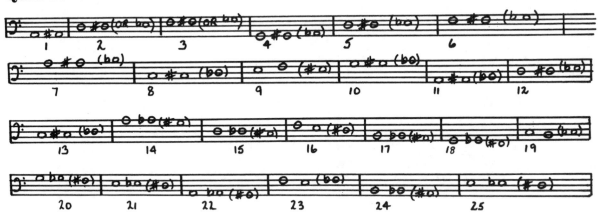

Quiz 10–8

1. A	11. D	21. B	31. A	41. G
2. C	12. F	22. A	32. G	42. C
3. E	13. A	23. G	33. F	43. D
4. G	14. F	24. F	34. A	44. E
5. G	15. B	25. G	35. F	45. F
6. B	16. G	26. D	36. E	46. A
7. D	17. B	27. C	37. G	47. C
8. F	18. C	28. B	38. E	48. E
9. A	19. F	29. F	39. B	49. B
10. G	20. B	30. C	40. C	50. A

Quiz 10–9

Quiz 10–10

Box A	Box B	Box C	Box D	Box E
1. C	11. C	20. F	30. B	40. B
2. A	12. A	21. A	31. C	41. H
3. D	13. E	22. B	32. A	42. A
4. F	14. B	23. E	33. E	43. C
5. E	15. G	24. C	34. D	44. E
6. J	16. D	25. D	35. G	45. G
7. B	17. H	26. C	36. H	46. F
8. G	18. F	27. I	37. F	47. H
9. H	19. I	28. J	38. J	48. I
10. I		29. H	39. I	49. K
				50. J

Boredom Buster 10–1

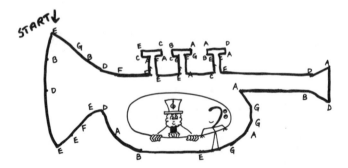

Boredom Buster 10–2

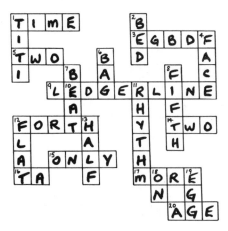

Boredom Buster 10–3

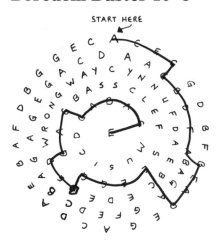

Boredom Buster 10–4

A gigantic cat with seven eyes, two tails and eight legs landed on earth in a field. Its spaceship was a cage of gold with big rockets. The cat had a tremendous thirst and crept towards the closest milk factory. When the cat arrived, it opened its huge mouth, stuck out its giant tongue and in one slurp, drank the entire factory. Then it ran back to its ship, sped away to Pluto and its path to Pluto was forever called the Milky Way. From then on other cats followed the Milky Way to earth every Friday afternoon to slurp factories.